HIGH PI
10 LIFE-CHAN
FROM HEAVEN . . .

"As someone who has had a life-changing near-death experience, I absolutely love this book. Jeff has captured many profound life lessons from thousands of NDErs and put them into a practical framework that everyone can benefit from. By applying these lessons, we make the world a better place. And to me, that's what this is all about. Acting upon the insights contained in this amazing book has the power to transform your life!"

JEFFERY OLSEN
Near-Death Experiencer, Author of *Knowing*

"I heartily recommend Jeff Janssen's *10 Life-Changing Lessons from Heaven* whether the subject of near-death experiences (NDEs) is new for you or it's an old friend. In clear yet beautiful language, Jeff leads you through learning about the life-altering wisdom of these profound experiences from both the vantage points of the experiencers themselves and through the filter of his own understanding. You'll gain greater insight into the depth and breadth of spiritual wisdom, and come away with ways you can bring this insight into practice in your own life."

NANCY RYNES
Near-Death Experiencer, Author of *Awakenings from the Light*

"*10 Life-Changing Lessons from Heaven* is both inspiring and practical. It's filled with fascinating stories from ordinary people who've had a near-death experience. They share in detail the wisdom they received. Jeff has powerfully summarized these experiences into actionable practices we can use in our everyday lives. He shows us how to bring kindness, love, compassion, and service into a world that truly needs it."

LYNN A. ROBINSON
Author of *Divine Intuition: Your Inner Guide to Purpose, Peace and Prosperity*

"The near-death experience is profoundly life-changing for the experiencer. What we know now is these lessons are not just for the experiencer but for all of us. In this deeply inspirational book, Jeff Janssen has collected near-death experiences and the lessons taught from them and categorized them into teachings that can change our lives in the here and now. There are practices you can take from this book and apply today. There's no need to wait until we cross over to get the lessons. We don't even have to go through the trauma of nearly dying. Whether you've studied near-death experiences for years, as I have, or you're brand new to the field, this book is one you should read."

BRIAN D. SMITH
Shining Light Parent, Creator of From Grief 2 Growth

"10 Life-Changing Lessons from Heaven is inspiring and a must read! This beautifully written book has given me many useful lessons and stories to ease the pain of those in the midst of grief and in the struggle of letting go. I would personally love for every pastor, along with those in similar positions of dealing with grief, death, and dying, to participate in a book study or workshop using these 10 Life-Changing Lessons! Regardless of one's current beliefs about heaven and hell, having these important compassionate views as possibilities of what awaits us on the other side are indeed life-changing, empowering, and comforting to the soul! Thank you, Jeff, for sharing these profound stories! My life is forever changed for the better."

REVEREND TINA BROWN
Unity Minister, Inspirational Unity Celebration Church of Scottsdale

"10 Life-Changing Lessons from Heaven is a great read that has really made me think before I react to certain situations and makes me want to treat others in my path better. I am growing in my understanding of being a spiritual being having this human experience. The experiences of the NDErs' changed my perspective. This is a book that you will want to refer to often to help you stay centered."

MICHAEL TOWLER
A New Way of Life

"10 Life-Changing Lessons from Heaven offers readers a view into another world. Jeff explores the fascinating realm of near-death experiences (NDEs) and addresses powerful and oft-asked questions. Digging deep into first-had accounts of NDEs, Jeff organizes their wisdom into an accessible resource."

JEFF O'DRISCOLL, MD
Author of *Not Yet*

"Jeff takes us on a journey of a host of individuals through their near-death experience and learnings. He synthesizes so many of the NDErs' experiences and makes them relatable for us. The lessons written so plainly, clearly, and heartfelt show what we can do to improve our lives and spiritual journey while staying on this side of 'the veil.'"

CHRISTINE MORIARTY
MoneyPeace

"Jeff Janssen's book is a delightful guide to the Afterlife! What did those who died and came back have to share? What can an NDE teach us? How can we enhance our lives by using these revelations in a practical way? The answers are transformational and contained in this enlightening book. I highly recommend *10 Life-Changing Lessons from Heaven!*"

REVEREND JAMES KING
Author of *Jesus Never Said That*

10 LIFE-CHANGING LESSONS FROM
HEAVEN

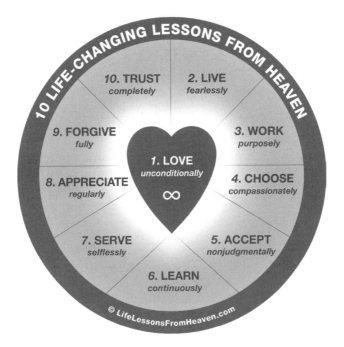

JEFF JANSSEN

Published by Life Lessons from Heaven
6841 Piershill Lane, Cary, NC 27519

Website: www.LifeLessonsFromHeaven.com

ISBN 978-1-7330850-0-7

DEDICATION

To my Archangel Soul Peeps: Tammy Shain and Cathy Shaw

*Words cannot describe how thankful I am for your support
and encouragement to share these life-changing lessons with the
world. You have been there for me from the very beginning of this
scary yet sacred and soulful journey, recruited others to the Soul
Peeps groups, and challenged and supported me every step of the
journey. I can't thank you enough. You will only know the true
difference you have made in my life and the lives of countless others who read this book when you experience the Ripple Effect of it
in your Life Review.*

THANK YOU!

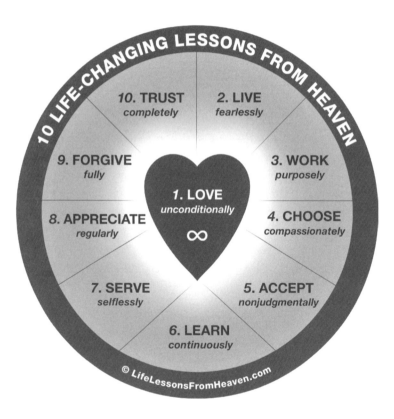

10 LIFE-CHANGING LESSONS FROM HEAVEN

10. TRUST
completely

2. LIVE
fearlessly

9. FORGIVE
fully

3. WORK
purposely

1. LOVE
unconditionally
∞

8. APPRECIATE
regularly

4. CHOOSE
compassionately

7. SERVE
selflessly

5. ACCEPT
nonjudgmentally

6. LEARN
continuously

© LifeLessonsFromHeaven.com

TABLE OF CONTENTS

VIP PASS TO VISIT
HEAVEN

This special VIP Pass to Visit Heaven entitles the holder to:

- **receive a personalized, grand tour of heaven**
- **see and interact with deceased friends and family members in the Afterlife**
- **meet with ALMIGHTY GOD and discover the many secrets of the Universe**
- **learn the meaning of life, why you are on earth, and discover your life's purpose**

VIP PASS

A SPECIAL VIP PASS TO VISIT HEAVEN

Imagine somehow receiving a special VIP Pass to Visit Heaven . . . Would you take it?

This special pass would allow you to visit heaven for a short time and come back to your earthly life. On your visit you would get the amazing opportunity to see and interact with your friends and family members who have passed away. You would get to feel their love once again and see they are blissfully happy, 100% healthy, and beaming with joy. You would also get your own personalized, grand tour of the awe-inspiring beauty of heaven conducted by an angelic guide who knows you even better than you know yourself. Best of all, you would get to see and talk with God, learn the many secrets of the universe and what life on earth is really all about, straight from the Source and Creator of All Things! And finally, you would receive several soul-satisfying answers to life's BIG questions like:

- *What is the meaning of life?*

- *Why am I here?*

- *What is my purpose?*

- *Where will I go when I die?*

Sounds heavenly doesn't it? Would you take this special opportunity if given the chance?

Most people would absolutely love to visit heaven, see their deceased friends and relatives, take the grand tour, and chat with God Almighty. And many actually have . . .

In fact, millions already have—they are called Near-Death Experiencers, or people who have died a clinical death, visited heaven, and then were revived and brought back to earth for another chance at human life. Though they had to virtually die to get there (the disclaimer is listed in very small print on the back of the pass), the privileged perk they received through their near-death experience was a visit to heaven—or what various cultures call the Afterlife, Nirvana, Paradise, the Promised Land, the Happy Hunting Ground, or the Other Side.

Wondering what their otherworldly visit was like and what amazing insights they learned while they were there?

16 to 19 Million Near-Death Experiencers

According to Gallup polls, approximately 16 to 19 million adults in the United States have had a near-death experience, or roughly 5-6% of the population. As a comparison, the number of people who have had a near-death experience across the U.S. is the same number as the entire population of the state of New York, the country's fourth largest state. This high number of people obviously means that you very likely know at least a few people in your own circle of friends and acquaintances who have had a near-death experience, whether or not they have told you about it. (Keep in mind the 16-19 million number is based on the reported near-death experience accounts of adults and is likely significantly higher because many go unreported and thousands of children also have near-death experiences.) With the advances in medical resuscitation, approximately 750 near-death experiences, or NDEs as we will call them, occur every single day according to the Near-Death Experience Research Foundation (NDERF), or over a quarter of a million people each year, just in the United States alone, which is a mere 4.4% of the world's population. So these "miraculous" experiences are becoming increasingly more common and accepted than many people might think.

Ordinary and Famous People with Extraordinary Experiences

As you might imagine, these ordinary people have extraordinary stories to tell from their visits to heaven. Even famous people like Tracy Morgan, Sharon Stone, George Lucas, Jane Seymour, Ernest Hemmingway, Johnny Cash, and George Foreman have had NDEs. These millions of near-death experiencers, or NDErs for short, represent men and women from all walks of life, all ages, races, religions, agnostics, and atheists, etc. Despite their different backgrounds and cultures, the stories of their visits to heaven are remarkably similar as has been documented in several books through the years, the first by Dr. Raymond Moody called *Life After Life* in 1975.

Since his seminal work, Dr. Moody and his colleagues have found that NDErs typically experience these common elements: dying a physical death, painlessly leaving their bodies and floating above the scene, feeling a strong sense of peace and unconditional love, entering and moving along a tunnel, seeing a bright, warm, irresistible, loving Light (God), seeing and communicating with deceased friends and family members and/or religious figures, having a panoramic review of their life, coming to a barrier or border they are not able to cross, and then returning, often reluctantly, back to their physical bodies. These are the classic, general characteristics of an NDE, though like each person is unique, so are the details of their NDEs.

Dying Provides Tremendous Insights for Living

By getting a glimpse of heaven and interacting with deceased relatives, heavenly guides, and even God Him/Herself, NDErs gain tremendous knowledge through their "death" of what it means to truly live—and many of their revelations from the Other Side will likely surprise you. Through their temporary physical death, they get a special pass to visit heaven, and an exceptional, behind-the-veil glimpse that many of us would love to hear about and learn from as evidenced by the many books written by NDErs on the *New York Times* Bestseller List. As you might imagine, they come back spiritually transformed people with sacred and profound insights that can help all of us understand how to truly live a life of success and significance from a spiritual standpoint.

The *10 Life-Changing Lessons from Heaven* book reveals the miraculous stories of NDErs' harrowing yet heavenly experiences, the life-changing lessons they learned while on the Other Side, and shows us all how to incorporate these powerful principles into our own lives, without having to nearly die to get them. Based on the knowledge gained from studying over 2,500 NDEs, this book highlights the inspiring and informative insights of over 130 NDErs and weaves them all into a practical guide for living and loving that those 95% of us who haven't had NDEs can benefit from in our daily lives.

But Are NDEs Real?

Some scientists, doctors, psychologists, and pastors have tried valiantly but unsuccessfully through the years to deny and debunk near-death experiences as the hallucinatory effects of an oxygen-starved brain (anoxia), the unconscious wishes of a dying person, the release of neurochemicals like DMT (Dimethyltryptamine), or even the diabolical work of the devil. However, given the sheer volume of the millions of people who've had them since as far back as the time of Plato and the Apostle Paul, the fact that they have been studied extensively for the past 40 years by highly reputable schools like the University of Virginia and the University of Connecticut, and the vast number of documented accounts (4,500 and counting on NDERF.org), there is both comprehensive and conclusive evidence that NDEs are indeed real. Further, respected brain surgeons like Dr. Eben Alexander and anesthesiologists like Dr. Rajiv Parti, who understand the intricate workings and abilities of the brain inside and out, say definitively there is no way the profound NDEs they experienced can be explained in any way by science.

So by picking up this book, I'm going to assume you are at least open to if not already believe in the validity of NDEs. But, if you are still skeptical and need more proof before proceeding, I encourage you to check out these highly credible resources before returning to this book.

The Evidence of the Afterlife: The Science of Near-Death Experiences by Dr. Jeffrey Long

Consciousness Beyond Life: The Science of the Near-Death Experience by Dr. Pim Van Lommel

The Handbook of Near-Death Experiences: 30 Years of Investigation by Dr. Janice Miner Holden, Dr. Bruce Greyson, and Debbie James, RN

The Self Does Not Die: Verified Paranormal Phenomena from Near-Death Experiences by Titus Rivas, Anny Dirvan, and Rudolf Smit

These doctors and scientists, who have extensively studied this phenomenon and authored these books, provide reams of evidence and veridical anecdotes that NDEs are real.

WHY LOOK TO NEAR-DEATH EXPERIENCES?

What makes NDErs such valuable and credible sources of knowledge about spiritual values and principles? Here are three primary reasons:

1. NDErs have been to heaven and experienced the Afterlife first-hand.

2. NDErs have heard it directly from the Source (God).

3. NDErs come back totally *transformed!*

1. NDErs have been to heaven and experienced the Afterlife first-hand.

Think of it this way: If you wanted to learn more about Dubai but you've never been there before, who would you ask to learn more about it?

Obviously, you wouldn't ask someone who has never been to Dubai or knew anyone who had because they would have no idea what the place is all about. Rather, you would seek out someone who had been there, seen the sights, heard the sounds, walked the streets, interacted with the people, and experienced it all first-hand.

Similarly with heaven, why not ask the people who have actually been to the Other Side to learn more about it? NDErs have directly experienced heaven and come back to tell about. They have seen, heard, and felt first-hand that life somehow goes on after our physical body shuts down. Consciousness indeed does continue after our heart stops and brain ceases to function. NDErs' dazzling descriptions of their visits to heaven are exactly why it is often referred to as paradise.

"Here was an endless vista of grass rolling away into shining, radiant hills. We have never seen green in our world like the deep, shimmering green of the grass that grew there. Every blade was crisp, strong, and charged with light. Every blade was unique and perfect and seemed to welcome me into this miraculous place. And the whole garden was singing. The flowers, grass, trees, and other plants filled this place with glorious tones and rhythms and melodies; yet I didn't hear the music itself. I could feel it somehow on a level beyond my hearing . . . I said to myself, 'Everything here seems to be singing,' which was woefully inadequate to describe what I felt. We simply don't have language that adequately communicates the beauty of that world." RaNelle Wallace

"Flower-filled grassy meadows spread out on the hills around me and huge deciduous trees in full leaf, trees larger and more grand than any here on Earth, surrounded the meadows . . . That was the visual. But there is more to Heaven than what we can see with our eyes. Below the surface visuals was a well of feeling fueled by love, peace, and an abiding Presence that I will call Spirit or God . . . The Beauty I felt really does deserve a capital "B". It wasn't just pleasing to the eye, there was something deeper to it, more harmonious, more blessed, more powerful. Everything felt tied together by love and peace, and the beauty of the scenes around me were the product of this unconditional love. While the beauty of Heaven took my breath away, the sense of love completely ensnared me and made me want to stay there forever . . . Each soul might see the 'landscape' differently, but all sensed and 'saw' the love that formed the basis for everything in the same way." Nancy Rynes

"Heaven isn't an abstraction; it isn't a dreamscape cooked up from empty, wishful thinking. It is a place as real as the room or the airplane or the beach or the library where you are right now." Dr. Eben Alexander

See Deceased Loved Ones in Heaven

Not only is heaven amazingly beautiful, NDErs often have joyous reunions with deceased family and friends on the Other Side.

"There were enormous shade trees scattered around and beyond the field was a small river about 30 feet across. On the opposite bank of this river was my father, who had died when I was seven, and my brother, who had been killed in a car accident when I was 23, and various aunts and uncles who had passed away. And even there were four people that I had never met in this life, but I certainly knew who my four grandparents were even though they died before I was born. It was this huge welcoming, homecoming, and family reunion feeling. They were as thrilled to see me as I was to see them." Karen Thomas

"When you die you are greeted by loved ones first so that you may understand what has happened. There is a big celebration, like a birthday party, heralding your arrival. Family and friends who have gone on before you are there to celebrate your arrival." Betty Bethards

Hi-Def Heaven Is Realer than Real

In fact, NDErs often describe their experience in heaven as the most authentic and real one they have ever had; it is hyper-real. The sights and colors are much more vivid, the sounds more melodious, and the feelings much deeper. In comparison, they say our earthly world seems drab, dull, and dreamlike. The difference between heaven and earth is like watching an IMAX, ultra HD, color screen and an old, fuzzy, black and white TV with rabbit ears and poor reception.

"Ultra-real, frequently mentioned in descriptions of NDEs, is a key concept here . . . I was astonished to find that more than half of NDErs report that realm to be far more real than this one . . . That realm is far more real than this murky, dreamlike material realm." Dr. Eben Alexander

"What we refer to as being dead is the most breathtakingly beautiful experience I've ever had. The afterlife is real, more real and more utterly magnificent than anything we could ever dream of on this side of the veil." Dannion Brinkley

"My experience [on the Other Side] was the most realistic event of my life. While I was on the Other Side all my senses were expanded beyond anything possible in mortal life. By comparison, earth life is the dream world." Dr. Joyce Brown

So the mysterious Afterlife realm that so many wonder about even existing is actually described by NDErs as being much more real and magnificent than earth itself. Our conjecture and confusion about the mystery of heaven even existing is similar to the parable of the twin babies in the womb who wondered if there was actually life after delivery, first written as short story by Pablo J. Luis Molinero and then condensed into a parable online.

Is There Life After Delivery?

As the story goes, there were two twin babies in the womb, a boy and a girl. The girl baby asks the boy baby if he believes in life after delivery. The boy thinks the concept of life after delivery is both crazy and impossible. The sister tentatively tells her brother she believes there is some kind of life after delivery and their time in the womb prepares them for it. She speculates after delivery they may even eat with their mouths and walk with their feet. Her skeptical brother thinks this is pure nonsense. He chastises her saying, "Walking is impossible. And eat with our mouths? Ridiculous. The umbilical cord supplies nutrition. Life after delivery is to be logically excluded. The umbilical cord is too short." He confidently informs her that delivery ends their life, there is just complete darkness, and that no one has ever come back after delivery. His sister persists telling him she hopes that after delivery they will see their mother who will take care of them. The incredulous brother thinks this fantasy is even crazier. He taunts her, "Mother? You believe in Mother? Where is she now?" The sister admits she doesn't know for sure but thinks their mother is all around them, that they live within her, and she is eager to take care of them after delivery.

Her doubting brother says he doesn't see this imaginary mother anywhere so it proves definitively she doesn't exist. His sister counters with, "Sometimes when you're in silence you can hear her, you can perceive her. I believe there is a reality after delivery and we are here to prepare ourselves for that reality when it comes. . . ."

2. NDErs have heard directly from the Source (God)

Many NDErs have the opportunity to communicate directly with God during their visits to heaven. As world-renowned psychologist Carl Jung, himself a near-death experiencer, once said, "I don't believe there is a God. I KNOW there is a God." NDErs come back not just *believing* God exists but *knowing* God exists because they have actually experienced His presence and amazing love.

> "The real value of the experience is in the fact that I encountered God . . . As for faith, it is no longer a matter of believing in or having faith in the existence of God and heaven. I know both God and heaven exist because I have been there and have seen the light of God's presence." John Wintek

> "With the eyes of my soul body, I looked to see what held me in such love and I beheld a radiant, Spirit being, so magnificent and full of love that I knew I would never again feel the sense of loss. I have no way of explaining how, but I knew the Spirit was Christ. It was not a belief, perception or understanding, but my recognition of Christ came from my new perspective of spirit . . .The radiant Spirit was Christ, the manifestation and expression of pure love. Because of my Christian education, I knew no other name to call what I felt as I looked at him. Others might have called him Buddha, or Yahweh, or Great Spirit in the Sky, but the naming did not matter, only the recognition of absolute love and truth was important. Safe in the gentle yet powerful embrace of his love, I rested, secure that everything was okay, exactly as it was supposed to be." Linda Stewart

> "All I could see was Light. Within the Light there was an intelligence . . . If I were Christian, I would call the Light 'Jesus'. If I were a Buddhist, I would call the Light 'Buddha'. If I were a Hindu, it would be 'Krishna'. Whatever— the Light becomes what we believe, what we associate with, and that's immaterial. It doesn't make any difference what we call the Light—because it's love." Roland Webb

> "I knew immediately I was in the presence of God. I have always referred to God as a him, and I guess I always will. But the being on my right was not a him or a her; it was just God . . . There was no distinct form, certainly no face or body, just a blinding profusion of brightness. I wasn't so much meeting God as I was recognizing Him. I already knew Him, and He knew me. I'd spent my life doubting His existence and disbelieving His love for

me, but in that instant I knew God had always, always been there—right there with me . . . This was the Creator of the universe, and I was in His presence! The sheer ecstasy of it! The beauty of it, the joy and the grace, the way my spirit soared and my heart burst—how I wish I had the words to convey just how miraculous this was." Crystal McVea

(**Author's Note:** Honoring the common understanding of NDErs and many religions that God possesses both masculine and feminine qualities, throughout the rest of the book I will refer to God in even numbered chapters as He and in odd numbered chapters as She. Also, keep in mind that NDErs use many different terms to refer to God including the Light, Spirit, Source, Creator, Great Teacher, etc. I will use the term "God" in the general sense for simplicity sake in an effort to encompass all these terms. I realize "God" means something different to everyone so if the word "God" concerns you, please substitute a different one—Source, Creator, Krishna, All-That-Is, Allah, Buddha, The Great Spirit, Universe, Supreme Being, Yahweh, Elohim, etc.—that better fits your viewpoint throughout the rest of the book.)

3. NDErs come back totally *transformed*!

Finally, we can learn from NDErs because after their visits to heaven they come back totally transformed and spiritually awakened people. This is not just a small, cosmetic, temporary change like getting a haircut. This is a significant, deep, and lasting change that alters a person's entire operating system and rewires them personally, socially, and spiritually. After experiencing the immense love, peace, joy, compassion, and bliss from the Other Side, NDErs want to emulate God's unconditional and universal love they experienced in heaven and implement it into their own lives as best they can and share it with others.

"These experiences are transformative. The people who have these experiences are never the same again. They are totally transformed!" Dr. Raymond Moody

"Before my NDE, my life was totally different . . . I despised myself when I was younger. I grew up very different from everyone else around me. I was a very introverted child who had almost no friends. Getting picked on and teased was a daily occurrence that drove my self-esteem to the point where it didn't exist . . . I was one of the most antisocial people that ever existed . . . I instantly changed from a pessimist to an optimist. There always seemed to be a brighter side to everything. I knew that everything happened for a reason . . . I felt like I now had a purpose, which was to help people and share my positive perspective . . . In doing this, other people around me began to accept me for who I was. I do not fear things anymore . . . I feel that my NDE was the best thing that ever happened to me." Neev

"Every belief, every value and every goal had to be re-evaluated after my luminous journey. The near-death experience was for me a great liberation—a rebirth—and its effects still can be felt in my daily life. Most of all, as a result of the experience, never again could I fear death. Never again could I look upon life as being anything less than a divine gift that transcends the limits of this physical realm." Reinee Pasarow

"Think of the aftereffects of an NDE like rebooting your computer. Except when you reboot from an NDE, your life is no longer version 2.0. Now it's version 20.0." Debra Diamond

In fact, because of the inspiring insights they gained in heaven, it is this kind of profound, powerful, and permanent transformation of being more loving, compassionate, caring, and confident that NDErs can be a valuable guide for all of us in living a more positive and productive life.

The Many Positive Life Changes After NDEs

Dr. Melvin Morse, who has studied and written about hundreds of NDErs, says, "We found that these people were transformed. They were transformed in physical ways and they were transformed in psychological ways. They are unusually psychologically healthy, they give more money to charity, they exercise more, they eat more fresh fruits and vegetables. So it's not just that their spiritual beliefs are different than the ordinary population, but their actual habits are different."

Nancy Clark, herself an NDEr, found numerous transformative effects in her study of dozens of other NDErs including the following:

- "The existence of Heaven, God and celestial beings was no longer a matter of belief, it became a self-evident reality.

- No longer fear death.

- Became more compassionate and loving individuals.

- A stronger desire to help others . . .

- Possessing more strength, power and grace to endure whatever was happening in their lives, regardless of the circumstances.

- A certain serenity that enabled them to know with certainty that the Creator's love is with them at all times.

- Deeper, more intimate connection with Mother Nature.

- Realizing the purpose of one's life.

- Feelings of interconnectedness with the global community.

- Acceptance of all religious paths toward the Divine.

- Understanding that we are more than biological beings; we are spirits of consciousness that continue to exist beyond the physical dimension . . ."

Obviously there are a lot of positives that can come from having such a profound spiritual experience. NDErs come back different, and dare I say, more loving and spiritually-evolved people for having gone through their harrowing yet heavenly experience.

> "It had put me on a new path that changed my personality, broke old patterns of living that were detrimental to me and my family, gave me greater compassion for others, and led me on a search for the spiritual instead of the material. Returning to the NDE state was like a course correction to keep me on the righteous path, a compass heading that led me to God."
> Dr. Rajiv Parti

The insights from the NDErs do indeed show us a path to better and more completely understanding God and our sacred purpose here on earth. Each of their separate experiences is a small yet significant piece in the complex puzzle of the meaning of life and what it actually means to be a spiritual being having a human experience. (Note about NDEr Names: Many of the NDErs are listed by their first and last names since their quotes are often taken from their books, presentations, and interviews. Some NDErs are listed by just their first name and last initial. These NDE accounts are often quoted from nderf.org, a terrific website of thousands of NDE accounts which only lists the person's first name and last initial for privacy reasons.)

10 Life-Changing Lessons from Heaven

After hearing, witnessing, and studying over 2,500 near-death experiences, a clear thread of *TRUTH* soon emerges about the real meaning of life, our sacred purpose within it, and how God calls each and every one of us to live and love. These powerful and profound principles, or what I call the 10 Life-Changing Lessons from Heaven, recur over and over again as people tell their stories, share their insights, and reveal the sheer wisdom of God and the Afterlife.

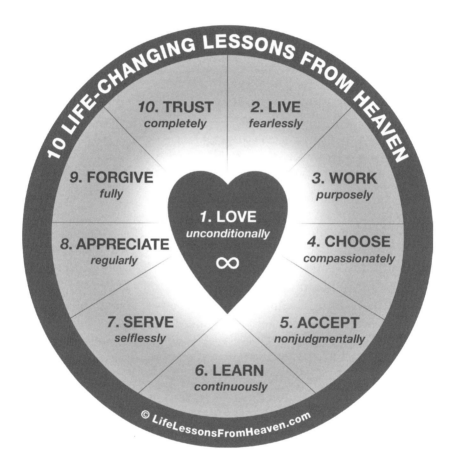

1. LOVE unconditionally

2. LIVE fearlessly

3. WORK purposely

4. CHOOSE compassionately

5. ACCEPT nonjudgmentally

6. LEARN continuously

7. SERVE selflessly

8. APPRECIATE regularly

9. FORGIVE fully

10. TRUST completely

By living and loving in these 10 ways on a regular basis, we are all able to bring a bit of heaven with us to earth. As you may notice, many of these 10 Lessons naturally align with what is taught by most religions. Truth is truth is truth. In many ways, these principles cut across and unite the beliefs of most religions and reflect the Universal Truths that form the foundation of most faiths.

However, I'll also bet there will be several interesting insights from NDErs' visits to heaven about how we are called to live and love that will surprise and even shock you—causing you to likely contemplate and possibly even change some of your current spiritual views, beliefs, and practices. The intent of sharing these profound and paradigm-shifting insights from NDErs is certainly not to deny or denigrate anyone's sacred religious beliefs—just to encourage you to examine them in light of what millions of people have experienced and come to understand on their visits to heaven and direct discussions with God.

Entire chapters will be dedicated to each of these 10 principles and the insights over 130 NDErs gained on how we can best implement them into our lives. I have also organized them into a framework and model to help visually communicate these 10 Life-Changing Lessons from Heaven. Since love is repeatedly mentioned as the central force in the universe, it is placed at the absolute center of the model. It is the core of God's existence and teachings and all the other nine Lessons are really subsets of and fully aligned with love.

*"What the caterpillar calls the end,
the rest of the world calls a butterfly."*

LAO TZU

NDErs Assure Us Death is Nothing to Fear

For many people, death is one of their biggest fears. Because it is so scary to them, death often becomes a taboo subject they don't like to think about much less talk about. However, as they say, the only certain things in life are death and taxes—so we all know some day our time on earth will come to an end. Fortunately, NDErs tell us one of the big takeaways from visiting heaven is that there is absolutely no need to fear death. They say death itself is beautiful, an easy transition, and one they actually look forward to because they get to go back to heaven and what they call their true "home" when it is their time. So NDErs assure us there is nothing to fear about death or the Afterlife.

> "I want to assure you, and all of us who have been out and back want to assure you, that the precise moment is nothing but pure bliss, pure release, pure joy, pure love, pure light. And if you can stand it, none of all these words together is enough to describe it." Lewis Brown Griggs

Ironically, when they are informed they need to return to earth, the vast majority of NDErs actually beg, plead, and throw toddler-like temper tantrums with God and the angels to stay "dead" in heaven because they realize what a glorious realm it truly is and they feel more alive than they ever have before.

> "If I lived a billion years more, in my body or yours, there's not a single experience on earth that could ever be as good as being dead. Nothing." Dr. Dianne Morrissey

> "I was just hoping I would not have to go back into that body. I was finally pain-free and furthermore, I had gained absolute knowledge about everything, absolutely everything about life, which was pretty amazing. Really, if this was death, I wanted to be dead forever." Marion Rome

> "The best way I can describe the transition from being 'alive' on the physical plane and the passage to the Other Side is like passing from one 'room' to another. You do not cease to be or lose consciousness; your consciousness simply shifts from one vantage point to another. The experience changes; your outlook changes; your feelings change. And the feelings I experienced were profound; for me, it most certainly became that peace that surpasses all understanding." Juliet Nightingale

> "I am no longer the least bit afraid to die. I know that I would not want to suffer, but I know that the actual dying process is nothing like I thought it would be, and that it was probably the most beautiful and peaceful experience I have ever had." Craig

"His love was so complete and unconditional. I yearned to go to Him. Although I had had a very happy life, coming back to life was as attractive to me as for a human to become a roach. I had gone through a metamorphosis and now I could not go back." Daniela

Suicide is NOT the Answer!

We can see by these quotes why death is no longer feared by NDErs, and shouldn't be by any of us either. ***Please understand that no NDEr advocates suicide or killing another person so they can get to heaven.*** While they are excited and eager to go back to heaven when it is their time, they know each of us has an important mission and purpose to accomplish here on earth before heading to heaven as we will see in our upcoming Work Purposely chapter.

> "One thing I can tell you is that suicide won't work. If you're thinking about that, you can just scratch that one off the list. Because it's not going to do what you think it's going to do. That was one of the things that I was shown is that there is no short way around." Raymond Kinman

> "You can't take your own life. Suicide isn't the answer. That won't do it. You have to go back and live your life's purpose." Laurelynn Martin

You Don't Have to Die to Learn How to Live

One of the main messages of the NDErs and this book is that you don't have to go through a near-death experience to learn how to live. While a visit to heaven is indeed a beautiful, surreal, and life-changing experience, most NDErs also endured unthinkable physical trauma via gruesome car accidents, painful plane crashes, ravaging end-stage cancer, electrocuting lightning strikes, death-defying drownings, etc., as their ticket and hefty admission price into the Afterlife.

If the initial trauma wasn't enough, most of them also suffered through excruciating and lengthy recoveries and rehabs when they got back. The intense physical pain they endured in the initial traumatic event or illness, the multiple surgeries, the weeks in hospitals, the months in rehab, their lasting scars, ailments, and/or amputations, etc., are obviously not something anyone wants to subject themselves to—nor even wish upon their worst enemies.

> "I don't want anybody to have to go through an NDE to learn this stuff because it's pretty hard, especially if you get struck by a truck." Nancy Rynes

Further, many NDErs took years to process these overwhelming spiritual insights before better understanding them themselves or being comfortable enough to share their spiritually supernatural experiences with others. As an analogy, an NDE is much like drinking from a fire hose rather than a water fountain; so much profound and mind-blowing spiritual wisdom bombards NDErs all at once during their visit to heaven that it takes time for them to process and actually recover from it spiritually as well as physically. (Seven years is the typical average to fully process their experience according to NDE researcher PMH Atwater.) So rather than wishing you had an NDE, which is obviously not likely nor desired with the accompanying physical pain, you can still benefit from NDErs' unearthly experiences by learning the lessons (one manageable yet potent sip at a time) and applying them to your life—without all the painful and prolonged physical and mental trauma that most endured.

> "You do not need to have a dramatic experience like an NDE to undergo this change in perspective. But I do believe that it is the duty of those of us who have undergone these more dramatic kinds of experiences to spread the word—to talk about where we've been and what we've seen, and to use every skill at our disposal to bring that message to life and translate it back to this world." Dr. Eben Alexander

> "Perhaps it was time to bring me back into the fold, to teach me the things I needed to learn in order to live an amazing life. But it took a horrendous accident and a near-death experience for me to see the light. No matter how it happened, I am extremely grateful that I received these messages. I hope that you don't need to go through something quite that traumatic to gain some benefit through these words." Nancy Rynes

If you are looking to make a positive and powerful change in your life and bring a little (or a lot) more heaven into your earthly existence, applying the life-changing lessons of the NDE is a great way to go. In fact, noted NDE researcher Dr. Ken Ring, in his excellent and highly recommended book *Lessons from the Light*, says everyone can benefit from learning the lessons of NDErs because they reflect what a spiritually-developed, highly-evolved human looks like. "Whenever the blessings of the NDE are fused properly into one's life, the individual comes to exemplify what a highly developed person would be and act like . . . The phenomenon of the NDE is a teaching about life, love, and human potential that all interested persons could draw upon actively now in order to enrich their lives and to hasten their own progress toward enlightenment."

"I'm showing more love to others now than before I started my near-death experience studies. My understanding of near-death experiences has made me a better doctor. I face life with more courage and confidence. I believe NDErs really do bring back a piece of the afterlife. When NDErs share their remarkable experiences, I believe a piece of the afterlife, in some mysterious way, becomes available to us all." Dr. Jeffrey Long

If you want to develop yourself spiritually and evolve into a better human being, studying the insights gained from those who went to heaven and heard directly from God is certainly an effective way to do it.

Life Transformation Without the Death-Defying Trauma

You can look at learning from NDEs without having to nearly die as "transformation without the trauma." Dr. Ring continues, "There is indeed evidence that merely learning about the NDE has similar effects reported by NDErs . . . We can experience some of the same benefits as those who have had NDEs and understand more clearly just what they have gained from their encounter with the Light, you, too, will have the opportunity to learn and grow as the NDEr has . . . to reap the seeds of transformation of the NDE, without having to nearly die first to do so . . . The lessons from the Light are not just for the NDErs of the world. They are for everyone. The NDErs are simply our teachers here, whose job is to remind us of the truths we may have forgotten."

Throughout this book you will learn from over 130 NDErs who graciously share their experiences and insights from their extraordinary visits to heaven through their talks, videos, books, and one-on-one interviews with me. I have included so many of their powerful quotes and testimonies in an effort to capture their profound experience as well as reinforce the principles from so many different perspectives.

Further, each chapter also includes a feature on a specific NDEr quoted in this book, starting with Dr. Eben Alexander, and a very brief overview of their remarkable experience. I highly encourage you to check out their resources to learn more about them and their incredible stories. In the back of the book I have included a Recommended Readings section for those of you who want to learn more and dig deeper into their NDEs and the insights they gained. I thank them for generously sharing their experiences and wisdom to enlighten all of us.

NDEr FEATURE

Dr. Eben Alexander: A Neurosurgeon's Life-Changing Visit to Heaven

Neuroscientist Dr. Eben Alexander's brain was ravaged and rendered useless by a sudden and severe case of bacterial meningitis from which only 10% of people ever recover. In a deep coma for seven days, Dr. Alexander had an intensive NDE where he experienced the innermost levels of heaven. He had a personal guide during his visit that only later did he come to understand her special relationship with him—I encourage you to find out exactly who she is and her shocking connection to him by reading his books, *Proof of Heaven*, *Map of Heaven*, and *Living in a Mindful Universe*. Because of Dr. Alexander's high-level training as a brain surgeon at Duke University, his time as a professor at the Harvard Medical School, and the severity of his meningitis, his NDE is highly credible evidence that NDEs are not caused by a dying brain. You can learn more about Dr. Alexander and his incredible NDE at www.ebenalexander.com

A Practical and Powerful Plan to Bring More Heaven into Your Life

This book is not more about seeing the Light at the end of the tunnel, or another guided tour of what heaven looks like, or anything like that. This book will also not try to prove to you that NDEs are real. In my humble opinion, we are way beyond that, so it is time to forge ahead and break new ground. It is high time we stop being merely mesmerized and intrigued by NDE stories and start putting their profound, powerful, and practical lessons into practice. This book does exactly that by providing you with an understanding of the 10 Life-Changing Lessons from Heaven coupled with a practical plan for putting these principles into place so you can have a much better life; be a more loving spouse, parent, son/daughter, brother/sister, etc., for your family, and how to be a better person for your community, business, school, church, and world.

> "My experience taught me volumes about death, but there was something else. It taught me how to live . . . how to truly and freely live and love like most have never imagined . . ." Robert Tremblay

"The true promise of the NDE is not so much what it suggests about the afterlife—as inspiring and comforting as those glimpses are—but what it says about how to live NOW . . . to learn from NDErs about how to live, or how to live better, with greater self-awareness, self-compassion, and concern for others." Dr. Ken Ring

Why Me as Your Author?

Why should you listen to me as your author? Honestly, I've asked myself that question numerous times because I would have never ever guessed I would write a book about NDEs during my first 40 years of life. Being a highly left-brained, practical person and business owner, I was pretty skeptical when it came to anything that seemed in any way spiritual or new age.

However, in 2011, at the relatively young age of 42, I was running on a treadmill in a doctor's office when I felt crushing chest pains, shortness of breath, and numbness radiating down my left arm. After quickly giving me a Nitroglycerin tablet and having me lie down, my doctor told me I was on the verge of having a full-blown heart attack and would need an immediate cardiac catheterization and possibly open-heart bypass surgery. Overwhelmed by the heart-stopping news, I hastily took stock of my life, told my wife and two children how much I loved them, and gave them the biggest and longest hugs I ever had because it was quite possibly the last time I would see them.

During the heart catheterization, the doctors discovered a 99% blockage in my coronary artery, often ominously and appropriately called the Widowmaker. I was 1% away from having a massive and likely fatal heart attack. Fortunately the severe blockage was in a location where they could use stents to open it up instead of needing to perform coronary bypass surgery. While I did not have a spiritual NDE like we're exploring in this book, coming that close to death at the relatively young age of 42 was obviously a powerful and profound enough experience to get me to seriously contemplate life's BIG questions like: *Why are we here? Where do we go when we die? What is the meaning of life? What is my purpose in life?*

Having been gifted with a second chance at life, I sought and found amazing, comforting, and soul-satisfying answers to these questions from NDErs and became highly intrigued by their wisdom and insights. Since my physical NDE, I have been on a personal spiritual quest to learn more and have read tons of NDE books and accounts online, watched hundreds of NDE videos, and regularly attended the local and national

International Association of Near Death Studies Conferences (IANDS) around the country and listened to the stories of NDErs and respected NDE researchers alike. I began interviewing NDErs and after befriending many of them and learning from over 2,500 accounts, saw several common themes relayed in this book that truly helped me answer life's big questions.

With a continuing effort to implement the principles, I made many positive and much-needed changes in my own life. I stopped taking so many things for granted and started appreciating all the big and little things I had. I decreased my obsession with work and increased my time with my family. I became much more tolerant and less judgmental of people. I initiated conversations with homeless people and generously shared a smile, money, and sometimes even a hug with them rather than just callously walking by. I asked for forgiveness from those I hurt and in turn became more understanding and forgiving of others. I valued all life going on around me and marveled at nature's mystery and beauty. I trusted God has a perfect plan. Although I still have a LONG way to go, I found myself becoming more of the loving, kind, generous, compassionate, accepting, forgiving person I want to be and less of the judgmental, stressed out, elitist, impatient, jealous, competitive, grudge-keeping, spiteful person I had many times been.

I felt called and compelled to write the manuscript for the *10 Life-Changing Lessons from Heaven* book and hesitantly began sharing it with only a super small group of highly trusted friends because, quite honestly, I was scared to tell people of my interest in such a "fringe" topic. I was afraid it would destroy my credibility and didn't want to take that risk.

However, after seeing the life-changing impact these paradigm-shifting principles began having on my friends, and them eagerly wanting to share them with their family and friends, I eventually realized the positive impact and ripple effect these ideas were having was so much more important and valuable than my selfish worries and fears about what other people might think of me. I made the difficult yet critical choice to Live Fearlessly, just as the NDErs encourage us all to do. I eventually realized that part of my life's purpose is to not only use these insights to help myself and a small group of friends, but to share them with others who had not had NDEs so that they could benefit from them as well.

Ironically, my father actually had an NDE from a heart attack when he was 54. He described the warm, loving, and inviting Light to me and although I believed him, I unfortunately didn't pay much attention to his experience nor ask the many questions I would have today. It's one of my biggest regrets because he passed away just three years later at the age of 57. Now I'm asking those questions, truly listening to those answers, trying to apply their wisdom to whatever's left of my own life, and most importantly, sharing them with you and others through this book. I hope they make the same positive impact in your life as they have in mine and so many others!

Whatever your religious background or beliefs, keep in mind that people from all religions as well as agnostics and atheists experience NDEs. Most NDErs become more spiritual after their NDEs and less tied to one religion. Most say the Higher Power they experienced far transcends and even unites all religions rather than favoring a specific one. NDEr Howard Storm asked God which religion was the best and was told: "The best religion is the religion that brings you closest to God." Ultimately, it is up to each of us to find the religion or spiritual practice that brings us closest to God.

Additionally, our beliefs impact how we view and interpret things. So too are the NDErs as they share their sacred stories and try to relate their otherworldly and ineffable experience in light of their theological beliefs. I too am not immune to this. So you know my past beliefs, I was raised Christian, attended a Jesuit college, drifted away from the church and became somewhat agnostic during my early adulthood, and now am a spiritual person who accepts and appreciates aspects of all religions. My intent is not to promote or criticize any religion. I feel all religions and spiritual paths can provide tremendous value to bring people closer to God. Thus, I have included quotes and examples from many religions in the book. Since the NDErs encourage us to love unconditionally and accept nonjudgmentally, my hope is that this book becomes a unifying message to respect all religions, agnostics, and atheists, even if their beliefs are different than our own.

So if you are ready to transform your life into something more positive and productive using the *10 Life-Changing Lessons from Heaven*, let's get started!

OPTIONS FOR GETTING THE MOST OUT OF THIS BOOK

Hopefully you will get a lot out of reading this book and applying the lessons. In piloting this book with various groups and individuals, we found that people like to learn and process the material in a variety of ways. Here are some options you might find helpful:

10 Life-Changing Lessons from Heaven Journal

If you prefer to reflect on the lessons, note your thoughts and feelings, and personalize the lessons to your life, we created a special *10 Life-Changing Lessons from Heaven Journal* with several soul-stirring questions as well as weekly practical implementation strategies for each of the 10 Lessons. The *Journal* provides you with a sacred space to record your thoughts and transforms the book into your own personalized Spiritual Development Program.

Create Your Own Book Club Discussion Group

We've found that significant spiritual growth and long-lasting impact occurs when you read and discuss the 10 Lessons with a group of people (friends, family, church members, etc.). You may wish to gather a small group and read and discuss a chapter a week. Having been a member of several of these groups in piloting the book, I can tell you it is a very powerful way of learning, implementing, and infusing the lessons into your life as well as connecting with your fellow participants on a much deeper level!

Join an Online Soul Peeps Discussion Group

We also facilitate online discussion groups for people who want to go deeper into the material. Led by author Jeff Janssen or one of his experienced team members, you can discuss your thoughts on each chapter with a group of fellow spiritual seekers. You can join as an individual or assemble your own group of family or friends to discuss the book and other spiritual topics with us and learn how to apply the 10 Lessons.

Since everyone learns differently, we wanted you to be aware of these options as you begin the book in case one of them better fits your preferred learning style. Additional information is available at the end of the book and at LifeLessonsFromHeaven.com.

1.

LOVE
UNCONDITIONALLY

*"The ultimate lesson all of us have to learn is unconditional love,
which includes not only others but ourselves as well."*

Elizabeth Kubler-Ross,
Author of *On Death and Dying*

NDEr FEATURE

Howard Storm: From Atheist to Ordained Minister

Howard Storm, a conceited college professor and chairman of the art department at Northern Kentucky University, was on a trip to Paris when he experienced terrible stomach pains. Unfortunately, he could not find a doctor to see him in a timely manner so he spent the day in excruciating pain, precipitating his NDE. He actually started his NDE by descending into a kind of a hellish realm until he called out to Jesus to save him by going to the Light. During his time in heaven, Howard learned that life was not all about material success but instead should be centered on the importance of love and making compassionate choices. After his NDE, Pastor Storm, once an atheist, became an ordained minister and has shared God's message of love with many. He describes his NDE in his excellent book, *My Descent into Death* and has several videos online. He has appeared on *The Oprah Winfrey Show* and *The Tonight Show*. You can learn more about him at www.howardstorm.com

Love Is All You Need

Unequivocally, the most important message NDErs come back from heaven with is that it is indeed all about love. Love is the basis of everything. God is love. We are love. Our lives should ideally revolve around love. NDErs are absolutely blown away by the amount of pure, powerful, and unconditional love they receive on their visits to heaven and come to understand that love is the foundation of the entire universe.

Because love is the central message of NDErs, it anchors the core of the 10 Life-Changing Lessons from Heaven model and everything else revolves around it. All of the other nine principles are obviously related to the main message of love. Since love is the basis of all the others, we naturally begin with it and will invest a significant amount of time on it in this first chapter because love is so foundational to everything else we will discuss.

In this chapter we will look at the many aspects of love that NDErs describe including:

- God's immense, intense, and indescribable love for us

- God's love is unconditional—absolutely no strings attached

- Love is the basis of everything

- We come here to learn all about love

- We must learn to love ourselves as well as others

- How the questions on "God's Final Exam" all revolve around love

God's Immense, Intense, and Indescribable Love for Us

Let's start by trying to get some kind of grasp on God's all-encompassing love for us. Some of the most beautiful descriptions from NDErs are of God's TOTAL and ALL-ENCOMPASSING LOVE for us—even capitalizing all the letters to emphasize its importance is grossly inadequate. Though most are at a complete loss for words when it comes to capturing the overwhelming and infinite magnitude of God's love for us, they do their best to try to explain it, clearly admitting that human language doesn't do it justice in the tiniest bit. God's love is that powerful and profound. Here's what NDErs say in attempting to describe it:

"The most amazing part was a pure feeling of the most intense love I can barely describe. It was just wave after wave of pure love. It was within me, it was around me, it was EVERYTHING. It felt like heartbeats of love, one wave of love after another. Yet there was love in the interim as well, then the wave would come with even more and more. It was endless, eternal and complete. I had no fear whatsoever, I had no feeling other than LOVE. I had no thought other than reaching the LIGHT. I felt pure happiness and joy. It was the most beautiful feeling that words could never even come close to describing. The closest thing I can think of to relate it to on this earth would be the moment I brought my child into this world. That moment of pure unconditional love that I'm sure most mothers and some fathers have felt. Still that is only but a very small fraction of what I am trying to explain. Words seem so small and insignificant in comparison to the experience." Nichole BD

"I felt the unspeakable, all encompassing, unconditional Love of God for me. It felt really 'personal' and because of its unconditional character it is almost incomprehensible. To the point where I thought: 'All this Love for me? Who am I? I am just a boy who grew up in a middle-lower class family, in a regular neighborhood, went to a regular school. I have no accomplishments. I've never done anything remarkably special. I'm just a regular guy, a normal human. What have I done to deserve this? Is ALL this

LOVE really for me?' The moment I finished that thought, I was instantly 'swallowed up' by this amazing Love. 'I' was completely GONE! There was nothing but Love. No me, no God: just eternal, incomprehensible, indescribable, total, complete, absolute LOVE." Carlos K.

"I had no idea I was that precious to anybody. It felt like I was being loved, held, and cradled as if I was the last newborn baby ever going to be born in the entire universe; being loved, held, and cradled by every mother in the entire universe . . . in the entire 13.8 billion year history of earth all at once. That does not even begin to come close to what God's love is truly like. I was just blown away." Tony Woody

Hopefully these multiple and moving descriptions give you some small sense of the sheer magnitude of the overwhelming LOVE God has for each and every one of us. Perhaps the best analogy for the power and intensity of God's love would be this: Imagine yourself standing right next to the sun and absorbing its direct heat and powerful rays 100% full on at point blank range. That illuminates what the power of God's radiating, intense love is like for each of us.

Unconditional Love

The most common quality of God's pure, powerful, and perfect love mentioned by NDErs is that it is unconditional. This concept is likewise one that can be hard to fully grasp the meaning of so let's again hear directly from some NDErs to better understand exactly what unconditional love means and feels like.

"The feeling of complete, pure, unconditional love was unlike anything I had known before. Unqualified and nonjudgmental . . . it was totally undiscriminating, as if I didn't have to do anything to deserve it, nor did I need to prove myself to earn it." Anita Moorjani

"Unconditional love was pouring into my soul the likes of which I have never experienced. No love on the face of the earth can compare with the unconditional love of the Light. Healed in a nanosecond of all illusions I'd previously held about myself—the low self-esteem, guilt, and inability to love myself fully—I now received the most precious gift from the Light: it showed me how LOVED I am, with no strings attached!" Nancy Clark

"God's love is infinite and eternal and unconditional FOR EVERY ONE OF US. It doesn't matter what our religion is or if we drink or smoke or curse. It isn't dependent at all on anything we do, and we can never lose it. It is a gift from God to us forever. TO ALL HIS CHILDREN everywhere." Tabitha

Plain and simple, unconditional love means God loves us simply because we exist. We don't have to do anything to earn God's love and we can do nothing, absolutely nothing, to ever lose it. NDErs remind us that God loves us regardless of what we think, say, or do. It is a complete, universal, no strings attached, and eternal love. This kind of unconditional love is so special because we don't often experience the purity of it on earth. Rarely is our human love completely unconditional. We usually love people because of how they make us feel, what they can do for us, or because they are related to us. Seldom do we fully and unconditionally love people simply because they exist.

> "Love is not as unconditional as we like to think. There are things we want in return for that love. We do this unconsciously. We have roles we expect others to play, and we will dole out respective levels of love because of our expectations. We're not going to automatically give everyone the whole scoop. We're going to give it out a little at a time, often just a spoonful at a time, because we feel we have to keep some love in reserve." David Bennett

> "My love for my fellow mortals was rather conditional. I was an all-or-nothing person: 'I love you or I hate you,' with no shades of grey . . . I cruelly lacked patience when it came to my interactions with others and, if I realized my mistakes in my dealings with other people, my pride used to get in the way of taking steps to restore harmonious relationships . . . If anyone hurt me in the slightest of ways, I would hold onto grudges for ridiculous amounts of time . . . I was simply very selfish and egocentric." Marion Rome

Without often realizing it, as humans we often place many conditions on the love we choose to share or withhold from others. We are picky and sometimes even discriminatory about whom we decide to love. For example, we might only fully love the people who are from our family, church, school, community, political party, or country. We might only love people if they are good to us. We might only love people if they love us back. This kind of conditional love is selective, fickle, and fleeting. People have to earn this kind of conditional love by believing a certain way, behaving a certain way, dressing a certain way, praying a certain way, etc. If they don't do what we want them to do, we don't love them. Our love then is obviously dependent on people meeting certain conditions. When viewed and understood in this way, most of our human love is conditional love and surprisingly little of it is unconditional.

"Unconditional love is larger than we are. We have trouble understanding it. Unconditional love is endless and unifies everyone and everything in this universe. It's hard for us to constantly feel unconditional love as humans; conditionally using love is easier, simpler. We keep adding a step to our love—wanting something in return or something else—and making it complicated. Maybe that's why so many think of love as troublesome. It would be much simpler to love unconditionally. If we expected nothing in return for our love, it would be a truer more powerful love, and more like the infinite power of the universe." David Bennett

"I was shown how much all people are loved. It was overwhelmingly evident that the Light loved everyone equally without any conditions. I really want to stress this because it made me so happy to know we didn't have to believe or do certain things to be loved. WE ALREADY WERE AND ARE, NO MATTER WHAT. The Light was extremely concerned and loving toward all people. I can remember looking at the people together and the Light asking me to 'love the people.' I wanted to cry, I felt so deeply for them . . . I thought, 'If they could only know how much they're loved, maybe they wouldn't be so scared or lonely anymore.'" Peggy P.

God's Love Is Unconditional. Period.

God's immense love for each and every one of us exists completely and eternally, without condition or question. No matter what we think, say, or do, God still loves us just the same. Sure we are going to make mistakes, and even some BIG blunders, but NDErs remind us that God loves us no matter what. This unconditional love obviously doesn't mean you should go out and rob a bank or harm anyone; that's not the point. God wants us to learn how to act in loving ways toward ourselves and others. But when we do screw up, which of course we will do many thousands of times throughout our life, God loves us regardless and always will, no matter what. Isn't that kind of unconditional love spiritually liberating and empowering? It encourages us to try to love others in the same complete and lasting way.

In discussing this chapter with others, most people regrettably come to realize that, other than their own children, the vast majority of their relationships are based more on conditional love than unconditional love. Many often cite their dogs, cats, and other pets as among the few relationships they have that are truly unconditional. Not surprisingly, many NDErs learned in heaven that our beloved pets are often in our lives to model unconditional love for us; and in case you're wondering . . . Yes, many NDErs talk about seeing their deceased pets in heaven in addition to friends and family members.

All About Love

Because love is so central to what God is all about, NDErs also tell us the entire universe is actually comprised of love and that it is the basis of all things. Hard to fathom but hear them out:

> "Love is, without a doubt, the basis of everything. Not some abstract, hard-to-fathom kind of love but the day-to-day kind that everyone knows—the kind of love we feel when we look at our spouse and our children, or even our animals. In its purest and most powerful form, this love is not jealous, or selfish, but unconditional." Dr. Eben Alexander

> "One of the most important lessons that was transferred to me by the Light is that love is all that matters . . . Every interaction is meaningless if love is not attached to it in some way. A prayer is meaningless without love. A sermon is meaningless without love. A religion is meaningless without love. If I had to sum up, the main lesson of my NDE is that God, or the Light, is a loving force that doesn't want people to harm others and wants us to feel joy and happiness in our lives. Love and kindness are the greatest gift we can give others. We are all a part of that Light, but we forget how to love because of fear." Tricia Barker

As Dr. Raymond Moody, the original pioneer of studying near-death experiences and the person who first coined the NDE term says, "There are a number of transformations we see from people who come back from near-death experiences. The most prominent one is that whatever they had been chasing before whether knowledge, or fame, or power, or money, or any of these other things, that when they come back, they say that the most important thing we can do while we're alive is to learn how to love. It's all about love and learning to love."

We Come to Earth to Learn Love

Because God is all about love and love is the key to everything, the overwhelming message NDErs share is that we come to earth to learn all about love. Our primary purpose on earth is to learn and practice love. It's as if our earthly lives were specifically created and constructed to provide us with millions of opportunities to learn and demonstrate love. We get to see and experience the power of love in action—and witness and feel the negative consequences of a lack of love. Learning exactly what it means to love ourselves and others, despite the many ups and downs of our earthly existence, despite interacting with people who sometimes act in unloving ways and even outright cruel ways, seems to be the primary purpose of life according to NDErs.

"Earthly life has been given to us to learn how to love! This is the message that was so infused in my consciousness when I was united in love with my Great Teacher. Every moment is an opportunity to learn that lesson . . . This profound wisdom is shared with you in the hope that you will choose to live lovingly while you have the many opportunities that appear before you. Perhaps listening to the vast numbers of individuals who have encountered the Divine down through the ages, saints, mystics, and sages of all religions, near-death experiencers, and others who have had spiritually transformative experiences, humanity can begin to comprehend the one message that echoes throughout the voices of all those experiencers—LOVE ONE ANOTHER!" Nancy Clark

"I learned that one of the main reasons we're here on Earth is simple: to love. That's it . . . Yes, we are here to enjoy our human selves, too, and perhaps even learn, but the heart of why we are here is love. While the message sounds pretty simple, as humans it's not always easy to put into practice. We're asked to love everyone regardless of their political persuasion, religious affiliation, their job title, annual income, skin color, age, and who they in turn love . . . It doesn't mean that we have to agree with everyone, but it does mean that through love and compassion, we work to overcome our differences and solve our problems, together, as one humanity . . . What is does mean, though, is that we recognize other people fully for who they are: someone who carried a spiritual spark of love at his or her core. It means that we show them respect, compassion, kindness, gentleness, and thus love." Nancy Rynes

"There is only one truly significant work to do in life, and this is love; to love nature, to love people, to love animals, to love creation itself, just because it is. To serve God's creation with a warm and loving hand of generosity and compassion—that is the only meaningful existence." George Rodonaia

"It occurred to me that the love from this Light was so overwhelming that this life must have something to do about learning to love like that. Or perhaps, even more to the point, learning to BE love like that." Dr. Ron Kennedy

Clearly, learning how to love and be love is our primary purpose for our human life. How can we learn to give and receive love no matter what situation we might face?

Earth School: A Spiritual Development Boarding School for Your Soul

Many NDErs talk about Earth as a kind of school or spiritual development camp we attend for the education of our souls. Like parents sending their kids away to boarding school, think of your earthly experience like God and you thinking it is a great idea for you to move away from your heavenly home for a while to attend a special boarding school (Earth) to learn much more about the important and complex topic of love. The primary curriculum and lesson plans for your evolving soul while at Earth School all revolve around love: how to be love, give love, and receive love. Every day you face numerous people, situations, challenges, and sometimes crises, where you can choose to respond with various forms of love like kindness, compassion, patience, tolerance, generosity, forgiveness—or respond with forms of fear like jealousy, anger, revenge, intolerance, or hatred. Through this special Earth School and all its varied experiences and lessons, you learn how to love others and how to love yourself. Not only do you learn it intellectually, you get the world's most intense and immersive internship experience in learning how to love by applying your education to your everyday existence and seeing the consequences of your choices.

"Earth life, I found, is designed as a university, a school where we learn from our choices and our mortal experiences. I recognized that my most painful experiences taught me the most. It was enlightening to understand the bigger eternal picture—to know that I was not a victim of circumstances . . . I learned that being charitable, patient, and forgiving toward others are some of the most important character traits to be acquired—learned in the school of life." Dr. Joyce Brown

"I was told that the earth is like a big school, a place where you can apply spiritual lessons you have learned and test yourself to see whether you can 'live' what you already know you should do. Basically the earth is a place where you can walk the walk and live the way it should be done. It was made clear to me that some people come to the earth to work on one or more aspects of themselves, while others come to also help the world as a whole . . . We're under continual pressure to make decisions that have a spiritual base. We may be taught on the 'Other Side' what we are 'supposed to do,' but can we live it under the pressures of the earth? From what I saw and hear on the Other Side, everything is about relationships and taking care of each other. We aren't expected to be perfect, but we are expected to learn. All of our experiences in a lifetime follow some sort of pattern, and we often learn the same lessons, but in a different way and under various circumstances. This is how we know what we are here to learn and test." Jean R.

"Earth is the hard part. This is the University of Earth. I was shown that I applied and was accepted to this school. God doesn't cause bad things to happen. Before we come here we pick our lessons and plan how we will live our lives—just like we do before we go to college. He is always

"The bottom line is that what it is all about is love—loving ourselves, loving each other, loving the Divine. There is no greater truth, no greater aspiration than this."

YVONNE KASON

with us. When we learn our lessons and finish the job we came here to do, we get to graduate and go back home. Whether we die quickly or slowly, we all have to review our lives before we get to graduate." Mary Beth Willi

Earth is not only a living laboratory where we can learn love theoretically, but actually put it into practice on a minute-by-minute basis—or not. We clearly get to see and emotionally feel the effects of our loving and unloving choices. We get to see the smile on the face of the elderly person when we help them carry their groceries and feel the warmth in their heart for helping out. We also get to see and feel the consequences of our unloving choices when we gossip about a friend and it gets back to them, hurting their feelings and damaging the friendship.

"The more we lend a hand to God by loving others, as well as ourselves, the more we grow spiritually. The problem is that most of us just don't know how to love, do we? We are full of pride, jealousy, lust, and an almost insatiable craving for money and power." Keith Keller

"A true heart which is motivated by loving compassion is what matters in life. Our job is to try to love one another no matter what. It matters very much if we can love or not because that is our job in this world. We must love! This is what we live for and it doesn't mean we must only love our spouse. It means we need to find out how to love our enemy because that is why we are here." Heather V.

"We were created to learn how to love. It takes more than a lifetime of experience to learn how to live lovingly. Every person will be given all the experiences one needs to learn how to love." Howard Storm

Handpicked Teachers for the School of Life

Further, many NDErs are convinced that certain people are purposely put in our lives so we can better learn how to love from them. It is as if God not only works with us to select the lessons and curriculum we should go through during the School of Life, but She also intentionally selects our teachers and instructors to best fit what we need to learn the most from life.

"God brought my wife and me together to learn love. I saw it in my life review. God gives us each other to learn how to love. They showed me how God had given us the opportunity to learn love by having children and raising them to be loving." Howard Storm

"I believe God brought my best friend into my life for us to learn about what true love is from each other. My children have taught me so much about love and all its challenges. Love is not an easy thing for me, as my nature is somewhat self-centered . . . I need more work on loving the 'unlovable.' That includes learning to love the 'unlovable' aspects of my-self." Karen M.

Don't Forget to Love Yourself Too

Understanding how to love others is obviously an important lesson to learn on earth but an often-overlooked aspect of learning how to truly love is loving ourselves as well. Many people initially balk at this idea. Love yourself? Isn't that selfish, egotistical, and narcissistic to love oneself? But before you jump to this conclusion, take a moment to hear what the NDErs have to say about self love when they got to see themselves through God's eyes:

"Until my NDE, I didn't love myself . . . I didn't realize that loving ourselves is actually the most important thing we can do, and that it's the key to liv-ing a blissful life . . . I saw myself through the eyes of God, and I realized that far from being unloved and unlovable, I was actually a beautiful child of the universe who was loved unconditionally, simply because I exist." Anita Moorjani

"I knew God was allowing me to see myself as He saw me. And in His eyes I was an absolutely perfect creation, and I would always be. All the things that happened to me on earth, all the bad decisions that caused me to hate myself—none of it mattered. I had believed that God couldn't possibly love me, not after what had been done to me, not after what I had done. But this belief was a lie, and God blasted the lie by showing me the intensity of His love for me . . . Seeing myself through God's eyes made me whole and set me free." Crystal McVea

"That being knew all of everything I ever was and loved me. Not just loved me but everything that defined me as myself, unique from any other bit of creation, was wonderful to it. It loved the way I was made, it loved that we were meeting, it loved me with all the love it had in it. Its love overpowered me. I knew that I was precious to it and treasured by it. I was perfectly what I was supposed to be and it loved me just that way. If I was a dia-mond, I was flawless, perfectly cut, beyond beautiful. I could not be loved more by that being. Not one thing in me needed to be changed for that being to love me. I was perfect—in its eyes—as I was made. I felt it think at me, 'As I made you, I did you perfectly!' With joy, it loved me, as I was, completely. I 'knew' that being loved me just as I was. I did not need to change one thing to be perfect. I was perfect to it. I knew it felt a true joy in being with me. I felt like it was just bursting with happiness because I was there. It was beyond glad to see me; it loved me. It thought I was just perfectly made and was thrilled that we were together . . . That huge and powerful entity made me feel like being with me made its life worth living, complete." D.S.Weiler

From God's important perspective, we are all so lovable. Despite our negatively skewed human viewpoint that typically focuses on our faults and imperfections, God doesn't care if we've gained a few pounds, lost some hair, or forgot to send a birthday card to a friend. God sees us for the wonderful people we are despite our human follies and foibles. She intentionally made us this imperfect way as humans but loves us all the same. We too need to cut ourselves some slack and better learn to love, care for, and appreciate the "perfectly imperfect" people we really are.

Don't Beat Yourself Up—Imperfect Beings Who Are Loved Perfectly

So many people find it much easier to love others than they can themselves. Some struggle to love themselves because their parents sent them direct or indirect messages that they weren't lovable. Others struggle to love themselves because they don't measure up to society's ideal of the perfect person, man/woman, spouse, friend, etc. They consistently dwell on their weight, wrinkles, knobby knees, or frizzy hair. Still others are in romantic and marital relationships that generate and perpetuate feelings of unworthiness. Others struggle to love themselves because of their own perfectionistic standards where they believe they are never good enough. Whatever the case, so many people in today's world don't love themselves in the least bit. This debilitating belief and lack of self love is at the core of serious challenges like depression, alcoholism, eating issues, suicide, self-mutilation, etc.

> "I can see the beauty of God so easily in others all around me, but it is much more difficult to see God's beauty in myself. I find, even now, I have to remind myself that I am special and that I am beautiful. Each and every one of us is special to God. He made us; He is in us. He doesn't make mistakes and he doesn't make junk. To Him we are all important, we are all beautiful. He sees us with perfect love. We are imperfect beings who He loves perfectly. Perfect love makes our souls shine so beautifully. What I had to learn was that real beauty shines from deep within the soul. External beauty fades with time, but real beauty comes from inside and never fades because it is internal and eternal. To God, I am me; that's all, just me. In His eyes, I am a perfect being 'just me'. My worth is in being who God made me to be. I don't have to make everyone else happy. What God wanted me to know was that He is always happy with me. What I have to do is be happy with myself and find Joy in my life." Sharon M.

> "I used to be a person who beat myself up for my mistakes. I used to feel that I wasn't good enough or smart enough or accomplished enough in

life. But now I realize that God accepts me for who I am and that I don't have to be an accomplished person by human standards. God's ways are not our ways. God doesn't judge us by our credentials or academic accreditations, certificates, or social status. God knows us for who we are in spirit." Sandy B.

We need to heed the messages sent to us by God and the NDErs that loving ourselves is not only permissible, it's absolutely essential. Without self love, we will continually feel bad about who we are and get stuck in an unhealthy cycle of despair and depression. Without self love, we won't feel worthy to contribute our precious gifts to the world. Without self love, we won't have the strength or stamina to fully love others. If we are going to love others, we have to first find it within ourselves.

"How many of us truly love ourselves? How many of us accept both our dark and light sides with compassion? How many of us look in the mirror and see a spiritual being staring back at us in our reflection? Each of us deserves to have the love, compassion and kindness of at least one person: ourselves. Unfortunately, loving ourselves may be the hardest task of all . . .It may be easier to love an enemy, but loving ourselves is something we should all make a priority. In the end, if we can learn to love ourselves unconditionally, loving everyone else will be easier." Nancy Rynes

"When we love ourselves, we can finally come to a place where we no longer focus on our imperfections, but instead, focus on our gifts. I had focused on my imperfections my entire life. These same imperfections would bring me my greatest spiritual growth. In fact, for the first time, I could really see how I had it all backwards. I realized I had tried to change myself to become worthy when I was already valuable in God's eyes. How could I be myself once more? To love myself is not to judge myself—it is to forgive myself and it is where I will find myself . . . What I needed was to embrace love and appreciation for myself and dare to be me. Only when I could truly be myself would I be able to discover my true value and heal my life . . . Without loving myself first, I'd never be able to go on to truly love or help others on the level that God had planned for me. For the first time, I felt as if I didn't need to worry about anything other than being who God made me to be. It was such a sense of relief to feel that I was good enough and to believe it with my heart." Erica McKenzie, RN

Don't Let Others Determine Your Worth

Many of us don't love ourselves because we think we are not worthy of it. Too many of us determine our self worth by what we think others will think of us. We worry about their judgments of us.

"I had to learn that my worth as a human being isn't dependent on what others think of me or whether they were happy with me or not. I also needed to learn that happiness doesn't come from an external source. In order to be truly happy, it has to come from inside my own heart. I have to stop worrying about what everyone else thinks. I need to see His beauty in myself." Sharon M.

"Your time is limited so don't waste it living someone else's life. Don't be trapped by dogma which is living with the results of other people's thinking. Don't let the noise of others' opinions drown out your own inner voice. And most important, have the courage to follow your heart and intuition, they somehow already know what you truly want to become. Everything else is secondary."

Steve Jobs, Apple Founder

We need to stop worrying about what others might think of us and letting others determine our worth. We need to remember that each of us is on our own spiritual path and journey in this life and we need to be comfortable being ourselves. We need to see ourselves the way God sees us.

Speaking of how God sees us, our last section of this chapter includes a rare, sneak peak at the all-important questions God will ask us as we stand at the gates of heaven . . . Curious what they will be?

What Are the Questions on God's Final Exam?

If you thought final exams in school were stressful, imagine having to answer directly to God at the end of your life! Talk about pressure! Wouldn't you love to somehow know exactly what the questions were ahead of time so you could prepare accordingly and be ready for your toughest test?

Because Earth is a school, we are evaluated on how much we have truly learned from all of our life's coursework and experiences. At the end of our human life, we all take Life's Final Exam, with God asking the probing and penetrating questions and the angels proctoring the test. During this comprehensive Final Exam covering absolutely every facet of our existence, we examine our entire life and all the lessons we learned through what many call a Life Review, which we will discuss in great detail in the Choose Compassionately chapter. Do you wonder what God's questions will be on the most important FINAL EXAM you will ever take? Our NDE friends reveal the exact questions they were asked—the same ones each of us will eventually be asked when we too take God's Final Exam.

> "What have you done for your fellow man? Had I given as much love as I had taken? Did I practice random acts of kindness? Was I responsible for making people feel good just for the sake of feeling good? These are the things on which I reflected." Dannion Brinkley

> "What have I done with my life? Where was my life going? What had I done to show love of God, love of my neighbor, love of myself? What had I done to be of service to mankind? These were the important questions I would have to consider." Ned Dougherty

> "A great question then emanated from Him to me so strongly it completely penetrated my being. 'In life, what did you do with what you had?' Rapidly the question engulfed me, commanding an answer. I began answering defensively with reasons and excuses, as I had in life when I felt I was being called to task for failure to reach a goal. I believed my excuses were good reasons to explain why I hadn't accomplished more: my difficult childhood, others getting in my way, my poor health, a broken home, my continual strife with my mother, lack of opportunities, and my growing family of children who held me back . . . I was stopped short in my thinking as I felt all my excuses melting in this Light of Truth. I felt the thoughts and words coming from this Being of Love and Light. 'The question has nothing to do with what you did not have in life or with your burdens or faults or problems. But rather, in life what did you do with what you did have?' I could not rely on or blame anyone else; this question was directed solely at me. I was being measured against no one else—I stood alone, on my own. What did I do with my life, with what I had, my opportunities, my time on earth? What had I done with what I did have?" Dr. Joyce Brown

> "Every detail of twenty years of living was there to be looked at. The good, the bad, the high points, the run-of-the-mill. And with this all-inclusive view came a question. It was implicit in every scene and, like the scenes themselves, seemed to proceed from the living Light beside me. What did you do with your life? It was obviously not a question in the sense that He was seeking information, for what I had done with my life was in plain view . . . Hadn't I ever gone beyond my own immediate interests, done anything other people would recognize as valuable? At last, I located it, the proudest moment of my life: 'I became an Eagle Scout!' Again, words seemed to emanate from the Presence beside me: 'That glorified you . . . What have you done with your life to show Me?' Already I understood that in my first frantic efforts to come up with an impressive answer, I had missed the point altogether. He was not asking

about accomplishments and awards. The question, like everything else proceeding from Him, had to do with love. How much have you loved with your life? Have you loved others as I am loving you? Totally? Unconditionally?'" Dr. George Ritchie

"God asked me, He said, 'Let me ask you one question. Have you ever loved another person the way you have been loved here?' The love I had received in that time was so overpowering—I had never felt anything like it so I answered God honestly. I said, 'No, it is impossible, I am just a human, you are God.' He gave me the illusion of a sweet protective chuckle. He then said, 'Mary, you can do better.'" Mary Jo Rapini

"The most important criterion for judging my life review was this: How well had I used my life to love myself and others? Was I a Light bearer, or a Light extinguisher?" Nancy Clark

"To what degree have you learned to love?" Jeff Olsen

Notice a common theme here? God's Final Exam questions have nothing to do with the amount of money in our bank account, the size of our house, or how many awards we might have won. NDErs tell us the value and significance of our time on earth all comes down to one thing: how well we have loved. Ultimately, God wants and challenges us to be love, give love, and receive love in everything we do. Earth is then indeed a spiritual development school where we experientially learn how to more fully and unconditionally love ourselves and others. It is our primary purpose in coming here and, in the end, we judge and grade ourselves on how well we have truly learned to give and receive love as we will discuss more fully Chapter 5.

Hopefully after seeing and contemplating the Final Exam questions that God will sooner or later ask you about your life, you too are more aware of and committed to ways you might share more love with the world. Rather than be surprised by the questions or wait until the end of your life to try to cram for them, why not ask yourself the same questions now and honestly answer them.

"After my experience, I understood that I was being challenged to extend love, compassion, and kindness to everyone." Nancy Rynes

"I felt compelled to ask . . . 'Why didn't I do more for You? Why didn't I accomplish more in Your name? Why didn't I talk more about You? Why didn't I do what you asked me to do?' It's not that I felt regret—regret is a negative emotion, and there is nothing negative in heaven—it's that I love God so immensely I felt like He deserved so much more from me." Crystal McVea

Love the One You're With

Rather than being overwhelmed by the challenge of loving others, it is simpler and more manageable than most of us think. In Howard Storm's NDE, Jesus told him the way to positively change the world was to simply love the person you are with.

> "Jesus: The way I want you to change the world is by loving the person you are with.
>
> Howard Storm: Wait a minute, that's a contradiction. You want me to change the world but you just want me to love the person I'm with?
>
> Jesus: Yes, that's the plan; that's The Big Plan . . . If you love the person you're with, then that person will go out and love the person they're with, and they will go out and love the person they're with and it will be like a chain reaction and love will conquer the world and everyone will love one another. That's God's Big Plan." Howard Storm
>
> "It's great that we serve the poor and feed the hungry and clothe the naked and do all the blessed things that Jesus talked about, but if you can't love the people that you're near, then you're not doing your job." Peter Panagore

With love at the center, Jesus simply asks us to "love the person you're with." While it sounds overly simplistic and too good to be true, God's Big Plan works if we can consistently understand and unconditionally apply exactly what it means with all people, in all settings, under all circumstances. Love the one you're with whether it is your spouse, child, relative, friend, neighbor, co-worker, pet, countryman, and even your enemy. By fully and unconditionally loving whomever we are with at each moment, we extend God's love out in to the world and inspire that person to want to pass along that same love to everyone they meet. When everyone truly loves the person they are with, without conditions, it brings the amazing power of love that NDErs are overwhelmed by in heaven down to earth for everyone to enjoy and share. As Jesus said, "Love one another, as I have loved you." (John 13:34)

"Every time I wonder who I should love and
for how long I should love them,
God continues to whisper to me: Everybody, always."
Bob Goff, Author of *Everybody Always*

With love firmly in place as the foundation or our lives, we move on to the next Life-Changing Lesson in our next chapter—Live Fearlessly . . .

LOVE UNCONDITIONALLY | MAJOR LESSONS

- God's love for everyone is intense, immense, and indescribable

- God's love is universal and unconditional—there are no strings attached

- Love is the basis of everything in heaven

- We come here to earth to learn all about love

- God handpicks the various people in our lives to be our teachers

- We must learn to love ourselves as well as others

- God's Final Exam questions revolve around how we learned to love ourselves and others

- No matter who is around you, love the one you're with

2.
LIVE FEARLESSLY

*"Every choice you make is either an expression
of love or an expression of fear.
There is no other choice."*

A Course in Miracles

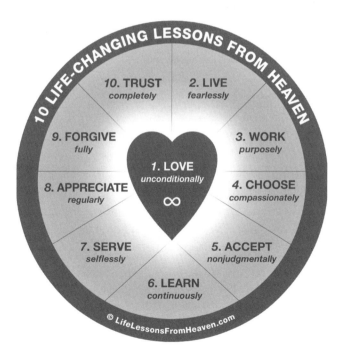

NDEr FEATURE

Anita Moorjani: "Go Out and Live Your Life Fearlessly"

Anita Moorjani admittedly lived much of her life out of fear. She feared failing, not being good enough, disappointing others, especially her family, and she certainly feared illness, especially cancer. This chronic state of fear Anita learned in her NDE contributed to her actually getting cancer (Hodgkin's Lymphoma). With lemon-sized tumors throughout her body, Anita was comatose and in total organ failure from end-stage cancer. Doctors thought her death was only a matter of hours. Anita drifted out of her body during her NDE and met her deceased father and deceased friend in heaven. They told her she needed to stop fearing what others thought of her, love herself more, and live life fully and fearlessly. Anita miraculously survived from the brink of death and fully recovered within a few weeks of her NDE, astounding her doctors, family, and friends. She now speaks around the world and encourages everyone to Live Fearlessly through her talks and books *Dying to Be Me* and *What If This is Heaven*. You can learn more about Anita's jaw-dropping story at www.anitamoorjani.com

Fears Often Rule and Restrict Our Lives

FEARS . . . We all have them—and most of us, lots of them! Whether they are the more typical fears of death, failure, public speaking, heights, enclosed spaces, open spaces, darkness, spiders, snakes, dogs, flying, drowning, needles, germs, clowns, etc., or the more rare fears of balloons, books, plants, trees, and even fog, as human beings we all deal with our own set of frightening fears and phobias. Before their NDEs, like us, most NDErs lived their lives primarily out of fear.

> "Before my NDE, I suffered a lot. I made myself small so others could feel big and I lived from a place of fear. I feared illness, not being good enough, I was a people pleaser. Everything I did and every decision I made came from a place of fear. That contributed to my suffering and getting cancer."
> Anita Moorjani

> "I understood what had become the greatest block to my growth in life: fear. It had plagued me all my years, had stopped my progress, cut short my attempts at working through problems. Fear had limited my enjoyment of life and it was blocking me now." RaNelle Wallace

So many of us live our lives based on unfounded fears or fear things that will never happen to us. Sure some fears are real and legitimate. We do need to fear things that could cause us bodily harm and injury and obviously need to protect ourselves against them. However, many of the fears we concoct, feed, and end up controlling our lives are merely illusions that exist only inside of our heads. Many fears are psychological in nature as opposed to real physical threats. As Mark Twain said, "I've had a lot of worries in my life, most of which never happened."

> "If I knew how much time I'd spent in my life fearing things that never happened, I would be stunned, I'm sure . . . At this point, I've probably spent years fearfully worrying about one thing or another. Yet, when I think back on it, a good 98 percent of what I was worried about never came to pass. And if the other 2 percent did come to pass, it just kept right on passing without too much consequence—or even left me better off than before."
> Robert Kopecky

"The most difficult times for many of us are the ones we give ourselves."
Pema Chodron, Buddhist Teacher

Facing My Own Fears of Publishing this Book
To be fully transparent and candid with you regarding my own fears, I struggled immensely in publishing this book since some people consider NDEs a strange, "fringe" topic. I was highly concerned about how people would view me both personally and professionally and wondered if they would lose respect for me or want to disassociate themselves from me. I battled these fears for over two years as I kept the manuscript shrouded in secrecy. I finally realized I was selfishly looking out only for myself based on my own self-created fears rather than willingly sharing these life-changing insights with others. Despite my fears, I eventually followed the strong and unrelenting calling of my heart and soul rather than worrying and obsessing so much about the opinions of others. Through much difficult soul searching, I finally felt like the 10 Life-Changing Lessons in this book were more important to share with the world than whether certain people liked, understood, or respected me. It was a prolonged, hard-fought "Battle Royale" in my own mind to finally overcome the formidable fear that held me and this book hostage for so long. The next quote inspired my critical breakthrough and inspired both me and this book to blossom.

*"And the day came when the risk to remain tight in a bud
was more painful than the risk it took to blossom."*
Elizabeth Appell, Author

So many people's lives are ruled, restricted, and unfortunately ruined by fear. Like I did for so long, millions of people remain bound up in a bud rather than taking the risk to fully blossom. NDErs learn in heaven that life is meant to be experienced, enjoyed, and lived all out—not feared or limited. How many of your own unfounded or made up fears have steered you in a direction that limited your life? How many times have you let fear dictate your decisions?

The numerous fears we experience cause anywhere from a bit of mild discomfort to full-blown panic attacks and even agoraphobia. Let's look at three ways fear holds us back from living an exciting and meaningful life so we can find ways to break through them and overcome our fears.

3 PRIMARY PROBLEMS WITH FEAR

1. Fear Holds Us Back and Limits Us

2. Fear Creates Fake Masks and Personas

3. Fear Makes Us Sick

1. Fear Holds Us Back and Limits Us

Fear limits us from being what we could be. Our fears become self-imposed shackles that hold us back and keep us from living a fun and fulfilling life. We settle for the safe path rather than the one that truly calls our soul and connects with our heart—the one that aligns with our true passion and purpose in life. If we live our lives primarily out of fear, we end up stifling ourselves with regrets because we settle for the easy and accepted route instead of breaking through, bucking the establishment, going for it, and building an exciting, fun, and fulfilling life that reflects our passions and shares our gifts with the world.

"Why do you stay inside when the door is wide open?"
Rumi, Sufi Poet

> "Most adults have the capability to live much better and much larger lives than we currently live. Often we allow others to dictate to us what we should do based on their own dysfunctions and fears. We allow society or religions to tell us what profession to enter instead of following the calling in our hearts . . . We allow the past to haunt our present by giving it too much weight and hanging on to it for dear life rather than letting go. We let irrational and non-existent fears to make our decisions for us. Any of these things can keep us from living our best lives . . . we each need to do what it takes to overcome our own learned and self-perpetuated inadequacies, our own fears, and our own judgments in order to live the amazing lives Spirit would love for us to live. We have everything inside of us or at our disposal to live loving, beauty-filled, glorious, full lives. The only thing really standing in our way is ourselves. Our own preconceived ideas and fears limit us. Many of us fall into the trap of thinking 'small,' of not believing that we have the capacity to live the full lives that our hearts crave. Instead we settle for a life on autopilot, one that is much less fulfilling than our hearts long for us to live. Our ideas of what life should be like, how this should work out, how people should be—these all limit us and keep us from living our lives to the fullest." Nancy Rynes

2. Fear Creates Fake Masks and Personas

Not only do fears limit us, they also are the root cause of us creating fake masks and false personas—inauthentic outer versions of ourselves because inwardly we fear being our real self is not enough; we fear we are not lovable enough, smart enough, attractive enough, etc. We hide our "perfectly imperfect" real self to others because we are afraid they won't like us or want to be seen with us.

> "I was a people pleaser and feared disapproval, regardless of the source. I bent over backward to avoid people thinking ill of me; and over the years, I lost myself in the process. I was completely disconnected from who I was or what I wanted, because everything I did was designed to win approval—everyone's except my own." Anita Moorjani

> "We spend a lot of time creating a persona so someone will either like us or leave us alone. Fear is one of the motivators to create this cloak, or persona." David Bennett

Whether we realize it or not, we often put up fake fronts by acting in certain ways, dressing to impress, applying makeup to cover up perceived imperfections, posting doctored pictures on social media, undergoing plastic surgery, embellishing our resumes, etc., all in an effort to appear worthy, desirable, younger, sexier, and as "perfect" as possible so we can win friends, spouses, jobs, etc. All of this pretending is tedious and tiresome and makes us live inauthentic lives. It is tough and disingenuous to be someone you're not just to hope people will like the fabricated you—not the real you. Even though fear motivates us to put on a persona to try to please others and protect us from our fears, ultimately we will stand transparent before God, perfectly imperfect.

"From one point of view we human beings can be characterized as creatures who spend a great deal of time hiding behind various masks. We seek inner security through money or power; we pride ourselves on our social class, the degree of our education, the color of our bodies . . . We adorn our bodies with clothes; we hide our inner most thoughts and certain of our deeds from the knowledge of others. However, in the moments around the time of death all such masks are necessarily dropped." Dr. Raymond Moody

"I felt totally exposed and transparent before God. You can wear masks before other people but you can't wear a mask before God." Ian McCormack

Rachel Farnsworth, known as the Stay at Home Chef at www.stay-athomechef.com, is an excellent example of a person who is not willing to succumb to society's warped, externally-based standard of beauty by changing her physical appearance to please others. Responding to a mean-spirited commenter on her blog who rudely suggested she dye her gray hair so she wouldn't "look like such an old hag," the 31 year-old Rachel, who has a rare autoimmune disorder that means she probably won't live to 70 said, "Every sign of aging that I have is a sign that I am still alive. A lot of people don't get the privilege to ever live to be old. And I probably won't either, which means that I don't have time to waste criticizing myself, and I don't have time to waste criticizing other people. I care a lot more about what my life is like right now. It has taken me more than a decade of really hard work to change how I felt about myself. I have a crooked nose with a hook in it, I've got freckles and bags under my eyes, I've got a yellow tint to my skin, I have hairs that grow in places I don't want them to. I fluctuate in weight and carry more pounds than I'd like to, sometimes. I've got wrinkles, and stretch marks, and sunspots, and scars all over my body. And I also have gray hair. And I love all of it. It's taken me a long time to learn that."

Rachel obviously learned to accept and love herself, gray hair and all, rather than create a false look and persona to try to please others. She continues, "The world needs people who will build each other up instead of tearing each other down. The world needs more men like my husband, who are willing to encourage women to embrace who they are. The world needs more women who are willing to rock their bodies exactly the way that God made them. Be that person." See Rachel's powerful and inspiring video at: thestayathomechef.com/be-that-person/

Similarly, men also put on masks in an effort to hide their insecurities and fears. Lewis Howes, author of *The Masks of Masculinity*, identifies 9 Masks of Masculinity including:

1. The Stoic Mask—insists that men should never show or share their feelings

2. The Athlete Mask—insists that men must be physically superior to their peers

3. The Material Mask—insists that men pursue material wealth and possessions

4. The Sexual Mask—insists that men must be promiscuous and successful with women

5. The Aggressive Mask—insists that men show aggression when they are angry

6. The Joker Mask—insists that men use humor to deflect and dodge real issues

7. The Invincible Mask—insists that men can never have anything go wrong

8. The Know-it-all Mask—insists that men be intellectually superior to their peers

9. The Alpha Mask—insists that men portray an image of dominance over their peers

Many men feel like they must continually put on and hide behind one or more of these Masks of Masculinity to be considered a "Real Man" by their peers, women, and/or society in general. However, these masks, which attempt to cover up deep-seated fears, often keep men from experiencing real emotions, real connection, and knowing and appreciating who they really are.

3. Fear Makes Us Sick

The dis-ease caused by fear also causes disease. When we are under continual stress and anxiety our mind and body cannot rest and relax. With our mind on continual high alert and in stress mode, our body releases cortisol and other stress-related chemicals that create a tremendous wear and tear on us. When we are under high and/or chronic stress, we are much more likely to develop a host of physical ailments like common colds and acne as well as much more serious diseases like ulcers, heart disease, and cancer.

> "The most frequent question people ask me is why I think I got cancer. I can sum up the answer in one word: fear. What was I afraid of? Just about everything, including failing, being disliked, letting people down, and not being good enough. I also feared illness, cancer in particular, as well as the treatments for cancer. I was afraid of living, and I was terrified of dying." Anita Moorjani

Of course fear doesn't cause all cancers and Anita acknowledges that in her books and talks. However, excessive fear and stress do often contribute to and exacerbate illnesses and diseases. People under stress are also much more likely to overeat, drink alcohol, smoke, and engage in other unhealthy behaviors. It is a vicious cycle that creates a whole host of problems. Fear is a natural and normal human emotion—but one we don't have to let rule our lives.

Break Through Your Fears Rather Than Running or Hiding from Them

NDErs encourage us to courageously examine, move towards, dismantle, and break through our many fears and eventually embrace them rather than run away from them. Instead of being petrified of and paralyzed by them, our fears are really signposts and doorways to some of our greatest personal and spiritual growth. As author Mary O'Malley says, "Whatever is in the way IS the way!" As scary as it seems, we are encouraged to find the courage within to tackle and overcome our fears rather than staying stuck in them.

> "Everyone is afraid and it's okay to be afraid. It takes great courage to walk through the fear and do it anyway. Victims stay stuck in the fear. You will never truly be who you are and realize your full potential if you remain stuck in fear." Mary Beth Willi

"Feelings like disappointment, embarrassment, irritation, resentment, anger, jealousy, and fear, instead of being bad news, are actually very clear moments that teach us where it is that we're holding back. They teach us to perk up and lean in when we feel we'd rather collapse and back away. They're like messengers that show us, with terrifying clarity, exactly where we're stuck. This very moment is the perfect teacher, and, lucky for us, it's with us wherever we are."

Pema Chodron, Buddhist Teacher

You Can Choose Love or Fear

Ultimately, earthly life gives us the chance to respond to life's stresses and predicaments with love or fear. Because we have the gift of free will and are not forced to act in certain ways due to God's unconditional love for us, it is totally up to us to choose how we want to respond.

"There are two basic motivating forces: fear and love. When we are afraid, we pull back from life. When we are in love, we open to all that life has to offer with passion, excitement, and acceptance."

John Lennon, Singer

Unfortunately, if we see ourselves only as frail and feeble humans, fear is the easy, default choice in many situations. It is easy to close ourselves off to difficult situations and people. It is easy to put the blame on others for problems rather than looking within ourselves to see how we might have contributed to the situation. It is easy to stay locked inside our self-imposed comfort zones and avoid going near, much less opening, the doors of opportunity that are all around us.

But this fear-based choice usually worsens and/or prolongs the problem and encourages others to respond in kind with more fear. Choices made from fear cause us to adopt a bunker mentality where we feel attacked and defensive—like the whole world is out to get us. That's exactly what marketers want you to feel so they can sell you their products (clothes, makeup, security systems, guns, etc.) to try to overcome your own irrational fears. Fear-based choices often lead to misunderstandings, arguments, and even outright conflict and war.

2. Live Fearlessly

"In my near-death experience it could not have been more obvious or more simple: Our purpose is to overcome fear, each one of us. We are supposed to utilize faith. We are supposed to let go, let God, trust God. The whole point is LOVE; to remember to choose LOVE instead of fear."

AMPHIANDA BASKETT

"When I was in that near-death state, the clarity was so incredible that I was not supposed to live in fear. I was supposed to make my choices based out of love and passion and I wasn't supposed to be suffering. And what I felt was, 'Why didn't I know this before? Why aren't we taught this as children?' That's when I realized that most of our suffering comes from being conditioned to believe in and do the wrong things . . . Another big thing I learned was to make choices from a place of love instead of a place of fear." Anita Moorjani

"When we act out of love, we create energy that is empowering and that raises the understanding to higher levels. Fear and all of the emotions that fall into its category like anger, resentment, no forgiveness, etc., are all destructive energies. They break down communication and growth toward higher realms where joy, peace, tranquility can be experienced." Teri R.

Choosing love is often the more difficult choice, but the one that does the most good if we see things from a spiritual perspective.

"I saw that God, in his non-judgment of us, lets us choose our own inner life path. The more that we move away from the spiritual love for ourselves and others, the more we move away from that which is the essence of God. He lets this be so, out of his unlimited capacity for complete and unconditional love. Part of that unconditional love is allowing all the use of free choice within our hearts. So therefore, we experience what we choose to carry within those hearts. God loves us enough to stand aside in that love and let us make our own choices." Deidre DeWitt-Maltby

Fearful Human Being or Formidable Spiritual Being?

One of the biggest reasons we have fear is how we see ourselves. Thus, one of the best ways to overcome our fears is to shift our perspective and paradigm to something greater. Many of us solely see ourselves as fearful, frail, and fallible human beings, which partly we are. However, because we come from God, we also have a spiritual side that is strong, powerful, and formidable. As Jesuit philosopher Pierre Teilhard de Chardin once said, "We are not human beings having a spiritual experience; we are spiritual beings having a human experience." NDErs tell us that we would be shocked at how powerful we really are when we fully understand our spiritual side that emanates from God Almighty.

"We are each amazing and powerful people buried there behind our fears and insecurities . . . Every person on Earth has amazing power and creativity. At our cores, we are shining beings of light, love, and energy who are living as humans in this time and place. Inside each one of us is a spiritual spark, a light-filled being capable of almost anything." Nancy Rynes

"There is nothing out there to fear. You are a divine, powerful being. We all are. We are all part of God. We are all part of love. That's who we are. We are the heart of God. And we are here to bring that to planet earth. To create heaven on earth. And we can do it. In love. That's why we are here." Ellen Dye

"We are the most beautiful creations. The human soul, the human matrix that we all make together is absolutely fantastic, elegant, exotic, everything. I just cannot say enough about how it changed my opinion of human beings in that instant. I said, 'Oh, God, I did not know how beautiful we are.' At any level, high or low, in whatever shape you are in, you are the most beautiful creation. You are." Mellon-Thomas Benedict

---

"Matter is energy. Energy is light. We are all Light Beings."

Albert Einstein, Physicist

The Statue of the Golden Buddha

Many years ago in a Thailand monastery there was a beautiful 10-foot tall, 10,000 pound statue of the Buddha made of pure gold. Unfortunately, the monks in the monastery got word that the Burmese Army had invaded their country and was on its way to raid the village. Fearing the Golden Buddha would be plundered and realizing they had little time to move the heavy statue, the monks quickly devised an ingenious plan to cover the Golden Buddha with clay to disguise its beauty in hopes the invaders would not realize its true value.

Sure enough, the Burmese Army soon ransacked the village, slaughtered all the monks, and took everything they saw of value. Because it was seemingly made of clay, the marauding army marched right past the statue and didn't touch or destroy it.

Almost 300 years later, in 1957 a group of Thai monks was asked to relocate the Buddha statue which they thought was made of clay. As they prepared to move it, one of the monks discovered a slight crack in the statue and spied a small gleam of light coming from it. Curious, he grabbed a hammer and chisel and carefully began chipping away at the clay. As he chiseled away the outer layer, the once drab statue grew brighter and brighter. To his utter amazement, he discovered the entire statue was actually made of gold that today is valued at over $200 million.

What looked to almost everyone on the outside as a basic, unremarkable, dull statue hid within a remarkably beautiful and highly valuable work of art. By covering up the statue with clay from the earth, the original monks disguised its immense beauty and worth right under people's noses causing them to ignore and disregard it. Only when one monk noticed a slim glimmer of light emanating from the statue and then painstakingly chipped away the outer layer of clay did people realize what an amazing treasure they actually had in their midst. How often do we too see ourselves only as the common clay-covered statue rather than glorious Golden Buddha within?

Now do you get the picture of how amazing our spiritual side really is? In every one of our souls is a fabulous, miraculous, powerful, golden piece of God, just waiting for us to recognize it and release it. Rather than seeing ourselves solely as feeble, frail, and fearful humans made seemingly of earthly clay, it's important we also understand and value our golden spiritual side as well. When confronted with earthly fears, we need to remember we are really strong spirits, made in God's likeness and image, who are fully equipped to take on and conquer life's challenges. We need to remember and see ourselves as formidable spiritual beings not mere feeble human beings. As Anne Frank once wrote, "Everyone has inside of him a piece of good news. The good news is that you don't know how great you can be! How much you can love! What you can accomplish! And what your potential is!"

The Hindu Legend of Discovering Your Divinity Within

According to an old Hindu legend, there was once a time when all human beings were gods, but they so abused their divinity that Brahma, the chief god, decided to take it away from them and hide it where it could never be found. Where to hide their divinity was the question. So Brahma called a council of the gods to help him decide. "Let's bury it deep in the earth," said the gods. But Brahma answered, "No, that will not do because humans will dig into the earth and find it." Then the gods said, "Let's sink it in the deepest ocean." But Brahma said, "No, not there, for they will learn to dive into the ocean and will find it." Then the gods said, "Let's take it to the top of the highest mountain and hide it there." But once again Brahma replied, "No, that will not do either, because they will eventually climb every mountain and once again take up their divinity." Then the gods gave up and said, "We do not know where to hide it, because it seems that there is no place on earth or in the sea that human beings will not eventually reach."

Brahma thought for a long time and then said, "Here is what we will do. We will hide their divinity deep in the center of their own being, for humans will never think to look for it there." All the gods agreed that this was the perfect hiding place, and the deed was done. And since that time humans have been going up and down the earth, digging, diving, climbing, and exploring–searching for something already within themselves.

"Finding yourself is not really how it works. You aren't a ten dollar bill in last winter's coat pocket. You are also not lost. Your true self is right there, buried under cultural conditioning, other people's opinions, and inaccurate conclusions you drew as a kid that became your beliefs about who you are. Finding yourself is actually returning to yourself. . . An unlearning, an excavation, a remembering of who you were before the world got its hands on you."

Emily McDowell, Artist

HOW DO YOU SEE YOURSELF?	
Fearful Human Being	**Formidable Spiritual Being**
Dull, unremarkable statue made of clay	Beautiful and valuable spirit made of gold
Human being having a spiritual experience	Spiritual being having a human experience
Cautious	Courageous
Separated from God's Love	Spark of God's Love
Fallible	Fabulous
Expiring	Eternal
Limited	Limitless
Passive	Powerful
Sinful	Sacred
Mundane	Magnificent
Isolated from everything	Interconnected with everything
Afraid to make a mistake	Excited to learn from experiences

*"There is no planet, sun, or star that could hold you
if you but knew who you are."*
Ralph Waldo Emerson, American Poet

Living with Little to No Fear Frees You

Living life with little to no fear is possible and frees you of many of the anxieties that limit you, cause you to fabricate a false self, and/or make you mentally exhausted and physically sick. Here's what the NDErs say about putting fear behind them after seeing that life, death, and the Afterlife are absolutely nothing to be afraid of.

> "I'm no longer scared of or worried about death. Actually, I'm not scared of or worried about much of anything anymore! I guess because I've died and it wasn't all that bad, not much of this world frightens me. This one aspect of my experience has liberated me from the burden of the fears and worries I carried with me for most of my life . . . I now realize that much of this drama that we deal with as humans isn't really all that important on a grand, spiritual scale, and in reality, we create most of it for ourselves anyway." Nancy Rynes

> "No longer having the fear of death offers incredible freedom, a freedom to live life unbridled and to its fullest, filled with joy and gratitude at each encounter and experience. Not fearing death also gives a sense of calm, which enables us to unwind; no longer caught up in the rat race." David Bennett

Doesn't it sound amazing to live freely without fear? You too can Live Fearlessly when you learn to break through your limiting fears, be your unique self and stop putting on masks, stop worrying yourself to death over unfounded fears, and see yourself as a powerful spiritual being who is ready, willing, and able to embrace and overcome every one of our human challenges.

"All healing is essentially the release from fear."
A Course in Miracles

Live Fully and Fearlessly

NDErs remind us to live fully and fearlessly. We need to confidently be the person we want to be, the person God wants us to be, and the person the world needs us to be.

"The most profound aftereffect of my NDE is that I now accept myself because of who I am. I am no longer bound by the preconceived restraints and conditions which others impose. I am no longer bound to do what others want; neither do I find the need to seek approval from others by measuring up to their standards. I have found a central core within me, a spirit, which knows what is best for me in all that I do. I trust this inner spirit and I listen to what it says, and I act on its directions. While I respect the opinions of others, while I appreciate the concerns of others for my well-being, I am no longer compelled to follow the dictates of others. I am secure with the inner knowledge of what is best for me. I no longer fear rejection because I do not seem to measure up to the expectations of others. I am growing, daily, in the knowledge that I am an individual unto myself and, as such, I am a fully functioning human being with a mind, a body, and a spirit of my own." Nel

"Our lives are huge gifts to be enjoyed, savored, and lived completely . . . Please don't waste this chance to savor your amazing life and all its nuances. Live your life wisely, lovingly, respectfully, and responsibly, but also fully in whatever way that means to you. Don't allow fear or others' desires for your life to stand in the way of making your life truly spectacular . . . We don't need to wait for heaven to experience love and beauty. We can create our own slice of heaven in our lives right now, and in doing so, we can bring a little of it into the lives of others too." Nancy Rynes

---

"Be fearless in the pursuit of what sets your soul on fire."
Jennifer Lee, Film Director

Every Successful Person Has Jumped!

Television host Steve Harvey has a tremendous book and video called *Jump* that my friend Cathy shared with me. Harvey reminds us that everyone experiences fear but successful people break through their fear and develop the courage to overcome it. He says, "I'm going to tell you something that every successful person in this world has done in his or her life or career. Every successful person has jumped! They have taken their hopes and dreams and took a leap of faith toward them. If you desire greatness in your life, eventually you are going to have to jump. You cannot just exist in this life and automatically find happiness. You have to live every moment to the fullest to achieve a life of abundance. If you are waking up thinking that there is more to your life than there is, believe that there is. But in order to get to that life of happiness and abundance, you are going to have to jump." Rather than let fear limit you, it is time to courageously jump.

"Start now. Start where you are. Start with fear. Start with pain. Start with doubt. Start with hands shaking. Start with voice trembling but start. Start and don't stop. Start where you are, with what you have. Just . . . start."

Ijeoma Umebinyuo, Nigerian Poet

How to Stop Living in Fear and Start Living Fearlessly

To summarize the main messages of this chapter, check out this table to help us apply the Live Fearlessly Life-Changing Lesson from Heaven:

STOP . . .	START . . .
living your life as a fearful human being	living your life as a formidable spiritual being
making choices from fear	making choices from love
limiting yourself	expanding your comfort zone
letting unfounded fears rule your life	realizing few of our fears ever really happen
fearing what others will think of you	appreciating your uniqueness and doing your thing
worrying yourself to death	trusting that all is well
taking life so seriously	having fun and enjoying the ride
turning to alcohol, drugs, smoking, eating	learning positive coping strategies
pulling back from life	opening to all that life has to offer
living fearfully	living fearlessly

"When I was in the other realm, where the layers upon layers of my values and beliefs were stripped away and I was left facing the truth of who I am at my core, I learned that two primary forces—love and fear—had been driving all my behaviors. One or the other of these two forces was behind every single action I ever took, and I could clearly see that I'd in fact spent most of my life being driven by fear, not by love. I understood with a sudden stunning clarity that to transform my life, whatever I said or did from that point on would need to come from a place of love instead of fear."
Anita Moorjani

2. Live Fearlessly

> *"Life begins at the end of your comfort zone."*
> **Neale Donald Walsch**, Author of *Conversations with God*

As you learn how to overcome your fears and Live Fearlessly, you are ready to take on your next spiritual assignment—to Work Purposely by discovering and living your life's unique and divinely inspired mission and purpose.

LIVE FEARLESSLY | MAJOR LESSONS

- Many of us live our lives out of fear

- Fear creates limits and regrets because we settle instead of breaking through our self-perceived barriers

- Fear creates masks and people-pleasing personas—we think we have to be a certain way to earn love, praise, attention, jobs, relationships, money, and be liked—we hide behind a false facade of success that is tough and tiring to maintain (keeping up with the Joneses)

- Fear fosters mental and physical disease

- Society, media, and some religious beliefs condition us to be fearful

- Most fear is false, exaggerated, irrational

- Life is not meant to be lived in fear—rather it should be lived in love

- Examine your fears and overcome them

- Know that deep down you are really a magnificent spiritual being with God-given gifts and talents who has willingly become human to see if you can know who you truly are

- Be yourself—be unique, be different, be who you really are

- Promise yourself to continually make decisions based on love and not fear

"Sometimes we allow fears to make our decisions for us . . . We allow fears of what others might think dictate the jobs we choose, the people we marry, or the places we live. We allow fear of failure to keep us from returning to school to finish our degree, or from writing that book we've been toying with for years. We're afraid of not having enough money or success and we choose careers that don't mesh with our true heart desires . . . Fear is an insidious and crazy thing, isn't it? Fear is a form of negative energy that sends ripples outward from us into the world. If we feel afraid, we'll act afraid and send that message through words and actions. Unfounded fears prevent us from truly enjoying the here and now of living this life. But examining our fears and respecting the message they are trying to tell us can be useful. We don't have to give in to the fear, but we can learn from it . . . Fear can help us if we use it wisely, but most of us allow unfounded fears to run our lives." Nancy Rynes

---

"Fear is going to be a player in your life, but you get to decide how much. You can spend your whole life imagining ghosts, worrying about your pathway to the future, but all there will ever be is what's happening here, and the decisions we make in this moment, which are based in either love or fear. So many of us choose our path out of fear disguised as practicality. What we really want seems impossibly out of reach and ridiculous to expect, so we never dare to ask the universe for it . . . My father could have been a great comedian, but he didn't believe that was possible for him, and so he made a conservative choice. Instead, he got a safe job as an accountant, and when I was 12 years old, he was let go from that safe job and our family had to do whatever we could to survive. I learned many great lessons from my father, not the least of which was that you can fail at what you don't want, so you might as well take a chance on doing what you love."

Jim Carrey, Actor/Comedian

3.
WORK PURPOSELY

"Here is the test to find whether your mission on Earth is finished: if you're alive, it isn't."

Richard Bach, Author

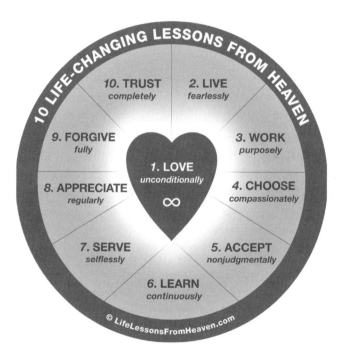

NDEr FEATURE

Dannion Brinkley: Saved by the Light

One of the more famous NDErs having appeared on *Oprah*, *The Tonight Show*, and *Larry King Live*, Dannion Brinkley had a rare total of three NDEs. Whoever said lightning doesn't strike the same place twice never met Dannion as he was hit by lightning twice, 23 years apart. His third NDE occurred during brain surgery. He relays the story of his first NDE in the *New York Times* bestselling book *Saved by the Light*, which was also made into a movie. A tough guy growing up and self-described jerk, his life changed significantly following his first NDE. He became a dedicated hospice volunteer and created the Twilight Brigade, a nonprofit organization of committed volunteers that provides end of life hospice care to thousands of dying veterans. Dannion wrote two other books about his NDEs including *At Peace in the Light* and *The Secrets of the Light*. You can learn more about Dannion and his story at www.dannionandkathryn.com

Born into this World with a Talent and a Task

NDErs are crystal clear that God has tasked each and every one of us with a special and specific purpose for our life on earth. Rather than just being here to hang out for several decades, twiddle our thumbs, punch a time clock, and die, God custom-designed each of us to do some of Her important work during our time here on earth and gave us the talents and aptitudes to achieve it.

> "Based on what I saw and heard in heaven, I believe every soul is born into this world with a talent and a task, a memory and a mission; everyone arrives with a gift and a goal. These talents and tasks are Spirit-given; they are our passports into the physical realm, for when properly expressed, they assure the continuation and evolution of the physical world . . . Through each of our efforts, as we put our talents to the wisest use, the world is made a more beautiful and harmonious place to be . . . Most of us were born with an abundance of gifts. One vital aspect of our physical journey is to consciously search for and fully develop these spiritually granted gifts for the purpose of manifesting the greatest potential for the good of all. Within this particular truth lies the greatest power . . . Comprehension and conscientious implementation of this truth literally puts you in control of your life and destiny . . . We are endowed with certain talents so that, in using them, not only do we find true happiness and meaning in life,

but we also authentically help others. Here again we see first-hand how everything in the universe is interrelated and interconnected, right down to the gifts we came into this world possessing. But the hitch in all of this is, how do you discover exactly what your personal gifts are? More than anything else, this process of discovery will hinge upon what you most sincerely want to accomplish in this lifetime . . . Your dreams and aspirations are the real clues that will lead you to your spiritual mission in this lifetime, a mission that can only be accomplished through the practical application of your inherent talents. In other words, whatever brings the greatest joy to your heart is the exact direction your life must follow." Dannion Brinkley

"'You committed yourself to giving your time and talents on Earth to further the work of the Lord. You need these people, and they need you. We are all dependent upon one another . . .' I saw that there was much I could do, sharing, sacrificing, offering what I have." RaNelle Wallace

Your Playing Small Doesn't Serve the World

Unfortunately, many of us are under the mistaken impression that our lives really don't matter. We don't often live with a deep sense of passion and purpose—looking forward to each day and eager to play our part and share our gifts. Instead, many of us sleep walk through life, do just enough to get by, waste away our days, squander our talents, and shortchange ourselves, our world, and God.

"If you're not doing what you're here to do you're like the walking dead. The walking dead are the millions and millions of people who are walking through their lives and they are not on point. They're off purpose. They're off course. They're the walking dead."

Oprah Winfrey, Talk Show Host

While some people worry about if there is life after death, the "walking dead" of the world should be more concerned about if there is actually life *before* death. If we sleep walk our way through life we aren't truly living but merely existing.

Marianne Williamson, author of *A Return to Love*, challenges us to courageously and fully live our lives and use our gifts to better serve the world: "Our deepest fear is not that we are inadequate. Our deepest fear is that we are powerful beyond measure. It is our light, not our darkness that most frightens us. We ask ourselves, 'Who am I to be brilliant, gorgeous, talented, and fabulous?' Actually, who are you not to be? You are a child of God. Your playing small doesn't serve the world."

Unfortunately, we sometimes struggle to find a critical sense of meaning and motivation in our lives. This mindset saps our enthusiasm and the energy of the people around us. We wander around aimlessly or waste time on trivial matters or mindlessly play games on our phones or binge watch series after series on Netflix or get lost in endless YouTube videos because we feel like our lives are going nowhere and we have nothing to contribute to the world.

> "I could have done more with my time on earth than I did . . . Time was to be used wisely and however it was spent, it could not be called back . . . I understood that each person has a definite purpose for living and only so much earth time to fulfill that purpose . . . I was filled with anguish for not having used my time on earth more productively . . . I knew that every day I lived on earth I had exchanged a day of my life's time for whatever I had chosen to do that day. Many days I had squandered my fortune of time and now I saw what I had thrown away. I had wasted precious time . . . Being in the presence of this Personage of Love and Light made me wish I had used every minute I had on earth planting love so I could reap the blessings." Dr. Joyce Brown

David Milarch's NDE and Life Purpose

Michigan native David Milarch had an NDE from kidney and liver failure. While on the Other Side he encountered two angels who showed him how our environment was being destroyed through deforestation. They told David he could make a huge difference by cloning the genes of the world's greatest, strongest, and heartiest trees. Despite scientists and tree experts telling him it couldn't be done, David and his family set out on their quest and created the Archangel Ancient Tree Archive. Over the course of 20 years, the Archangel Ancient Tree Archive replicated and reforested many of the world's oldest trees including redwoods and sequoias, 96% of which had been deforested. They have cloned over 140 species of trees and planted over 10,000 trees across the country. David's remarkable story is documented by *New York Times* author Jim Robbins in the book, *The Man Who Planted Trees*. "I'm pretty sure what I saw on the Other Side was an archangel. And when they call on you, they need something done, and you're gonna do it because they ask with positive attention and love . . . One person can make a difference, a big difference . . . Find your passion, go towards it, and don't look back," said David about his divinely inspired tree-saving and planet-saving mission.

*"If the success or failure of this planet, and of human beings,
depended on how I am and what I do;
How would I be? What would I do?"*

Buckminster Fuller, Architect and Author

We Need You!

Like David and everyone else, you too are here for an important reason. Don't waste your precious time or squander your opportunity to
make a real difference here on earth. As multiple NDErs have said: *You
play a critical and essential part in this world.* People's lives will not be
the same without your contribution! WE NEED YOU! Your family
needs you! Your friends need you! Your office needs you! Your community needs you! The world needs you! No one else has the special ability
to contribute what only you can. DON'T LEAVE US HANGING!
Don't let false fears, frustrations, or failures prevent you from playing
your particular vital role.

> "If one of us were to fail in his or her mission, all of us would be hurt in
> some way. If one succeeded, we would all benefit. It was as if we were
> part of a puzzle with millions of pieces. It was put together perfectly, but
> if one piece were removed, we all would be lacking and would not be
> content until that piece was found and returned to its rightful place. We
> needed each other. We still do, and always will." RaNelle Wallace

> "I now know I have to play my part in contributing to this world like ev-
> erybody else. I have to fulfill my mission before I can take the heavenly
> reward . . . God wants me to use my talents for Him, to help people get
> beyond this world and know Him. To give them the hope I have. And the
> worse this world gets, the more important that is." Karola

> "I was floored at how important we all are to God—especially how impor-
> tant I was to God. I didn't think He knew I even existed. All the years I was
> beating myself up and His question to me was, 'Why would I go through
> all the trouble to make you just the way you are if I wanted you to try and
> be like someone else?' No one else could do the job I came here to do the
> way He wanted me to do it! That is why it is so important that we not be
> so judgmental of each other. Some of us are here to teach, some to learn,
> and some to do both." Mary Beth Willi

> "I know, that whomever is reading this, you are deeply loved. Your life is
> deeply important to God. God is greater than anything you could ever
> even fathom—too great for me to even experience. I just felt the presence
> of God and His love. You, my dear person reading this, are important. Your

3. Work Purposely

"You are here to enable the divine purpose of the Universe to unfold. That is how important you are!"

ECKHART TOLLE

life is critical. The love you have inside you is beautiful and brilliant and it is needed on this Earth. You can change this world with your love, which is entirely particular to you only. You have your own song." Heather V.

"I am not afraid. I was born to do this!"
Joan of Arc, French Military Leader

YOU are on a Divine Mission from God!

As the numerous NDErs remind you: *You are on a Divine Mission from God!* Let that sink in for a minute . . .

Everyone is on a Divine Mission from God—or they wouldn't be here. The Creator of All Things, Lord of Lords, Yahweh, Great Spirit, Source, I Am, etc., has a specific job for you to do in this Universe, or "dharma" as Hindus, Buddhists, and Sikhs call it. You were indeed born to do this!

Like She did with Mary Beth, Heather, Juliet, David, and all the NDErs you have heard from, God factored you (yes, little old you) into Her Master Plan and wants you to play your part. You get to co-create with the Creator of All Things to make the world a better place simply by being yourself! You really are that important in the grand scheme of things!

By playing this special, custom-designed role just for you and serving your unique purpose, you not only help God, you help others, and you help yourself grow and develop spiritually. It's a Win/Win/Win proposition—what could be better than that?

So what are YOU waiting for? Our Universe needs you, your family needs you, your neighbor down the street needs you, your community needs you, and God needs you to discover your purpose and do your part!

"Don't be afraid of your dreams. Your dreams have chosen you for a reason. Because you are the perfect person to fulfill them. Yes, YOU. You just have to say yes. And then the universe will respond . . . Playing small serves no one. When you shine your light, it reminds those around you of the very same light inside themselves. You being yourself fully is the greatest gift you can give the world."
Kute Blackson, Author of *You. Are. The. One.*

---

3. Work Purposely

Don't Think Your Part is Big Enough?

Whether large or small, your role is critical. You may not have the notorious and seemingly glamorous role of governor of your state, pastor of your church, principal of your school, or president of your company, but even so your role is just as valuable and important.

> "Each of us has a purpose that is as critical as everyone else's; there are no 'small or insignificant' lives; we are all connected. Like having a small role in a play; it might not be as noticeable as the lead but the play as a whole needs every player to do their specific and equally critical role . . ." Lisa B.

No matter what your part might be, whether it is a custodian for a miniscule non-profit organization or CEO for a massive Fortune 500 company, your role is critical. Lisa continues:

> "I knew I had a clear purpose and was shown this purpose so I could understand how needed I was . . . But what I connected with was just the importance of my life purpose . . . And that I could only serve this purpose . . . I feel like a spiritual being who is on a human mission." Lisa B.

A Spiritual Being on a Human Mission

Once again NDErs remind us about the powerful and paradigm-shifting thinking of seeing ourselves as magnificent spiritual beings having a human experience rather than the other way around. We can't see ourselves as merely feeble humans—but strong spiritual beings with a specific and mission-critical purpose for our time here on earth. We are "spiritual beings on a human mission" as Lisa so inspiringly puts it. There are people in your corner of the world who need your help . . .

> "You have a specific purpose. You're going to see people that I'll never see. You're going to touch lives that I'll never touch. You're on your own mission. And no one else can fulfill your duties but you. That's what's so beautiful about you being you. You are special. But there is a fulfillment there that you've got to find—for your sake, His sake, for the world's sake. You were put here for a reason—to help." Oliver John Calvert

It's true—you will directly impact people I will never see, and vice versa. You will see them on your street in your corner of the world. You will connect with them in your office, school, or church. You will pass by them on your way to the grocery store, post office, and bank. You will see them struggling and in need of a helping hand. It is up to you to choose love and help them rather than ignore them and pass by. It doesn't need to be some huge act as we will learn in the Serve Selflessly chapter, just a simple gesture of acknowledgement, love, and respect. If not you, then who? If not now, then when? If we all commit to do our part to positively impact the people we each come in contact with, to love the ones we're with—together we can make a big difference.

> "One thing I learned was that we are ALL here to do an 'assignment of love.' We don't have to do it at all, or we can do as many as we like. It's up to us. Our 'assignment' is programmed in at birth and it is the very thing or things we love most. I was such a bozo. I always thought doing what you loved most was selfish. I can remember how amazed and happy I was when this information came into my mind . . . 'That is the most unselfish and constructive thing you can do for the world because that is your assigned energy and you will be happiest doing it, best at it, and most respected for it!'" Peggy

What is Your Particular "Assignment of Love"?

Don't you love Peggy referring to everyone's unique mission as a pre-programmed "Assignment of Love"; for that truly is what our earthly mission entails. Life on earth is an experiential way for us to learn love by serving humanity and God. Amazingly and conveniently, the pre-programmed yet initially secret Assignment of Love lines up exactly with what we LOVE to do; so it should be extremely easy for us to do it, once we find it.

Your Assignment of Love might involve parenting, mentoring, or helping children—your own, and/or other people's children. NDEr Jeff Olsen realized one of the main reasons he survived a horrific car accident was to be there for his young son Spencer. "I knew why I had survived. It was for him. It was for no grander reason than to simply be his dad. And what grander reason is there?"

For many of us, one of our primary "Assignments of Love" is to parent our own children—to teach them love, to encourage them to break through their own fears, and to help them discover their passion and work purposely. Parenting is one of the most experiential ways to give and receive love that impacts our children and their children and on and on for multiple generations.

Still not completely convinced each of us has a specific Divine Mission given to us by God?

3. Work Purposely

You Must Go Back, Your Purpose is Not Complete

To further underscore the importance of fulfilling your unique purpose, here are some more powerful examples of NDErs who were either told to or chose to come back to earth rather than stay in heaven because they had not yet fully realized their earthly purpose. In essence, they came back or were "kicked out of heaven" as some NDErs jokingly call it, because of unfinished earthly business, because they hadn't completed their critical human life's purpose.

> "Then I heard the voice again. This time the Light said, 'You have to return, you have a PURPOSE.' The word purpose kept echoing in my true being . . . I couldn't argue because I understood the truth within it . . . Resonating within me was the question: Purpose, Purpose, Purpose? What Purpose? I have a Purpose? I only knew I needed to survive because of that word. I knew there was some purpose to my being alive, living my life." David Bennett

> "I was told, 'It's not your time and you must go back.' And I threw a spiritual temper tantrum. I said, 'No, I'm not going back. You've got this all wrong.' And then once again, I was told, 'You must go back. It's not your time. But you can come back any time you want once you've fulfilled your purpose.'" Raymond Kinman

> "I was told that it wasn't my time, that I'd been granted a visit 'back home', but that I had to fulfill my purpose and do the work I myself had chosen to do on earth. The being of light reminded me that my purpose was to learn more about love, compassion, and how to express them on earth, and that my work was to help other people in any way I could. I had chosen this myself. And it told me that I would be back in the world of light in no time." Lisa M.

> "He asked me if wanted to stay on earth or go with Him . . . He showed me what I still had left to do—the whole reason I came to earth—the job I asked Him for!!!! His question to me was, 'Can you do this?' I remember saying so matter of fact, 'I can do that!' His next question was, 'Do you want to do this?' My answer was, 'That is so cool; I would really love to do that!' . . . My main reason for staying was that I didn't want to let God down. I wanted to finish the job I had come here to do. I wanted to show Him that I'm not a quitter . . . I felt like I had no other choice than to stay. I replied, almost in a whisper and very, very reluctantly, 'I really want to go with you—but I have to stay.'" Mary Beth Willi

Clearly, each of these NDErs had a specific earthly task and purpose that needed to be fulfilled before leaving earth and staying in heaven. Either God needed them to stay to complete it—or they themselves, like Mary Beth, knew their lives would be incomplete without accomplishing it.

NDE researcher Dr. Ken Ring says people come back to earth from heavenly bliss most often because of one of two highly compelling reasons. "Whether an individual feels he chose to return or was sent back, the reasons given usually have to do with one or the other of two nonindependent considerations:

1. The 'pull' of loved ones—usually children or spouses—who are felt to have need of the respondent or

2. A sense that one's life's tasks and purposes are not yet accomplished—a feeling of 'unfinished business.'"

One of the most powerful NDE passages from RaNelle Wallace clearly illustrates both of these compelling reasons. Like most NDErs, RaNelle clearly did not want to return to earth to her battered and burned body after her plane crash and pleaded with her deceased Grandmother to help her stay in heaven:

> "Grandma waved her arm and the ground opened before us. I looked and saw a person lying on a hospital bed surrounded by doctors and nurses. The person's face was bandaged. "You will never be the same, RaNelle," Grandma said. "Your face will be altered and your body filled with pain. When you go back, you will have years of rehabilitation . . ."

> "When I go back?" I looked at her. "You expect me to go back?" Sudden understanding came, and I looked at the person on the bed. The arms were spread wide, and both arms and hands had been sliced in several places to allow the fluids to drain into plastic bags. "Is that me?" I was horrified.

> "Yes, RaNelle, it is you. You will be badly scarred." I became frantic. "Grandma, I'm not going back."

> "Your children need you, RaNelle."

> "No, no they don't. They're better off with someone else. I can't give them what they need."

> "It's not just your children, RaNelle. You have things to do - things that aren't finished yet."

> "No, I'm better off here. I don't want to go through all that." I pointed to my body. "I refuse. I want to stay here." I sensed my grandmother's awareness that time was growing short. "You must go," she said. "Your mission isn't complete."

"No, I'm not returning to that body! I'm not going back." In response, my grandmother swept out her arm and commanded: "Look!" A rift opened in the space before us, and I saw a young man walking toward us. At first he didn't seem to understand why he was there. Then he saw me and looked stunned. "Why are you here?" he said almost in disbelief. As I remained silent, his disbelief changed to grief, and he began crying. I felt his grief, his sadness, and I too began crying. What's the matter?" I asked. "Why are you crying?" I put my arms around him, trying to comfort him. "Why are you here?" he repeated. Then I understood that my refusal to go back to Earth was causing his sadness. I belonged on Earth for him, I understood, and I immediately felt guilt for my selfishness. His name was Nathaniel, and he hadn't been born on Earth yet. He said that if I didn't go back, his own mission would be hindered. Then he showed me his mission, and I saw that I was to open doors for him, to help him, to encourage him. "I will complete as much of my mission as I can," he said, "but I will never fulfill it without you. I need you."

I thought my heart would break. I was a part of his puzzle, and I was hurting him and everyone he would help by refusing to go back to Earth. I felt a great love for this young man, and I wanted to help him in every way I could. "Oh, Nathaniel," I said, "I swear to you that I will help you. I will go back, and I promise that I will do everything I can to do my part. I will open those doors for you. I will protect and encourage you. I will give you everything I have. Nathaniel, you will complete your mission. I love you."

His grief was replaced with gratitude. His face lit up, and I saw the great spirit he was. He was crying now with gratitude and joy. "Thank you," he said. "Oh, I love you."

My grandmother took my hand and drew me away. Nathaniel watched me leave, still smiling, and I distinctly heard him say, "I love you, Mom."

Despite being told she would never be able to have children again because of the severe injuries from her plane crash, seven years after her NDE, RaNelle did indeed have a son, and named him Nathaniel. Hopefully these many powerful examples have convinced you that you too have a specific purpose in this life—even if you have not yet fully discovered it.

Talents and Gifts Tailored to Your Task

In addition to our essential purpose, God also blesses us with special talents and abilities that, when discovered, developed, and deployed, help us complete our mission and service here on earth. During her NDE, God provided Erica McKenzie with a great visual of the many unique gifts available to us when He showed her thousands of gift-wrapped presents on rows and rows of shelves:

"On the shelves appeared gifts, presents, like those we give and receive at Christmas. There were so many gifts on all the shelves that they filled each and every space available. But not one gift looked like the other. Not one was the same. God said, 'When you are born I give each of you gifts. When you were born, Erica, I gave you the gift of patience and the gift of beauty. In life I have more gifts for each and every one of you. All you have to do is ask, and then be prepared to be quiet and listen, to be able to receive the gifts.' Sometimes it's hard to see the gifts we possess. I thought of my gift of beauty and realized how impossible it was for me to see it in myself because I looked to mankind for my value instead of God. I had stifled the very gifts He had given me . . . It took dying to make me realize that my uniqueness was my value and my value was my contribution on this Earthly Journey." Erica McKenzie, RN

What a beautiful image to remind us that God provides each of us with gifts and talents to enjoy and help us successfully complete our task here on earth. Erica continues:

"We have been given a unique suite of gifts that makes each of us special and in turn makes our lives unique. We've been asked to use these gifts to their fullest as an expression of gratitude and love . . . When we use our gifts to better ourselves and the world, to live full and joyous lives, our souls rejoice, and so does the spiritual world. It is as if we are sending a huge 'thank you' to the universe. With our lives we are saying: I love what I have and am using my gifts to their fullest, in love, in joy, and in beauty. Thank you!" Erica McKenzie, RN

"We have different gifts, according to the grace given to each of us. If your gift is prophesying, then prophesy in accordance with your faith; if it is serving, then serve; if it is teaching, then teach; if it is to encourage, then give encouragement; if it is giving, then give generously; if it is to lead, do it diligently; if it is to show mercy, do it cheerfully."

Romans 12: 6-8

Our gifts and talents are designed to help and serve others. In doing so, we not only do God's important work and contribute to the world, we also help ourselves grow and develop.

"Sometimes we may want different gifts or try to hide the ones we have, but we each have something unique to offer. Just as each one of the billions of people on this earth has a unique fingerprint and genetic code, we each have a unique combination of talents and gifts that can be used for God's glory." Dr. Mary Neal

What are your unique gifts that you have been given? Some people have the gift of connecting with people, others are better at analyzing complex tasks, some have certain gifts of cooking, or woodworking, or a green thumb. All of us have been given certain skills that we do well and often enjoy doing. It is up to us to find them.

Identify Your Gifts and Talents

Take a moment to identify your specific gifts and talents. Although this exercise is uncomfortable for some people to do because they think they are bragging, it is actually a critical part in discovering your purpose. The things you enjoy and come somewhat naturally to you are the gifts and talents you have been given to develop and contribute to the world. Be proud of these gifts and feel good about them because they were given to you by God to make a difference as part of Her Divine Plan. Hiding these gifts or not using them fully would be like rejecting a hand-selected gift given to you by God—which in actuality, it is.

> "God has given us individual talents, some more and some less according to our needs. As we use these talents, we learn how to work with, and eventually understand, the laws and overcome the limitations of this life. By understanding these laws we are better able to serve those around us. Whatever we become here in mortality is meaningless unless it is done for the benefit of others. Our gifts and talents are given to us to help us serve. And in serving others we grow spiritually." Betty Eadie

As Betty reminds us, these gifts aren't ours to hide or hoard—they are to be given generously to others to make a positive difference in our lives.

Just as the whole universe is intelligently designed by God to work effectively, so too are the tasks and talents She gives each of us. They are all meant to intersect so that they help God with Her Divine Plan, help and serve humanity, match up with our talents and passions, and stimulate our spiritual growth in the process. Your purpose is where your talents, your passion, the area of your spiritual growth, what serves others, and God's Divine Plan all intersect. That's a pretty ingenious and integrated system when you look at it this way.

> "The Light seems to be telling us, each of us, that we have a unique gift, an offering to make to the world, and our happiness and the world's are both served when we live in such a way as to realize that gift, which is no less than our purpose in life." Ken Ring

Our role in this then is to contribute to the world by finding our passion and purpose, discovering our gifts, developing our gifts, and deploying our gifts to help humanity and enact God's Plan.

> *"The meaning of life is to find your gift.*
> *The purpose of life is to give it away."*
> **David Viscott**, Author

YOUR PURPOSE: DISCOVER IT, DEVELOP IT, DEPLOY IT

As several NDErs have said, God wants you to discover your purpose, develop your purpose, and deploy your purpose—to help your family and community—as well as to enjoy it yourself.

1. Discover Your Purpose

You must first start by putting in the time to discover your purpose. Like panning for gold, you often have to sift through a variety of things before you can discover your true and ultimate purpose. It very likely won't happen overnight.

If you have not pinpointed your purpose, that's certainly okay. There are a lot of people who take a while to find their purpose. Like entering an Escape Room that requires you to search for a number of clues in order to solve the problem, your purpose doesn't just magically appear but requires effort, exploration, and ingenuity on your part and will be eventually revealed to you over time through a series of clues and challenges. Expect it to take time and digging on your part.

"God's plans often challenge our feelings of comfort and contentment. By challenging our comfort zone, the journey almost always leads to personal growth, greater love, service to others, and a future that is often better than what we might have imagined for ourselves." Dr. Mary Neal

Unearthing your purpose is all part of the adventure and mystery of walking life's labyrinth. Some of the best ways to discover your purpose fortunately line up well with your interests and passions. Consider the following questions to help you find your purpose.

- What fascinates and excites you?

- What makes your heart sing and fills you up?

- What could you get lost in doing for hours?

- What would you eagerly do whether or not you were getting paid for it?

- What makes you come ALIVE!?!

Hopefully in answering these questions either in your mind or in the *10 Life-Changing Lessons from Heaven Journal* you have found a consistent theme. It is likely that your answers to these questions will bring you much closer to discovering your purpose in life as you traverse life's labyrinth.

"Don't ask what the world needs. Ask what makes you come alive, and go do it. Because what the world needs is people who have come alive."

Howard Thurman, Author, Theologian, Civil Rights Leader

"Listening to my heart and soul, and then following them gives me such joy in my life. I have been asked, 'How do we really know that we are doing the right job?' I learned the answer is 'this is it' if we can say to ourselves 'I cannot believe they are paying me to do this job!'" Mary Beth Willi

If you are still struggling to find your purpose, ask your friends and family to share what they see as some of your talents and the things that make you most come alive. You can also talk with a career counselor to get their advice and see if there are any career aptitude tests you can take to narrow down your interests.

"The two most important days in your life are the day you are born and the day you find out why."

Mark Twain, Author

---

2. Develop Your Purpose

Once you think you have discovered your primary purpose, your next step is to develop it. Spend time honing your purpose through practice. Set aside dedicated time each week to master your craft. You can seek out and talk with others who might be further along the path in developing a similar purpose to learn what they did that was helpful. You can also read books and watch videos on your purpose. Invest the time to develop your purpose. It will be fun for you because you enjoy doing it and it will be that much more helpful when you share it with others.

3. Deploy Your Purpose

Finally, commit to doing, deploying, and delivering on your purpose on a regular basis. As spiritual teacher Wayne Dyer said, "Don't die with your music still in you." If your purpose is part of a career, be sure to find or craft a position that allows you to spend most of your time on it, working in your sweet spot where your talents, interests, passions, and purpose all meet. If your purpose is a hobby or a volunteer position, be sure to build it into your weekly schedule so you can contribute it often. Not only will it help others, but it will be great for you too as you share your interests and gifts.

> *"When your life is on course with its purpose, you are your most powerful."*
> **Oprah Winfrey**, Talk Show Host

Summary

This chapter obviously focused on the importance of purpose—your purpose. NDErs are adamant that we are all here on earth for a specific reason. This important purpose not only helps you grow and develop spiritually, it also serves others, and helps God achieve Her greater plan. Invest the time to discover, develop, and deploy your purpose. It will make your heart sing, make the world a better place, and do God's important work.

"Tell people they are special and unique, each one. God made every one of His children to have a divine purpose, which only they can accomplish in the earth." Gary Wood

3. Work Purposely

WORK PURPOSELY | MAJOR LESSONS

- We are spiritual beings who have chosen a human experience and mission on earth

- We each have a divine, specific, unique, preprogrammed purpose/task/calling/mission

- Every person has an essential and specific role and purpose to benefit the whole

- Our purpose is an assignment of love—we don't have to do it but are strongly guided/encouraged to pursue and complete it for our good and the good of the world

- Our purpose conveniently aligns with what helps us develop, is aligned with our gifts/talents, and coincides with what is needed in the world (highest good)

- Using our talents provides personal meaning and motivation

- We must discover our purpose—follow our joy and bliss, the things that come naturally

- We are most happy when we contribute our gifts, when we find meaning and motivation

- Our purpose unfolds over time, we discover it by learning what makes our heart sing, what we love to do, and what we're passionate about

- When we fully embrace and align with our purpose, we co-create with God—God works through us, we have the energy, insights, support, and the Universe moves with and through us. Synchronicities occur because the Universe has our back

- People are often sent back to earth if they have not yet finished their life's work or completed their purpose—if we are still alive there is more work for us to do

- Our primary purpose can involve learning, teaching, or both

- Part of our purpose is positively parenting and loving our children (if we have them)

- God provides us with specific gifts and talents that help us achieve our purpose/mission

- Our job is to discover, develop, and deploy our gifts to help ourselves and others

---

"The person born with a talent they are meant to use will find their greatest happiness in using it."

Johann Wolfgang Von Goethe, Author

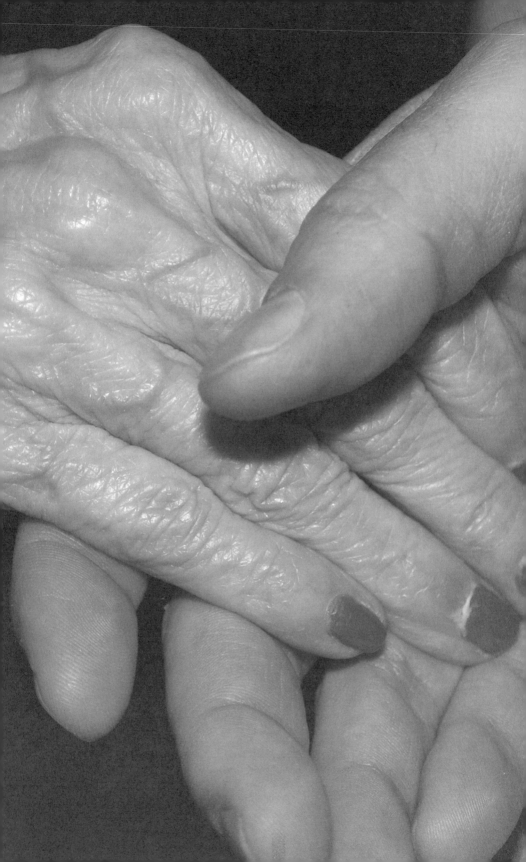

4.
CHOOSE COMPASSIONATELY

"After your death, when most of you for the first time realize what life here is all about, you will begin to see that your life here is almost nothing but the sum total of every choice you have made during every moment of your life. Your thoughts, which you are responsible for, are as real as your deeds. You will begin to realize that every word and every deed affects your life and has also touched thousands of lives."

Elizabeth Kubler-Ross, Author of *On Death and Dying*

NDEr FEATURE

Marion Rome: What We Do Unto Others We Do to Ourselves

Londoner Marion Rome experienced a profound NDE where she left her body and entered a spiritual dimension where she was able to see and feel into the minds and hearts of her friends and family in the past, present, and future. Her Life Review is one of the most detailed you will ever come across and her excellent description of it (partially included in this chapter) is one of the best to truly feel what it is like to experience how we positively and negatively impact others with our words and deeds. Marion shares her remarkable NDE in her book *Beyond Sight* and also wrote about the aftereffects of her NDE in her book called *Through the Light*.

God Grants Us Choices and Free Will

Choices are critical to our lives on earth. We are presented with millions of choices throughout our lifetimes. These choices range from seemingly mundane decisions like the clothes we wear each day, the kind of toothpaste we use, and our path to work in the morning to major things like where we go to school, who we marry, where we live, what we do for a living, whether or not we have children, how we raise our children, what religion we espouse, what politician we vote for, and our overall philosophy of life. As a multitude of situations come up every single day, we almost always have a significant degree of choice in how we want to handle the situation. Here's what the NDErs say about the value and impact of our choices:

> "Every word, thought, and action, no matter how small, affected everyone and everything. I had no idea of the power and consequences of my thoughts, my words, and actions . . . I had it all wrong! I hadn't given importance to the 'little things' and how each of my words, thoughts, and actions affected others." Erica McKenzie, RN

> "I saw the choices I'd made in my life. Those choices, like the ripples, made little waves in the world around me. They affected other people. They affected my future. And somehow affected my past, too. Good or bad, my choices had an impact. We have the power to change the world immediately around us through the effective use of our own thoughts, words, feelings, and actions. If we choose to use all of these carefully, with

love in our hearts and positive intentions, we can have powerfully positive lives. But if we make choices with an uninformed, negative, or malicious state of mind, or negative intent and not aligned with Spirit, our choices can easily hurt or destroy ourselves or others." Nancy Rynes

NDErs remind us that our choices do indeed have significant power over our lives, even the seemingly subtle and insignificant ones. Day after day, week after week, month after month, year after year, and decade after decade, these millions of choices end up determining our current situation in life—and the lives of others. Or put simply, choices have consequences. It is up to us to recognize, value, and consistently make wise and loving choices that benefit both ourselves and others. Every time we interact with people, we can choose to treat them poorly and have them resent us or choose to treat people kindly and have them respect us.

God's Gift of Free Will

Fortunately, God provides us with the amazing gift of free will to make choices on how we want to live our lives, how we want to treat people, and how we want to exist in our earthly environment. He unconditionally loves us so much He allows us to choose our own thoughts, feelings, and reactions to whatever comes our way—and these choices largely dictate our overall happiness, physical health, financial wealth, quality of relationships, and satisfaction in life. We can either choose to respond out of our ego (fear) or out of our Essence (love).

> "We were given agency to act for ourselves here. Our own actions determine the course of our lives, and we can alter or redirect our lives at any time. I understood that this was crucial; God made the promise that he wouldn't intervene in our lives unless we asked him. And then through his omniscient knowledge he would help us attain our righteous desires. We were grateful for this ability to express our free will and to exercise its power. This would allow each of us to obtain great joy or to choose that which will bring us sadness. The choice would be ours through our decisions." Betty Eadie

> "I learned that literally everything is a choice. The only rule in the entire universe actually was 'free will and choice', but without judgment, only in unconditional love." Jeff Olsen

Don't Play the Victim

When we feel like we don't have any choices we actually allow ourselves to become a victim of the circumstances we are in. However, NDErs tell us that we always have a choice in how we want to handle situations, even the toughest ones like losing loved ones.

> "I learned that my choices were mine alone to make. I got to decide how I felt, and that made all the difference in the universe. Even in this tragedy, I got to determine the outcome. I could choose to be a victim of what happened or create something far greater." Jeff Olsen

> "I heard His voice say, 'Don't waste your life thinking you're not loved.' Don't waste your life meant that I was creating the situation; that I was not a victim of my circumstance, that I had a choice, that I had choices all the time, that every thought was a choice." Yolaine Stout

No matter what kind of situation you might find yourself, use the power of your free will to choose your response to it. Rather than playing the passive victim and thinking you are doomed, accept the situation for what it is and decide how you are going to overcome it and use it to make you a better and more loving person.

Why Is There Evil? Evil is an Unpleasant but Necessary Side Effect of Free Will

God's gift of giving humans free will also helps explain why there is evil in the world. While God obviously wants us to learn to make choices that are based in love during our time on earth, as humans we still have the freedom and latitude to make choices based on fear, jealousy, and hatred. When we make choices based primarily on our fearful ego, we look out only for ourselves thereby making life difficult for others. This selfish and fearful environment is the perfect breeding ground for evil thoughts, words, and actions.

> "Evil was necessary because without it free will was impossible, and without free will there could be no growth—no forward movement, no chance for us to become what God longed for us to be . . . That evil could occasionally have the upper hand was known and allowed by the Creator as a necessary consequence of giving the gift of free will to beings like us." Dr. Eben Alexander

> "War exists in the world because humans come here and make free choices to learn and evolve. Unfortunately, this creates a mess and war is a part of that mess. But the same free choice principle is instrumental in cleaning it up." David Oakford

Rather than blaming God for the "evil" in the world like war, violence, hatred, intolerance, etc., we need to ask ourselves why we create and allow these things. A big part of our growth then as humans is learning to choose a loving response even though many fearful, victim-prone, unloving responses are readily available to us as well. God provides us with numerous opportunities throughout our lifetime to make loving choices—but ultimately it is up to us whether or not we want to choose to help others or just help ourselves.

"I saw a woman whom I had been asked by our local church leader to visit periodically. I was just to check up on her and see if she needed any help. I knew the woman quite well but was afraid of her constant pessimism and negativity. She was locally renowned for her bitterness. I didn't think I could handle the depressing influence she would have on me, so I never went to see her. Not once. I saw now that the opportunity to visit her had been orchestrated by Higher Powers, that I had been just the person she needed at that time. She didn't know it, and I didn't know it, but I had let her down. Now I lived her sadness and felt her disappointment and knew I was a cause of it. I had fallen through on a special mission to her, a responsibility that would have strengthened me over time. I had retreated from an opportunity for growth, both for me and for her, because I was not caring enough to fight through my petty fears and laziness. But the reasons didn't matter; I could see that, even now, she was living in sadness and bitterness, living through it just as I now experienced it, and there was nothing I could do to go back and help." RaNelle Wallace

Intent of Choices is Key—God Knows Our Hearts

NDErs tell us that what is most critical and revealing about the choices we make is our intent; the real reason behind our actions. Even though our fellow humans can often be fooled and manipulated by our dishonest words and deceitful actions, God always knows what is in our hearts. As Thomas á Kempis once said, "Man sees your actions. God sees your motives." NDErs say there is no fooling God when it comes to the intent and motives of our thoughts and actions.

"What was important were the choices I made. And what was more important than the choices I made, were my motivations and intent, and really the state of my heart in doing any single action . . ." Reinee Pasarow

"Choice making is a serious challenge, one that requires great patience and wisdom from us. It also requires a clear vision of our intent. Sparkling clarity is vital if we are to use the power of choice in a manner that guarantees the greatest good of all concerned. Whether our intent is the salvation of the world like the valiant efforts of a Mother Teresa, or just personal happiness, during the panoramic life review, we will see clearly the real intentions of our choices . . . The reason we do something is far more important than the act itself. The intention motivating us to take action

4. Choose Compassionately

determines the spiritual effectiveness of that action . . . When the intention is pure, not meant to be harmful in any way, the result of an action will always be measured before the action is." Dannion Brinkley

"I realized that we don't have to be perfect during earth life; just sincerely caring and making an effort to become more loving, charitable, and forgiving—and less judgmental. The desires and intent of the heart are so significant." Dr. Joyce Brown

What is most critical about the choices we make in life is our intent. We may serve at a soup kitchen, which others might see as noble and honorable, yet God will see right through it as a sham if the main reason we do it is for a good photo opportunity to make ourselves look better. We may try to lie, cover up, or justify to others our motives for certain choices, but God always knows what is in our hearts and understands the true motivations behind our actions. Thus, it is critical to be honest with ourselves, others, and God about why we make our choices; because all of our motives will eventually come to light in our Life Review.

THE LIFE REVIEW: The Ultimate "This is Your Life" Experience

One of the most powerful teaching tools for helping us learn to Choose Compassionately is what NDErs call the Life Review. A Life Review involves actually reliving all the events of our life from birth to death to see and learn how our actions impacted others. Amazingly, we not only see and feel the events of our life from our own perspective, but also from the perspectives of every person we ever come in contact with throughout our lifetime.

"A brief scene flashed before me. A series of pictures, words, ideas, understanding. It was a scene from my life. It flashed before me with incredible rapidity, and I understood it completely and learned from it. Another scene came, and another, and another, and I was seeing my entire life, every second of it. And I didn't just understand the events; I relived them. I was that person again, doing those things to my mother, or saying those words to my father or brothers or sisters, and I knew why, for the first time, I had done them or said them. Entirety does not describe the fullness of this review. It included knowledge about myself that all the books in the world couldn't contain. I understood every reason for everything I did in my life. And I also understood the impact I had on others." RaNelle Wallace

Hands down, the Life Review is one of the best teaching tools for spiritual development because we actually see and feel exactly how our choices, actions, and inaction impacted others and the greater world during our lifetime. The Life Review is an intensive, instructive, ingenious, and integral part of the Divine's master plan for our spiritual development while we are on earth. Because it is such a pivotal part of the NDE, let's take an in-depth look at the mechanics, motives, and undeniable outcomes of the Life Review process and how it masterfully helps us understand why Choosing Compassionately is such an essential part of our time on earth.

LIFE REVIEW FEATURES: Hi-Def, Panoramic, Multi-Player, Immersive Experience

The Life Review is truly an amazing experience that even the highest-budgeted Hollywood special effects team couldn't touch in production quality and impact. Here are the many key elements of the Life Review as described by our NDEr friends:

Your Entire Life Flashes Before Your Eyes

A Life Review is the experience of having your entire life appear before you in what seems like merely a matter of seconds or minutes. It's the concept of "your life flashes before your eyes" as many people talk about in the near-death state.

> "In my near-death experience (NDE) I was given a life review. I relived all 32 years of my life. In earth time it took 20 minutes, but I experienced it as though it was all happening again just as it had the first time." Barbara Whitfield Harris

> "I was suddenly able to think hundreds or thousands of times faster—and with greater clarity—than is humanly normal or possible . . .Time itself suddenly became infinite or irrelevant. In 'earth time' only about ten seconds had gone by until my heart re-started beating, but I was also in 'zero time' (for lack of a better word), or actually outside of time . . . There was an automatic review of my entire life—every event ever experienced complete with emotions (but viewed objectively)—rolling in front and around like a panoramic movie. From birth to death in linear fashion, observed without sadness or remorse. Yet in 'earth time', it only took a quarter second. Yet it seemed to be weeks spent replaying my life." Daniel A.

NDErs tell us that time is much different in heaven than it is on earth; it's as if time were suspended in heaven, or happening simultaneously all at once, instead of the linear, second by second process we experience here as humans. Somehow, during their Life Review in heaven, NDErs can review their entire life, which in many cases may take several decades to live out on earth, in the matter of what seems like mere seconds or minutes in the timelessness of heaven.

Panoramic Experience of Your Whole Life

Think a massive IMAX theater with 3D technology and the latest THX sound system is impressive? Or a sports bar with dozens of large screen TVs all over the walls showing every sports game imaginable is pretty cool? Nothing compares to the Life Review.

> "The heavenly structure resembled an amphitheater similar to those found in ancient civilizations. This amphitheater was made of a brilliant, crystal-like substance that radiated multi-colored waves of energy throughout its form . . . A shimmering, luminescent sphere enveloped me, making me feel as if I had stepped into a crystal globe . . . My life review was about to begin. Since the crystalline sphere was not encumbered by the limiting properties of time and space, I was going to re-experience my life with the same intensity with which it was originally experienced. My life review began as the surface of the sphere came alive with a vivid and lifelike scene that took me back to my infancy. The scene was not just life-like; it was reality itself." Ned Dougherty

> "As I got closer to the light, all of a sudden I popped into a giant sphere. It was about the size of a basketball coliseum. And I was suspended in the middle of this sphere. All around me, in all parts of the sphere—up, down, sideways, left, right, all over—were miniature motion pictures of my lives and what was going on. And I could see, I could touch, I could feel, I could sense every emotion that was taking place in all of those lifetimes. When I would concentrate on one, I would immediately be there; I would be reliving what I had lived and I would remember the reliving. Then I would think about another area. I would pop into another movie. And I would do this for some period of time." Andy Petro

> "Scenes from my life became visible in front of us, as though projected onto a large three-dimensional multisensory screen . . . The scenes moved quickly past, from right to left in sequential order. It was like swiping through the chain at the bottom of 'all photos' on an iPhone. This forward motion intermittently slowed when Jesus reached his hand forward to pluck a scene from the strand of my life. Rather than just seeing the scene in front of me, I would immediately re-experience it with absolute understanding, and from every vantage point." Dr. Mary Neal

For many NDErs, the Life Review experience is as if they have entered into a large spherical dome and all around them are millions of scenes of their lifetime from birth until their very last breath. Somehow every single one of our thoughts and experiences during our lifetime is captured in a kind of cosmic, universal, massive database that is played back to us at the end of our lives. Some call this exquisitely detailed heavenly database the Book of Life or the Akashic Record. Whatever the case, when we arrive in heaven, our whole lives have been recorded, available on demand, and simultaneously played back to us so that we can review them to see and learn from how we interacted with people, animals, and even our environment.

> "Realize that every single thing that you do in your life is recorded and that even though you pass it by not thinking at the time, it always comes up later. For instance, you may be . . . at a stoplight and you're in a hurry and the lady in front of you, when the light turns green, doesn't take off right, (she) doesn't notice the light, and you get upset and start honking your horn and telling them to hurry up. Those are the little kind of things that are really important." Dr. Ken Ring

> "I saw me as I was as a baby, a child, a teen, and adult, all at once. At the same time, I saw everything I ever did, everything I ever thought, everything. I saw events and people in my life that I previously considered important. Also, I saw many things that seemed not so important. I was aware of everything in my life all at once and I was aware of every response that others had to what occurred in my life. It was all there for me to understand . . . everything 'good', 'bad', or 'indifferent.'" Grace Bulbulka

Further, you don't just sit back and passively watch your Life Review with a bucket of popcorn, a box of Junior Mints, and soda like you would at a movie, you actually physically, mentally, and emotionally relive all the same thoughts and feelings you had at the time—so it is a fully immersive experience as well. But there's much more as NDErs further tell us.

Your Life on Fast Forward but with Pause and Zoom

Not only is your entire life recorded, but you can fast forward, pause on certain situations, and zoom in to get a closer examination of any or every life experience you ever had.

> "It was like watching my life from start to finish on an editing machine stuck in fast forward. The review took me from conception . . . through my childhood, to adolescence, into my teens, and through my near-death experience over again. I saw my life. I relived my life." Neev

> "Although moving with incredible speed, as though someone had put my life review on superfast forward, I quickly discovered I could linger on any scene that caught my interest, re-experiencing it moment by moment if I desired. My life review was extremely enlightening . . ." Dr. Joyce Brown

> "We just watched my life from beginning to the end. Some things they slowed down on, and zoomed in on, and other things they went right through. My life was shown in a way I had never thought of before." Howard Storm

Ultra-High Definition

If that's not enough, everything in the Life Review is displayed in ultra-high definition—millions of times more magnified and vivid in both senses and emotions than our most advanced, high pixel density screens. Here are some excellent examples of this unfathomable feature in the following Life Review descriptions.

> "When you have a panoramic life review, you literally relive your life in a 360-degree panorama. In astonishing detail, you see everything that has ever happened. For example, you can count the number of hairs in the nose of the doctor who delivered you at birth. You can even see how many leaves were on the tree in the front yard when you were six years old playing in the dirt. You literally relive it all." Dannion Brinkley

> "I relived every exact thought and attitude; even the air temperature and things that I couldn't have possibly measured when I was eight years old. For example, I wasn't aware of how many mosquitoes were in the area. In the life review, I could have counted the mosquitoes. Everything was more accurate than could possibly be perceived in the reality of the original event." Tom Sawyer

> "I felt everything I ever felt before. When I say 'everything' I mean every cut, pain, emotion, and sense associated with that particular time in my life." Neev

The level of detail of the Life Review experience is obviously astounding! And not just from our own perspective.

Experience Your Life Through Other's Eyes

If you aren't already awestruck by the intensity, intricacy, and impact of the Life Review, this next aspect will undoubtedly blow your mind . . . The Life Review is multi-perspective, meaning you don't just see and feel your life from your viewpoint, but also from every other person's viewpoint you ever interacted with as well!

> "During a life review, many of us don't just experience our own feelings; but we also experience the feelings of everyone else, as though all other people participating in our lifetimes are joined. This gives us an immediate and powerful understanding of the effect that all our words, actions, and behaviors have had on those around us . . . Some of it felt good and some of it felt awful. All of this translated into knowledge and I learned. Oh, how I learned!" Barbara Whitfield Harris

> "I was able to feel exactly what others around me had felt during my life. I understood how everything I did, said, and thought, had touched others around me in one way or another. I was able to enter the minds and

emotional centers of many who had been around me, and understand where they were coming from in their own thinking. I could see how their own personal views and life experiences had shaped their lives. I felt their struggling and their fears, their own desperate need for love and approval, their confusion, and more than anything, I could feel how child-like everyone was." Amy Call

"The review was everything that had ever happened to me . . . I saw it from three perspectives simultaneously. It was as though I was looking through my own eyes as I was experiencing it again as I first had. And then I was experiencing it through the eyes of everyone with whom I had ever interacted. And then it was this sort of omniscient viewpoint where I could see everything." David Beckman

"At the same time, I saw the effects of my life on the people around me . . . I felt all that they felt and, through this, I understood the repercussions of everything I did, be it good or bad. The life review was the most beautiful thing I had ever seen, and at the same time, the most horrifying thing I was ever to experience." Neev

Amazingly, in our Life Review, we feel the same physical sensations and exact emotions we led others to feel depending on how we treated them. Whether good or bad, happy or sad, pleasure or pain, valued or useless, we feel ourselves precisely how others felt when they were with us during our lifetime. For example, here is a very physical example as described by Roland Webb in his Life Review:

"I saw myself at five years old. I was in the neighborhood where I grew up in Washington, D.C. I was with my brothers and sisters and my neighborhood friend, whose name was Hydie. Hydie was maybe a year younger than us. We lived in an apartment building at the time. On the bottom floor of the apartment building, there was a beehive on the windowsill. I said, 'Hey Hydie! Pick up that stick and whack that beehive and we're gonna run and see if we can beat the bees.' So Hydie, listening to me, I don't know why, picks up the stick and whacks the beehive and we all took off running. The apartment building had a really dark green door. Everyone got into the apartment building and the last one to approach the door was Hydie. I had a devious thought in my mind: 'I'm going to hold the door and not let Hydie in, and see what happens to Hydie.' All those bees from that beehive stung the daylights out of Hydie. Every single bee sting I felt. I felt every sting, the burning sensation, and the swelling. His mother came out of the apartment building scared and frightened. I felt all her fear, all her fright, and all her rage. His father came out, trying to figure out what happened. I felt it all—it rippled. I felt every single thing. All the bees, how angry they were. I felt it all, every aspect. I felt everything." Roland Webb

"I was able to feel exactly what others around me had felt during my life. I understood how everything I did, said, and thought, had touched others around me in one way or another."

AMY CALL

Another powerful example of the physical impact of the Life Review comes from Tom Sawyer (yes, that really is his name), as he relived a brutal fight he had with another man from that man's perspective.

"I also experienced seeing Tom Sawyer's fist come directly into my face. And I felt the indignation, the rage, the embarrassment, the frustration, the physical pain . . . I felt my teeth going through my lower lip—in other words, I was in that man's eyes. I was in that man's body. I experienced everything of that inter-relationship between Tom Sawyer and that man that day."

In addition to the physical impact of our actions, we will also experience the emotional impact of our words and deeds on others. Some of the best examples of the emotional effect of the Life Review come from Marion Rome's descriptions in her fabulous book *Beyond Sight*.

"I had been shown my entire life from birth to my 'death.' During this life review I saw the consequences of my actions for other people . . . Throughout my life, I have done many things I regretted. Like anyone, there have been times when I have made poor choices and bad decisions . . . There was a time when a classmate of ours got a Superman outfit on his birthday. Every little boy at the party wanted to try it on and so did Oliver. Alas, he was too heavy for the costume and, when his turn came to put it on, he couldn't close the zipper. Everyone was laughing and I said: 'He's not Superman, he's Superfat,' and I kept repeating this over and over again, along with the other kids, amid the general laughter. Now my soul could feel every single bit of his pain. Emotion by emotion—and in a much more powerful way than we can experience it on earth—I could feel everything he felt that day because of me: sadness, shame, distress, anger . . . I could see him after the party crying alone in his room, wondering why other kids always made fun of him. It broke my heart in a way I can't begin to explain . . . What was strange—although it seemed totally normal and natural while it happened—was that I was both actor and spectator. I was everything at the same time. I was me but I was also the sadness of Oliver." Marion Rome

Fortunately and mercifully, we do not only feel all the hurt and sadness our words and actions cause others but also the happiness and support we provide them as well. Marion also shares a positive, feel-good example from her Life Review.

"I was viewing an occurrence that had happened in the earthly life just a few weeks before my NDE, in a practically empty train station. I was walking up an escalator that was out of order when I saw an old and frail lady trying hard to make her way to the top. I was carrying numerous shopping bags as well as my own large handbag and a huge backpack. That woman looked exhausted . . . I told her to stop there, that I would help her . . . As my soul was witnessing the whole scene I felt her smile . . . I FELT it in an incredible and magical way. I felt like I was hugged by it. Her smile was pure joy, tremendous happiness, and relief. It screamed: 'Thank you so much for helping me. That is so kind of you, you really have no idea.' What I was made extremely aware of during my NDE was the simple fact that I had taken time for her filled her with enormous joy . . . In that amazing afterlife, her joy was now my joy, too. My entire being was filled with every bit of it in such an intensified way and it is a sensation I'd give anything to feel again." Marion Rome

"With that, placed in front of me to see and feel was a review of my life in color. I had to see and feel all the good I had done (and the good I didn't even know I did). I actually could feel the joy each person felt when I touched their life in a loving way. I was getting 'caught' doing something right for once in my life. During the good He was telling me 'I am so proud of you!' I felt such joy for making Him so proud because I never realized what that felt like because I always felt like I couldn't do anything right. Reviewing my random acts of kindness gave me the most joy because I was able to feel the difference I made in someone's life that I hadn't realized at the time." Mary Beth Willi

What We Do to Others We Do to Ourselves: The Golden Rule Exemplified

We quickly discover that the Life Review exemplifies the Golden Rule of doing unto others as we would like to have done to ourselves. As we experience our Life Review, the Golden Rule becomes much more than a mere platitude we casually utter, we actually feel the effects our words and actions caused others and realize its undeniable truth.

"Through my NDE I figured out that anything we do to others we ultimately do to ourselves once we access that other amazing dimension. However, over there, we experience it in a much more powerful way and that's the reason why I believe we better do something good. Believe it or not, I think of my encounter with Oliver in that magical world nearly every day. Maybe that one affects me more than the others because I made him suffer while he was an innocent child. Yet, even though I was totally forgiven both by him and the light, I could still feel his pain—and not like we feel emotions here, but in an enhanced way that was particularly painful to me . . . My NDE made me understand the true meaning of life and of human relations . . . I am much more aware of the effect of every single one of my words and actions will have on others on a deep soul level, and also because I now know with absolute certainty that ultimately it's me that I am hurting in an unimaginable way from a human perspective." Marion Rome

"No matter what I did to any person—no matter what that action might be, good or bad—that action would react not only upon me but also on the others around me. I knew that every action was its own reaction. What we do for or against another, we do to ourselves. I fully understand what Jesus meant when He said, 'As ye do it unto the least of these, you do it unto me.'" Minette Crow

"Every act, every thought, every feeling, every emotion—directed toward another—whether you know the person or not—will later be experienced by you. What you send out, returns . . . What could be a more perfect form of justice than this; everything you do becomes yours. It is not that we are rewarded for our good deeds or punished for our cruel ones; it is simply that we receive back what we have given out, and exactly as we have done it." Dr. Ken Ring

"What we do to others, we do to ourselves. To hurt another is to hurt ourselves; to judge another is to judge ourselves; to hate another is to hate ourselves; and to love another is to love ourselves." Helen S.

Let the gravity of these comments sink in . . .

Whatever we do to others—*we ultimately do to ourselves.*

Whenever we hurt others—*we ultimately hurt ourselves.*

Whenever we help others—*we ultimately help ourselves.*

What better way of showing us exactly the importance of compassionately choosing our thoughts, words, and deeds than having us experience the actual consequences of those choices on ourselves in full force? This may just be the perfect example of karma.

Completely grasping this concept of the Golden Rule should motivate us to extend an extra amount of compassion, patience, understanding, and love to our fellow humans knowing that we will eventually feel those *exact same things ourselves.* And, understanding this concept also makes us think twice about the potential mental, emotional, and/or physical pain we might intentionally or unintentionally inflict upon someone else if we know we will ultimately experience it ourselves.

Finally, if experiencing directly ourselves how we treat others isn't enough to convince you about the sheer power of your choices and their consequences; as the annoying TV infomercial announcers say, "But wait, there's even more . . ." And there is!

Experience the Ripple Effects 25 Times Removed

Not only do you experience the impact of your actions on others, you also see and feel the long-term impact and implications of your actions

4. Choose Compassionately

many multiple times removed from the initial event. NDEr Dr. Mary Neal describes it well:

> "Then I went through a little bit of a life review—not so much looking at events in isolation but looking at the unseen ripple effects of those events, how an event had an impact not just one or two degrees removed but 16, 20, 25 degrees removed. This was another profound aspect of the experience. It made me truly understand that every action, every decision, every choice, every human interaction really does matter. You may not know it, and almost always you don't recognize the impact. But everything really, really does matter." Dr. Mary Neal

In our Life Review, we don't just see and feel the immediate impact of our actions, we also get to see the long-term consequences of our actions as they ripple outward to other people, over time, and even across generations. Like a long chain of dominos, our simple and singular actions create an often unseen, virtually unending chain reaction that causes multiple events to occur impacting numerous people, over time, and across space.

Known often as the Butterfly Effect, which refers to the idea that a small action of a butterfly flapping its wings in one location can eventually cause a hurricane on the other side of the world, we will eventually see in our Life Review how a simple action can indeed cause a real, three-dimensional ripple effect across people, places, and even generations.

> "Everything we do, including the words we speak, our actions, our thoughts, has an effect on both ourselves and the world around us. We can liken these effects to energy radiating outward from our centers. Our words and actions do not affect just us, they travel outward and touch others, too. And the sphere of that impact can be quite large." Nancy Rynes

> "Each one of us has his place in the world. Each one of us has things we need to do. And every deed that we do affects the whole world; every deed, every action that we do—negative or positive—affects the entire universe. That's the power we have. We have the power to completely change and affect the universe." Alon Anava

> "[In my life review] I'm driving across this bridge with my windows down and I open up some gum, put it in my mouth, and I flick out the silver wrapper. I watch in slow motion this silver wrapper spiraling slowly all the way down into the river. I watch this gum wrapper go down the river being met by trash, Burger King, McDonald's, Wendy's [wrappers], needles, cat litter, you name it. All this pollution was being accompanied by my silver wrapper. And as this collected more and more trash going down the river I

saw it going through lakes and I saw it passing an oil refinery. And I watch all the toxic energy, all this murky stuff come from the refinery and meet all this trash . . . And what I saw were children swimming in the river and the lakes. I could see these children who had died because of toxic waste. It made me realize that my one wrapper affects everyone. One action. I learned at that moment in life that my small action did affect someone, somewhere, somehow." Peter Anthony

Suicide survivor and NDEr Angie Fenimore saw in her Life Review how taking her own life would have negatively impacted her five-year-old son and eventually cut short his life at the age of twenty, rather than him going on and becoming a nurse and positively impacting thousands of people.

"It's so far reaching because it's not just the people in YOUR life, it's those people who are impacted by your death . . . they don't do the things they were meant to do. For example, one of the people that I saw in my near- death experience was my son, my oldest boy, and he was five years old at the time. I saw his life go all the way up to about twenty years old. And what I saw was that he was rendered completely incapable of doing the things he was meant to do here in this life by virtue of his mother ending her life. So I would not only be responsible for my son's heartbreak and the breakdown in his life, but all the people he was meant to impact for good. And then all those people who he was meant to impact for good who would go out and impact other people for good. And you should know this boy is now going to nursing school. He is meant to do great things in this world and I would be responsible for all of that lack of good that would happen in the world by virtue of my son being disabled by what I did. So I was there in order to get the impact of my actions on other people."

Here are some more practical and powerful examples of how the Butterfly Effect plays out across a person's family and even their lifetime.

"The life review continued all the way down to third grade . . . I was teasing a smaller girl . . . I'm feeling how it feels for her to receive my actions that are very hurtful. And I am not only feeling her sorrow and her pain, but I am also sensing and understanding how my actions are impacting her future life. I'm now seeing, sensing, and feeling that she will become much more shy and introverted for the rest of her life because of my actions. But not only do I sense and feel that, I also feel the pain and sorrow in her parents because she's now going to turn out a more shy and inward person. So I'm really feeling the full consequences—not just how my actions are changing the life of this little girl, but I am also feeling . . . how my actions caused ripples far away, not just in her life, but in her parents' lives, in her whole family, also in everyone around her. So I get the full spectrum of the

"Just as ripples spread out when a single pebble is dropped into water, the actions of individuals can have far-reaching effects."

DALAI LAMA

full consequences—all the links in the chain . . . spending a few minutes in a schoolyard teasing a girl." Rene Jorgensen

"I experienced in a holographic awareness that was instantaneous how every action that one takes is like a stone cast in the water. And if it's loving, that stone . . . goes out and touches the first person that it's intended for and then it touches another person and it touches another person because that person interacts with other people. And so on and so on. And every action has a reverberating effect on every single one of us on the face of this planet. So if I had committed a loving action, it was like love upon love upon love. A purely loving action was the most wonderful thing I could ever have achieved in my life . . ." Reinee Pasarow

"Now, in the life review, I was forced to see the death and destruction that had taken place in the world as a result of my actions. 'We are all a link in the great chain of humanity,' said the Being. 'What you do has an effect on the other links in that chain.' Many examples came to mind, but one in particular stands out. I saw myself unloading weapons in a Central American country . . . My task was simply to transfer these weapons from an airplane to our military interests in the area. When this transfer was complete, I got back on the airplane and left. But leaving wasn't so easy in my life review. I stayed with the weapons and watched as they were used in the job of killing, some of them murdering innocent people and some the not so innocent. All in all it was horrible to witness my results of my role in this war." Dannion Brinkley

Even though he didn't actually pull the trigger, Dannion's Life Review showed him that his role in delivering the weapons still contributed to the murders of innocent and not so innocent people. That is a sobering reminder of the Ripple Effect our actions can have directly and indirectly on others.

Putting almost all the elements of the Life Review back together, here is a great overall description from NDEr Tom Sawyer:

"I wish that I could tell you how it really felt and what the life review is like, but I'll never be able to do it accurately. I'm hoping to give you just a slight inkling of what is available to each and every one of you. Will you be totally devastated by the crap you've brought into other people's lives? Or will you be equally enlightened and uplifted by the love and joy that you have shared in other people's lives? Well, guess what? It pretty much averages itself out. You will be responsible for yourself, judging and reliving what you have done to everything and everybody in very far-reaching ways. You do have an effect on plants. You do have an effect on animals. You do have an effect on the universe. And in your life review you'll be the universe and experience yourself in what you call your lifetime and how it affects the universe. In your life review you'll be yourself absolutely, in every aspect of time, in every event, in the overall scheme of things in your lifetime. Your life. When you waved a loving goodbye to a good friend the other day, did you affect the clouds up above? Did you actually affect them? Does a butterfly's wings in China affect the weather here? You better believe it does! You can learn all of that in a life review! As this takes place, you have total knowledge. You have the ability to be a psychologist, a psychiatrist, a psychoanalyst, and much more. You are your own spiritual teacher, maybe for the first and only time in your life. You are simultaneously the student and the teacher in a relationship. My life review was part of this experience also. It was absolutely, positively, everything basically from the first breath of life right through the accident. It was everything." Tom Sawyer

Reviewing the Life Review

We obviously spent a good deal of time on the Life Review because it is one of the most awe-inspiring, paradigm-shifting, and powerful aspects of an NDE, thoroughly and convincingly demonstrating the importance of Choosing Compassionately. As Neev says so well, "The Life Review is the ultimate teaching tool."

> "I wish everyone could have one—it would change the world! Everyone would understand each other, there wouldn't be conflict, and there wouldn't be chaos, and there wouldn't be greed and war . . . The Life Review is the ultimate teaching tool." Neev

NDE researcher Dr. Ken Ring expands on the comprehensive and compelling educational value of the Life Review as well.

> "Life reviews teach us how to live. It is as simple as that. There are certain values—universal values—we are meant to live by, and life review episodes contain vivid and powerful reminders of these values. No one who undergoes one of these encounters can avoid becoming aware of these teachings, because they are shown to be self-evident and it is impossible not to be affected by them. You see, you remember, and you change your life accordingly. Nothing compels like a life review . . ." Dr. Ken Ring

> "As you can imagine, an experience like that changes you. I'm not the same person I used to be. I experience much more grace toward others, even in minor situations. When I feel cheated or taken advantage of, when an erratic driver cuts me off in traffic, I am able to feel a gentleness toward the perpetrator that I didn't before. When someone treats me rudely or disrespectfully, I remind myself that the person is, at that moment, the sum total of all his or her burdens and joys, successes, and failures . . . My life review had come to a close, but its impact would ripple through my life in countless ways." Dr. Mary Neal

Rather than providing punishment and torture as might seem to be warranted when reviewing our unloving behavior, the sole (and soul) intent of the Life Review is for spiritual growth and development. The focus is to help us continuously learn from all of our experiences, both loving and unloving.

> "The life review is not punishment or torture and the only reason to fear it would be if you are afraid to confront truth and afraid to grow more loving. The word 'sin' is the farthest thing from what I experienced during my life review. Everything that I was re-experiencing during my life review totally related to my goals for my life experience and where I was meeting those goals or missing obvious opportunities . . . I felt nothing but unconditional love and understanding from those helping me review my life. It was no feeling of judgment, just an internal feeling of, 'I know I can do better than that!'" Karen Thomas

> "I saw my life. I saw things that I thought were mistakes. But in those loving arms it was flowing: There are no mistakes. Everything's in perfect order . . . All that was flowing to me was: Look how much we love you. Look how much we honor your choices. Look how much we honor your life." Jeff Olsen

> "I got a life review without any judgement whatsoever but my own life seen against a backdrop of pure unconditional love, which made everything that was NOT love in my life stand out like blobs of ink against a white paper. It was entirely up to me what to do with it and how to assess it, and I measured my own actions against the perfect unconditional love I was shown." Lisa Meyler

> "A voice in my ear said, 'Remember, here you are learning.' Now I'm waiting for the yardstick that I remember from my Catholic school education, and I was waiting for it to hit me right on the back of the head. What hit me on the back of the head was the statement—here I was learning." Tom Leach

What Do You Want to See and Feel in Your Life Review?

Knowing that you too will likely have an intensive Life Review with God at your side when you get to heaven hopefully encourages you to consider and reconsider every one of your earthly thoughts, words, and deeds before acting. Before we fly off the handle with a friend, scream out in anger at our spouse, criticize a coworker, cutoff a person in traffic, gossip about a neighbor, or jump all over our children for an innocent mistake they made, we should strongly consider exactly how we would want to experience this very same situation ourselves in our Life Review—*because eventually we will.*

Many NDErs encourage us not to wait for the end of our lives to have our Life Review. They advocate that we do a mini Life Review on a daily basis so we can catch ourselves now, learn lessons from our behavior and how it impacts others, and make more compassionate choices.

> "On an almost daily basis I consciously have a life review. This doesn't mean that the life review I have is the intense variety I had during my two near-death experiences. What I do to have a life review is reflect on my daily actions. By having this sort of pre-death life review, I am able to strip away the ego, through which so many of us filter our actions, and look honestly at who I am. I often joke that we are having a near-death experience right now because we are living our life review right now. That makes the life review the most obvious aspect of the near-death experience to use in building your empathy, sensitivity, and direction on a daily basis. It also means that we don't have to wait until we die to receive the benefits of a life review." Dannion Brinkley

Last but certainly not least, there is one more critical aspect of the Life Review that we haven't discussed or answered: Who is the ultimate judge of your life and your Life Review? As usual, the answer NDErs give us will most likely surprise you and we will cover it in our next chapter . . .

CHOOSE COMPASSIONATELY | MAJOR LESSONS

- Because God loves us so much, we have the gift of free will to make choices

- God wants us to make the loving choice but gives us free will to decide

- These choices determine our life—the big ones and little ones

- Your choices impact your life and many others around you both near and far

- Intent is key in choice making—God knows your heart's intent with every choice

- Life Review—best teaching tool for how your choices and decisions impact others

- You relive and experience every thought, word, action from birth to death—everything is recorded, seen in super high definition, and can stop and zoom in and zoom out

- See it from your perspective, see and feel it from others' perspective, see it from a higher perspective

- You will feel the effects of all of your choices and actions on others

- Anything we do to others we ultimately do to ourselves

- You will see and feel the Ripple Effects of your choices 25 times down the line. It is not just the single domino, but all the dominoes. You will experience all the ripples—both positive and negative

5.
ACCEPT NONJUDGMENTALLY

"Judge not, that ye be not judged."

Matthew 7:1

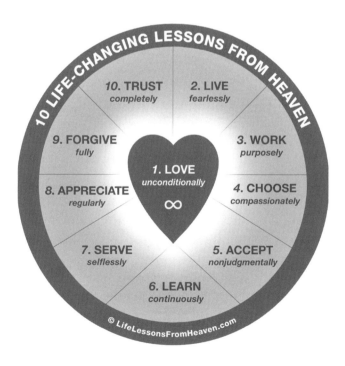

NDEr FEATURE

Nancy Rynes: The Atheist Who Went to Heaven

Known as the atheist who went to heaven, Nancy Rynes was cycling on a street near Boulder, Colorado when she was hit by a SUV driven by an inattentive, texting driver. She was dragged under the vehicle and suffered severe damage to her back and spine, necessitating a complicated surgery where she had her NDE. Brought up as a Catholic, Nancy's scientific mind didn't see any tangible evidence for God so she became an atheist as an adult. Upon entering the Afterlife in her NDE, Nancy surprisingly learned that not only did God exist, but He loved and accepted her just the same despite the fact that she hadn't believed in Him. Nancy's profound NDE featured a lengthy tour of heaven with a spirit guide who shared numerous practical and powerful lessons with her. Her guide told her to implement the ideas in her own life and share them with interested others so they could benefit from them as well. Her fantastic book, *Awakenings from the Light*, shares the amazing insights she received on her extended visit to heaven. You can learn more about Nancy, her message of awakened living, and her other resources at nancyrynes.com

God Loves All of Us Equally

NDErs consistently tell us God universally loves everyone equally and doesn't play favorites in any way. Because She made each of us and considers all of us Her precious creations, God loves us all just the same. It makes no difference whether we are young or old, male or female, rich or poor, black or white, gay or straight, religious or non-religious, saints or sinners, etc., She loves us all completely and unconditionally, no matter what.

"Too often we claim God's love for our closed group. We exclude everyone outside the group as being outside God's love. This is opposed to God's will. God loves everyone beyond anything we can imagine. God loves atheists, agnostics, murderers, prostitutes, thieves, drunks, drug addicts, homeless people, and liars . . . God loves every man, woman, and child on this planet more than we love our own children. God wants all people to have food, shelter, meaningful work, and an opportunity to be creative, to learn the truth, have freedom from fear, have self-esteem, be procreative, live in community, find complete joy, trust in God, and become the wonderful people that God created us to be. Our purpose is to know and do God's will in this life, and we do this when we love one another as God loves us. Every person without exception needs to be loved by us. This is the most difficult and important lesson of our life." Howard Storm

"My experience on the Other Side taught me that there is no room there for petty things like intolerances such as only Christians can go and meet Jesus Christ, and that only via him can one reach the Other Side, heaven. That this place is only for Baptists, or Mormons, Catholics, and other western type Christian-based faiths to the exclusion of Buddhists, Muslims, Native Americans and the countless other flavors of spiritual believers. There is no intolerance whatsoever. It is and remains about love and service, that is it! The choice of whether to live with and by such a belief is very much our own choice. There is no favoritism." Devin

"There were no churches there. It wasn't about just one way. And it wasn't about doctrines and books. But just about a universal compassion and love for everything, for everyone." Anne Horne

Contrary to the opinion of some, NDErs tell us that heaven is not an exclusive, restricted, members-only club available solely for a select group of "chosen" people. God doesn't favor anyone over anyone else. Despite our many differences in appearance, attitude, profession, nationality, sexual orientation, and religion, NDErs remind us that we are all God's treasured children and She loves us all for who we are, not what we look like, who we pray to or worship, who we love, who we vote for, or what country we live in. As we discussed in the beginning, God loves ALL of us universally and unconditionally.

God Doesn't Judge Us

Further, because God loves each and every one of us equally, immensely, and unconditionally, She does not judge us. This revelation shocks most people because we are often taught that God will come at the end of the world on Judgment Day to "judge the living and the dead." Surprisingly, NDErs inform us that God loves us instead of judges us. When you think about it, it actually makes sense because judgment and unconditional love are as incompatible with each other as oil and vinegar. Here's what the NDErs say:

"I was delivered into the hands of God, and I remember waiting and thinking, I haven't been judged yet. I was imperfect! Shouldn't God judge me? Isn't that what I deserve? On earth, I had been judged by people for making mistakes, not being skinny enough or not wearing the right clothes, just being different from everyone else. I waited to be judged by God. I was sure it was coming. But as I waited to be judged the most unexpected thing happened. God, once again, began to fill me with unconditional love. As love flowed through me, it washed away any thoughts and feelings of judgment and disappointment. I never felt judged but I should have been judged. Yet he did not judge me. He loved me!" Erica McKenzie, RN

"I had spent a lifetime of fear of judgment and now, standing with God, I had been known completely and found faultless. I knew God regarded me as perfect. God loved me because love is the totality of God. God loves without limit. Finally it all made sense. God could only love me because God is only love, nothing other than love. The only reality is God; there cannot be another and GOD IS LOVE." Linda Stewart

"The Being was not judging me in any way during the life review, even though I saw a lot of shortcomings in my life. It simply showed my life the way it had been to me, loved me unconditionally, which gave me the strength I needed to see it all the way it was without any blinders, and let me decide for myself what was positive, negative, and what I needed to do about that." Lisa M.

While some people may portray God as an angry, vengeful, and vindictive judge eager to banish all the sinners and evildoers to hell for eternity, NDErs tell us they experience the exact opposite. They only experience God's unconditional love, infinite compassion, and unending forgiveness. Much like the Biblical story of the Prodigal Son, they were joyously welcomed home to heaven with open arms regardless of their mistakes and missteps in life. Their "sins" and wrongdoings weren't held against them but were lovingly shown to them in their Life Review so they could learn from them. Don't misunderstand, God certainly wants us to make choices based on love, compassion, and kindness rather than fear, jealousy, and hatred, but rather than judge us, She unconditionally loves us and ultimately wants us to learn from our less than loving choices.

"I had to see and feel all the hurtful things I had done . . . I had to feel the persons' hurt I caused. But you know how we are taught that we will stand before God and be judged one day? God was not judging me. I was looking at my actions with God at my side loving me while I was judging myself . . . and believe me, no one can judge me any harsher than I already judge myself. It was like getting 'caught' by my parents when doing something wrong, only worse. During the hurtful review I was so ashamed and there was no hiding. My immediate thought, and I said it out loud, 'I'm ready. I belong in Hell. I don't deserve to go to Heaven!' But it felt like He took hold of my arm as I was making my way to Hell and said, 'Wait a minute young lady you get back here! You don't understand and I'm going to explain this to you.' He was asking me, 'What different choices could you have made? What are you learning from this?' Not yelling at me and say-ing, 'How could you do that!?' or, 'You're going to Hell!' This was clearly not the punishing God I had been taught to believe in. The hardest part of this was realizing He had already forgiven me." Mary Beth Willi

If God Doesn't Judge, We Shouldn't Either

Not only does God not judge us, She also wants us to stop judging each other. If we seek to learn and emulate God's unconditional love, then we too should not judge each other. NDErs tell us God wants us to be much more tolerant of each other's differences rather than judge them.

> "Before my NDE, I was much more intolerant and impatient toward other people than I am now. I thought I knew how you should live your life and how you shouldn't. I thought that if you face some great troubles in your life, you can blame only yourself. They are consequences of your own lazi-ness and stupidity. Now I try not to judge people by first sight. I try to think that there might be some greater tragedies that have caused the troubles in their lives . . . I now have more tolerance. I felt in heaven God's and Jesus' love and compassion to me. I know that they don't judge you and that they love every one of us equally, whatever we are like. I know that they are happy when you treat other people well and show their 'children' the same love and compassion that they show you." Mia

> "Tolerance allows you to see that others have their own goals and their own paths . . . I thought it was normal to try to change others . . . That type of behavior shows a complete lack of tolerance, even if you feel it is for a good purpose, aim, or goal. In this physical life we are unable to see the big interconnected picture of the universe, so how can we know what is good for another individual. I was still able to choose whether a person's actions were something I wanted to be around, but that involved changing me, not the other person . . . I had a way of recognizing and respecting the beliefs and practices of others." David Bennett

> "I've learned not to judge others' lives or compare them to mine. I have no idea what their journey is about. I know that each soul is on his or her individual path. They have come here to learn in their own way, on their own terms." Jeff Olsen

> "I knew that diversity makes the world an interesting and colorful place. More knowledge came to my mind that there are immeasurable benefits for not judging people's actions, looks, or differences. I understood that when people felt accepted and were permitted to make free-will choices, they could more easily grow to their personal potential." Dr. Joyce Brown

Clearly, tolerating each others' differences is a key aspect of demon-strating unconditional love for others and God. Since God made each of us, and sees each of us as Her beautiful creation, She wants us to accept each other and understand that everyone is on their own unique path back to Her.

"No one is born hating another person because of the color of his skin or his background or his religion."

Barack Obama, American President

Outward Appearances Can Be Deceiving

When you think about it, many of the judgments we make about others revolve primarily around their outer physical appearance. Many of us make snap judgments about people within the first seconds of seeing them. We quickly stereotype people based almost solely on their exterior attributes: their looks, clothing, shoes, skin color, age, sex, height, etc. When they do not look like us or the way we want them to, we have a tendency to judge them, pigeonhole them, disregard them, and sometimes even demonize them. Psychologists tell us we make almost instantaneous judgments of people based solely on their appearances that significantly impact how we treat them.

The Undercover Reverend

Interestingly, a new church pastor named Willie Lyle felt called by God to spend five days as a homeless person in Clarksville, TN before starting at his new church in the area. In temporarily transforming himself from a respected pastor to a reviled homeless person, Reverend Lyle learned first-hand what it felt like to be ignored and treated with disrespect and disdain by others because of his perceived lot in life. Few people paid attention to him, reached out to him, or cared to learn his story. "Generally speaking, people are not kind to the homeless." Lyle said.

Fortunately he found a place that served hot meals to the homeless, called Loaves and Fishes, where two volunteer teenagers especially stood out. "These two high school boys called me 'Sir,' introduced themselves to me, shook my hand and wanted to know how I was doing. They treated me with respect and dignity," Lyle said. So many others didn't simply because of his appearance.

On the day Reverend Lyle was to be introduced to his new church, he lay outside of it in his homeless overcoat, unshaven face, smelly body, and disheveled look. On their way into church, some of the people spoke with him and offered assistance, but the vast majority just callously passed by him without a word or glance of acknowledgement. When the service began, Lyle walked up to the front of church and began to preach, still looking like a homeless man. As he did, his daughter helped shave off his scruffy beard, he changed his shoes, and he took off his dirty overcoat to reveal his suit and tie underneath. Before his people's eyes, he transformed his outer appearance from the homeless man they just ignored on the front lawn of the church to its new pastor.

"If I made someone squirm, then so be it. Sango UMC is not going to be a congregation that talks about issues and solutions. We are going to be part of the solutions to the problems we face in our community . . . I wanted everybody to know what I had been through, what I had learned and the physical and emotional discomfort I experienced . . . We look at the outside of others and make judgments. God looks inside at our heart and sees the truth," Reverend Lyle said. Lyle's undercover operation not only helped him better understand the plight of the homeless, it challenged his entire church to change how they judged and ultimately treated others based solely on how they looked physically rather than getting to know the true soul inside of them.

Our Body is Our Overcoat

What's really interesting is that many NDErs soon come to realize that we are far more than our human body. Rather than solely identifying with our body as who we really are, they quickly learn that our body is merely a temporary outer shell that effectively houses our spirit for our time on earth.

For example, as death nears, virtually all NDErs spiritually separate from their physical body. Their spirit lifts up and out of their body and they often are able to see their body from a third-person perspective, as if they were up in the corner of the room looking down on the situation. Strangely, they often have a detached view and nonchalantly look at their own body as simply a kind of outer covering that people wear. In fact, some NDErs, upon leaving their physical body, even talk about viewing their body as an old familiar coat, jacket, or even a costume they happily discard at death—and have to stuff their spirits back into when they return.

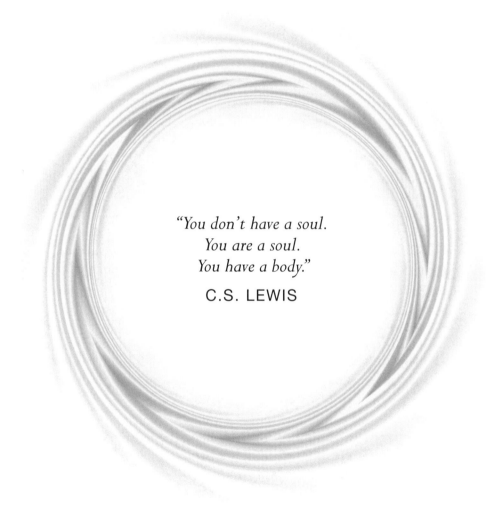

"You don't have a soul.
You are a soul.
You have a body."

C.S. LEWIS

"I looked at my body, the body I knew so well, and was surprised by my detachment. I felt the same sort of gratitude toward my body that I had for my old winter coat when I put it away in the spring. It had served me well, but I no longer needed it. I had absolutely no attachment to it. Whatever constituted the self I knew as me was no longer there. My essence, my consciousness, my memories, my personality were outside, not in that prison of flesh." Kimberly Clark Sharp

"I came up to a man, or a body, laying on a gurney and so I stepped closer and took a look and realized, oh my goodness, that's me! But it wasn't me. I was having this incredible connected experience but there was my body, there was that skin suit that I had been wearing around life." Jeff Olsen

"I found myself excited to be out of the meat jacket I had been wearing . . . They made me come back. I felt the pull so fast and the next thing I knew I was back in my body. The meat jacket. All of the pain and misery was back." Tonja B.

In fact, the word "incarnate" literally means to become flesh or "wear a coat of meat." So it is not surprising that NDErs, once separated from their skin, view the physical body as an outer covering for their soul. They surprisingly say the body is not who they really are but come to realize that it is a protective covering for their soul for their time on earth; much like a deep sea diver wears a diving suit and helmet underwater or an astronaut wears a space suit in outer space. The body is a helpful and functional covering for the soul but doesn't define who we are at our essence. Obviously, this is a strange concept for many to consider because most of us are so intricately tied to our body, how it looks, and how it functions. We have been conditioned to think we are our body because we intimately feel everything we touch, taste, see, hear, and smell. But NDErs inform us that we are so much more than our physical looks and body.

"I became aware that the thing on the sidewalk, that thing that suddenly became a piece of meat to me, was what I had identified as myself before, but had no connection with it other than that I had been with it for a very long time. But it had nothing to do with me because suddenly, I was more of a person than I had ever been before. I was more conscious than I could ever be. I was free of the limitations of being a physical being." Reinee Pasarow

"When we have done all the work we were sent to do,
we are allowed to shed our body, which imprisons our soul
like a cocoon encloses a butterfly."
Elizabeth Kubler-Ross, Author of *On Death and Dying*

Thus, if the body is indeed basically an outer covering for our soul, rather than judging people on what we see on the outside, we need to remember that each person's soul on the inside is what really matters—not the brown, black, white, big, little, new, old, dirty, or clean corporal coat they might have on them. Deep down, underneath the jacket of the human body, people are all essentially the same with similar fears, frustrations, hopes, dreams, and a unique and important purpose. Underneath the bodily overcoat they wear for their earthly journey, everyone is a child of God. Honor, respect, and love them as such rather than judging them.

"No longer did I see people as strangers to me in the physical realm, I was now seeing them in their true form, as I was. They were all beings of spiritual Light at the core of their being. Their human body was simply a protective covering that is used to enable the soul to function well in the physical realm." Nancy Clark

"The real me was not attached to that body. I honestly didn't think I could shove myself back into what had once felt so familiar, but now I identified as foreign . . . I knew that body wasn't me! I was limitless, powerful, filled with God's love and light . . . I was a spiritual being, not that limp, worn out, abused body on the gurney. It was too confining and claustrophobic to even consider trying to stuff myself inside it. My body felt heavy and confined as if I'd been zipped inside a jacket two sizes too small . . . It wasn't me at all! I had lived as a multidimensional being, basking in the love of God's presence only to be forced back into the stark reality of a three-dimensional body. How could I possibly go back to that?" Erica McKenzie, RN

"You are more than your physical body. You almost have to get out of your body to realize that. My body is my physical façade that I present to everyone. Once you have this type of experience you don't see any differences in people, no matter what the color of their skin is. We are all one. We're all part of the same family, from the same origin." Juliana

---

"These bodies are perishable, but the dwellers in these bodies are eternal, indestructible, and impenetrable."

Bhagavad Gita, Hindu Religious Text

Instead of immediately and unfairly judging people by the outer bodily coat or costume they wear while here on earth, understand and respect that they are a fellow spiritual traveler that is much more similar to you than different. Accept everyone nonjudgmentally as a fellow beautiful soul, rather than quickly judging and possibly rejecting them as a different-looking human.

> "We are here to have love for every person born on earth. Their earthly form might be black, yellow, brown, handsome, ugly, thin, fat, wealthy, poor, intelligent or ignorant, but we are not to judge by these appearances. Each spirit has the capacity to be filled with love and eternal energy." Betty Eadie

> "What I learned on the Other Side, there is no gay, there is no black, there is no Muslim, there is no Christian, there is no wealthy, there is no poor. There is spirit. All those categories that we've been taught, for century after century, that's not what you see on the Other Side. What you see on the Other Side is spirit. What you feel is the essence of love. That's it. What I learned when I came back, those people, those leaders, and those who abuse power are the ones who divide us by putting us in these categories." Peter Anthony

> "It changes the way you look at people. It changes the way you accept people. It changes the way you view the world because if you view each person instead of their body being who they are, if you view them as their soul instead, then you overlook height differences, weight differences, color, religion, anything. It totally changes your outlook. Each person is just another soul. When you look beyond the exterior and you look for who they are, it's way more beautiful to find who they are inside rather than just seeing the outside of the person and judging that." Barbara Bartolome

We all know people who might initially look gruff and tough and intimidating on the outside, but after we get to know them, we discover they are this sweet, gentle, teddy bear of a soul on the inside. Similarly, some people might appear meek and mild on the outside but after talking with them we find out there is an intense, passionate, and relentless tiger on the inside. Just as you don't judge a book by its cover, you also don't want to judge people by their outer covering. Get to know the real person and spirit within.

5. Accept Nonjudgmentally

*"My soul is not contained within the limits of my body.
My body is contained within the limitlessness of my soul."*

Jim Carrey, Actor/Comedian

The Interconnected Web of Humanity

Not only are we much more than our physical body, another real reason NDErs remind us not to judge, hate, or persecute people is that we are all one big interconnected family of humanity. Despite being separated into different and distinct physical bodies, NDErs repeatedly mention they see how all of us are interconnected at a deeper spiritual level.

"What if I could feel the unconditional love I was now experiencing for every soul? I marveled at my perceptions. Most of my life I had actually avoided people. Now, everyone I saw was truly my brother or sister. In fact it went even deeper than that. They were, in a strange sense, me! We were all connected pieces in a huge puzzle of oneness. Words Jesus had said rushed to my recollection: 'Inasmuch as ye have done it unto the least of these my brethren ye have done it to me.' Was he talking about the awareness I was experiencing? Did he feel the same thing I was feeling? Was this how he walked the earth, in the consciousness of knowing each individual soul at this deep level of love? I realized he didn't see himself as better than the beggar or the prisoner; he knew he was one with them . . . We are all linked and equal in God's eyes." Jeff Olsen

"The most important thing I have learned since my experience, the message I want to share with the world, is that we are all connected. Life, at least in Western culture, teaches us to be independent . . . We build fences and walls, both literally and figuratively, to keep others out. This independence is confusing and contrary to what our spirits need and desire . . . I am linked in spirit with the criminal, the beggar, the infirm. It is by recognizing this truth that I realize that I too could have gone the way of the thief, the impoverished, or the afflicted." Penny Wilson

"We're all interconnected. Every little action we do, every thought, every word affects so many things around us and we have to remember that. We need to actually start loving each other and caring for each other and being there for each other. It's hard, we're in this 3D, heavy world, this existence and we've kind of forgotten about where we're from and who we are and what we're about which is love . . . We need to wake up and we need to be good to each other. It's about love." Heidi Craig

NDErs liken the connections we have with each other to an invisible spiritual web, much like the fine stands of a translucent spider web, that holds us all together as one big web of life.

"As I looked around the room, I saw these silver cords that are attached to each person's solar plexus and attached to one another. They were thin, silver cords almost like a thick piece of wire. Each one was attached to another like a spider web. And I could feel each person in there. I could feel all their emotions, everything they were thinking. It was crazy—it was great!" Kathy Baker

"Interconnectedness exists between all living beings and the Divine Consciousness at all times. We are always connected to everyone else . . . Once you feel this interconnection you cannot help but know compassion for everyone. Compassion leads us to truly care for the wellbeing of any person, regardless of race or background. As compassion grows within so do patience, understanding, and tolerance in every situation we experience . . . I recall my life review and seeing those ribbons and slivers of light that connect us to one another, how my actions and life experiences affected others." David Bennett

"All forms of life—plants, rocks, animals, people—are interconnected; they come from the same source of light. Everything is united by a transparent net, or web, and each thread shines with great radiance. Everything pulses with the same luminosity—a magnificent light of unparalleled brilliance." Josiane Antonette

Although almost all of us can't physically see the connections between us, we can certainly feel them, especially when it comes to family members and close friends. Each of us likely feels a very deep heart connection with our close loved ones. Our deep love for them pulls on our heart-strings and feels like we are connected heart to heart—which NDErs tell us we really are. I can remember getting and giving hearty and heart-warming hugs from my young daughter when it felt like our hearts sent out tendrils that wrapped themselves around each other. Ironically, I actually called them "Heaven Hugs" at the time because at that moment the palpable love I felt between us seemed as amazing as what the love would be like in heaven. It was so easy to feel the loving connection between us—even though I couldn't physically see it.

In addition to our connections with family and friends, we also have connections with our greater humanity as a whole. Though we probably don't notice them nearly as much, they are still there and can be strengthened by fully accepting others for who they are and extending love to them. NDErs tell us we are all parts of the greater human

*"Humankind has not woven
the web of life. We are but one
thread within it. Whatever we
do to the web, we do to ourselves.
All things are bound together.
All things connect."*

CHIEF SEATTLE

body and each play a role in God's Divine Plan as we mentioned earlier in the Work Purposely chapter.

Taking this interconnection a step further, we are all part of the same body of humanity. Thus, just as our fingers may look different and perform a different function than our toes, we still don't judge our toes and put them down for being different than our fingers. We are all part of the same body with different appearances and functions. We need to respect and value the differences of each of our body parts because together they make up a fully functioning body. Similarly, we need to value and respect all people and cultures because they each make up a different part of our humanity. Judging, ridiculing, and harming them ultimately hurts all of us.

"A human being is a part of the whole called by us universe, a part limited in time and space. We experience our self, our thoughts and feelings as something separated from the rest, a kind of optical delusion of consciousness. This delusion is a kind of prison, restricting us to our personal desires and to affection for a few persons nearest to us. Our task must be to free ourselves from this prison by widening our circle of compassion to embrace all living creatures and the whole of nature in its beauty."

Albert Einstein, Physicist

Accepting Nonjudgmentally Means Loving Everyone

Ultimately, we are challenged to love and accept everyone universally and unconditionally, just as God does, regardless of their appearance, skin color, beliefs, values, politics, and behavior. This doesn't mean excusing their bad behavior, letting criminals roam the streets, or staying in abusive relationships, it does mean though that we need to recognize everyone as a fellow child of God who is likely acting in unloving and harmful ways either out of ignorance, emotional pain, fear, a chemical imbalance, or a lack of self love. Rather than seeking revenge and retribution, we should try to help them if at all possible. Helping might mean hospitalizing or incarcerating them for a time to keep them from doing further harm to others while they rehabilitate themselves. We are to see each person as an aspect of God, because truly they are.

"Spiritual love doesn't mean loving just those people in our families, or simply loving people we agree with, but loving everyone and everything. That's Big Love, and it is not always easy for us humans to live this way. Each person has a spiritual spark inside. Each person is an expression of Divine love—not just those people we count as family or friends, but everyone. When we look into the eyes of another, we are also looking directly at Spirit. Each person is an expression of divinity, a window into the Creator, no matter the color of his skin, her religious affiliation, politics, or financial status. How could we not love each person we see, and thus love Spirit more fully through them? . . . My Guide insisted that we try our best to extend love to everyone and everything on Earth: to you, your spouse or partner, friends, your siblings, the unfriendly neighbor down the street, the politician we don't agree with, those people across the sea that your country invaded last year, the folks with the skin color a shade or two different than your own, those who worship in a slightly different way from you, fans of the opposing team, and even the animals. All are a part of God and God loves them all." Nancy Rynes

"I knew that accepting people at their own level of growth and patiently letting them learn from their choices can bring peace and joy beyond description. Acceptance would bring a form of freedom—freedom from pettiness, from prejudice, from judging and being judged. The freedom I felt was wonderful as I understood that each person has different interests and goals and was to be permitted to learn from the results of their choices." Dr. Joyce Brown

Judgment vs. Discernment

Does acceptance mean we have to agree with all the unloving things people say and do and put up with things that clearly go against our morals and values? No, of course not. NDEr David Bennett distinguishes between the concepts of judgment and discernment to help us understand the difference.

"The more I was able to observe, the better I became at allowing people to be where they were on their path, even though I might not agree with them. I found that even in a conflict, I was able to distance myself and use discernment instead of judgment to help me decide if I wanted to interact or not. The lack of judgment in my life reviews brought me to explore the differences between judgment and discernment. I found that in discernment, you are not adding labels. You are not seeing it as good or bad, you are saying, 'Is this a part of my path? Or is this something I do not need to be involved in.' Through discipline it simply becomes perception in the absence of judgment."

So look at different and difficult people and situations with discernment. It is more than okay to have preferences and believe things and do things differently than others; that's both normal and natural because each of us is obviously unique. The key, however, is not to belittle, exclude, or attack others simply because they are different. Seek to understand their viewpoint, even though it might be drastically different than yours. Whenever possible, use open-minded discernment to see if something fits for you rather than discriminating judgment to label it as good or bad whenever possible. In short, just because something might not be your way doesn't mean it is the wrong way.

We Judge Ourselves

If God doesn't judge us and we are not supposed to judge others, is anyone ever held accountable for their unloving and bad behavior? The answer is an emphatic YES! NDErs tell us we ultimately judge ourselves, and often are our harshest critics. We actually hold ourselves accountable because we judge and learn from our behavior and empathically feel the impact we had on others in our Life Review.

> "Guess what? When you have your panoramic life review, you are the judger . . . You do the judging. If you doubt me, believe this: you are the toughest judge you will ever have. The concept that we are our own judges is a difficult one for most people to grasp. In the Western world, many have come to believe that God will preside over our eternal fate, sitting like a judge on the bench, deciding if we are good enough to join him in heaven or are so bad that we warrant an eternity in hell . . . I found that I sat in judgment of myself. I did not receive a stern rebuke from the Being of Light, which initiated my life review. Instead I felt the love and joy that a wise grandfather might radiate to a grandchild who has not yet gained the wisdom of long life. 'You are the difference that God makes,' the Being of Light communicated to me. 'And that difference is love.'" Dannion Brinkley

> "Even at the end of it, no one is going to judge you but yourself. You will be accountable for everything you've done here. But not accountable like you are going to be punished. It is not going to happen like that. You are going to be accountable [because] you will understand and see what you did and what you should have done. And you, from the love of who you are; the immense love that you are, you will want to do something about it and you will not allow it to not be corrected and fixed by yourself . . ." Julie Aubier

> "In our Life Reviews, it's not God that's judging us, it's not the ascended masters, it's not our loved ones, it's us. We're not judging ourselves

harshly or negatively or mean. We're just looking at it as, 'Oh, wow! So because of that action I caused that.' We're looking at it with compassion and with love so that we can learn and we can grow. But it's us—we are the ones reviewing our own life. We're not really judging it, we're having to process it to learn from it." Heidi Craig

"Nothing about my life was secret to God, nor to the spiritual beings, yet I did not perceive that I was being judged . . . There was no one among the assemblage of spiritual beings who was about to cast the first stone at me. I was going to need support to give me the courage and strength to review my life . . . I realized it was I who would be conducting the review." Ned Dougherty

Ultimately, we judge ourselves. We unmistakably and indelibly learn the impact of our loving thoughts and actions as well as our fearful and hateful thoughts and actions because we completely experience their full impact in our Life Review as if we did them to ourselves. While we often feel tremendous remorse and regret for our unloving thoughts and actions, God loves and accepts us through it all, rather than judging us. She doesn't replay our own unloving behaviors to torture us, even though it may initially seem that way as we feel the intense pain we caused others, but to help us see and more importantly feel how our thoughts and actions impact others, like Marion Rome's "Oliver/Superfat" story; to learn how interconnected we truly are. The purpose is to help us learn and grow by seeing how we indeed are so closely connected with our earthly brothers and sisters that we get to see and feel how our lives impacted them.

"The purpose of the review is not for punishment, but for spiritual growth through understanding the ramifications of our actions, thereby gaining increased compassion for others." Ron K.

"At the end of this life screen event, I was not left with anyone telling me, 'You sinned! You're a sinner! You did this and this and this that was bad and against the Ten Commandments!' Rather, I was left to form an opinion of the life." Brian S.

ACCEPT NONJUDGMENTALLY | MAJOR LESSONS

- God loves all of us immensely and equally—there are no favorites

- Because God loves us unconditionally, She doesn't judge us. She simply wants us to learn from our life experiences, not to punish us

- Because God doesn't judge us, we should not judge each other

- There is no room for intolerance based on anything—religion, sexual orientation, politics, gender, etc.

- Love others the way God made them, each person is on a different path with different things to learn and different gifts to share—we don't know the challenges they've faced or the path they are on

- Most of our judgments are superficial based on a person's outer appearance—however we are not our bodies but the spirit that animates them—at our core we are each portions of God's light, with the same human attributes and challenges

- We are all interconnected and our success is bound together— we are all parts of the same body of humanity, even though we look different, we are all a part of the human family

- Discernment rather than judgment—we may prefer certain things but we don't have the right to judge others

- Ultimately, we judge ourselves and hold ourselves accountable

Proverbs

Birds of a _____

A man's best ____ are his ten

An ___ of pluck is _____ a ┼

_____ wind that blows┼

is never ___ late ___ mend

nobody
feather
together

6.

LEARN CONTINUOUSLY

EARTH TEACH ME TO REMEMBER

Earth teach me stillness, as the grasses are stilled with light.
Earth teach me suffering, as old stones suffer with memory.
Earth teach me humility, as blossoms are humble with beginning.
Earth teach me caring, as the mother who secures her young.
Earth teach me courage, as the tree which stands all alone.
Earth teach me limitation, as the ant which crawls on the ground.
Earth teach me freedom, as the eagle which soars in the sky.
Earth teach me resignation, as the leaves which die in the fall.
Earth teach me regeneration, as the seed which rises in the spring.
Earth teach me to forget myself, as melted snow forgets its life.
Earth teach me to remember kindness, as dry fields weep with rain.

John Yellow Lark, Lakota Chief

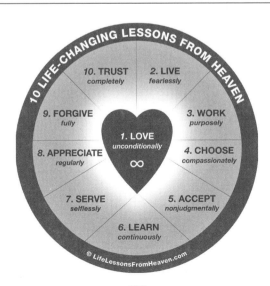

NDEr FEATURE

Jeff Olsen: Things Happen for a Reason, There Are No Accidents

Jeff Olsen experienced his NDE when the vehicle he was driving at 75 mph on an interstate highway rolled eight times with his family inside—instantly killing his wife Tamara and 14-month-old son Griffin, while barely sparing Jeff and his seven-year-old son, Spencer. Jeff's NDE included his deceased wife Tamara pleading with him that he couldn't come to heaven with her because Spencer needed a father on earth. Severely injured, Jeff had his left leg amputated and endured months of rehab to recover from the terrible crash. Yet as life-changing as the horrible accident was, Jeff transformed the hardship into a powerful message of hope. He is an inspiring speaker with a moving message. He shares his story through his excellent book *Knowing*. Learn more about Jeff at www.envoypublishing.com.

We Come to Earth to Learn Lessons

As we discussed in the initial Love Unconditionally chapter, one of the primary reasons we are here on earth is to experientially learn lessons. Just as we send our kids to school to learn lessons about math, science, history, etc., God also sends us to school to experience and learn life lessons, many of them revolving around love. NDErs come back with the messages that God, with our consent, basically enrolls each of us in "Earth School" to provide us with millions of experiences to help us learn how to give and receive love. We learn these various lessons as we face different experiences and tests in life, learn from different mentors and teachers as we progress, and learn by studying religious texts like the Bible, Qur'an, Bhagavad Gita, Vedas, Tripitaka, I Ching, and many other sacred books. The primary educational approach of Earth School is active, experiential, and ideally, service learning. The main point of our time on earth is to learn by doing through making choices, reflecting on their impact and consequences, and absorbing the lessons as we make our way through the curriculum of life.

God Expects Us to Make Mistakes as We Learn

Just as we know our own children will make mistakes as they learn to walk, ride a bike, play a sport, and study in school, God also expects us to make mistakes in our lives and loves us regardless of them. He knows that providing us with the opportunity to try things on our own, make mistakes, and see the results of our choices, is the best way for us to learn and grow spiritually. So God knows we will make mistakes; He just hopes we learn from them so that we don't have to continually repeat them.

> "You will make mistakes. That is how you learn and grow. If you didn't make mistakes, you would either be perfect or dead. God created a world where you learn by your experience. The important thing you need to learn is to stop repeating those same mistakes over and over again . . . God wants you and every person to succeed in your spiritual growth . . . When you make a mistake, you need to consider what you did and why you did it. You should seek a better alternative. Tell God in the clearest way you know how what you did, why you did it, and what you are going to do about it. Do you think we expect you to be perfect? When you make a mistake, ask for forgiveness, and before you utter it you are forgiven, but you must ask for it. Try not to repeat mistakes. Learn, move on. The purpose of your life is to learn how to make your will God's will." Howard Storm

There are No Mistakes, Only Lessons

Fortunately, God doesn't even really consider our mistakes as problems. He sees our mistakes as natural and normal lessons—just as we know our children will fall down numerous times when learning to walk but love them just the same. As we discussed in the previous chapter on Accept Nonjudgmentally, God does not judge us regarding the choices we make; we judge ourselves. So in God's view, NDErs tell us there really are no mistakes, just lessons.

> "There are no mistakes, only lessons. We come here to learn lessons, teach lessons, or both. I was shown that I chose the lessons I wanted to learn before I came here. We will keep repeating the same lesson until we learn it—and sometimes we need to back up, rethink our decisions and then make different choices and then move on. In the midst of my worst 'mistakes' were the best lessons. Change is to be embraced not feared—it is how we move forward." Mary Beth Willi

In this way, God really isn't looking to punish us when bad things happen in our lives or we make unloving choices. As the Divine who loves us unconditionally, He simply wants us to learn lessons from our experiences, whether they happen to be positive or negative.

Making Sense of Life's Hardships and Heartaches

"Into each life, a little rain must fall," Henry Wordsworth Longfellow once said. For some of us, the hardships of life might seem like a drizzle or light rain. However, for others, the hardships seem like a hurricane with torrential rains, gale force winds, and massive flooding that seems like it will never subside. We wonder if, like Noah, we should have built an Ark.

Life's hardships, crises, and catastrophes, often called Dark Nights of the Soul, are without a doubt always excruciating to experience, understand, and explain, especially when they almost drown us and it seems impossible to keep our head above water. Whether it is a category five hurricane devastating a country, a terrible terrorist attack wielded on innocent bystanders, or a raging forest fire torching habitats and homes, national and international crises impact virtually all people. On a much more personal level, the difficult death of a loved one, an unexpected job loss, cancer diagnosis, messy divorce, or bankruptcy is always tough to understand, deal with, and recover from. We all experience many adversities and hardships we must endure throughout our lifetime.

From a human perspective, life's hardships often feel like hell on earth. These inexplicable hardships often shock us, scare us, devastate us, cause tremendous upheaval in our lives, and rock us to the core. We often question whether we will make it through them and if we somehow do, wonder if our lives will ever be the same again. Life's hardships break us open, expose us, and often have us feel so vulnerable, alone, and helpless. Sometimes, things seem so dire that people even contemplate and complete suicide because they can't bear the heartache anymore. In no way should we ignore or minimize or erase the extreme human pain and misery that life's hardships can cause. They hurt deeply and the pain is real—very real. However . . .

Stronger Where We've Been Broken

As Ernest Hemingway once said, "We're stronger in the places that we've been broken." An unmistakable and undeniable message NDErs come back to share with us is that our broken moments in life do often initially break us down only to eventually build us back up and make us stronger. "The wound is the place where the Light enters you," said Sufi poet Rumi. NDErs validate the saying, "What doesn't kill you makes you stronger" with their insights on handling hardships.

"While in the presence of the Light everything made sense. I feel that our suffering is the greatest of all blessings. We learn the most from that which nearly kills us." William C.

"As I reflect on the past forty-three years of my life, I realize these experiences were not mistakes, but opportunities for learning. They appeared as cancer, eating disorders, drug addiction, peer pressure, bullying, learning disabilities, endometriosis, early menopause, a career, being a parent, feeling judged and unaccepted, loneliness, heartache, anger, depression, challenging relationships, uncertainty, frustration, poor health, a near-death experience and more. At times, these experiences were overwhelming and I felt they were potential roadblocks. From my near-death experience, I learned that these potential roadblocks were actually incredible learning opportunities and by embracing the lesson in each experience they would never manifest into roadblocks. Rather, they presented an opportunity for me to choose to change something that would result in powerful healing and awakening in my life." Erica McKenzie, RN

Beauty Can Come from Brokenness

The Japanese art of kintsugi is a perfect example of how life's hardships and scars can actually be transformed into immense value and beauty. Kintsugi, which means "join with gold," is the ancient art of repairing broken ceramics with a golden glue. Much like our lives seem irreparably shattered when hardships hit, damaged ceramics can break into numerous jagged and imperfect pieces. Rather than lamenting the loss, believing the item no longer has any value, and discarding the broken pieces, kintsugi artists embrace the brokenness, incorporate the shards into the grand design, and lovingly join them back together by binding them with a beautiful golden glue. Instead of hiding and disguising the cracks, the artists illuminate and adorn them with gold to signify the beauty that can come from the times when our hearts feel crushed and cracked open. The reassembled pieces remind us of life's fragility, that we can recover from tragedies and become whole again, that our scars can be a proud part of our history, and that unforeseen beauty can come from brokenness. It's actually the imperfections and scars that make it much more unique, beautiful, and strong. Ironically, the seemingly "broken" ceramic painstakingly mended by kintsugi is often many times more valuable and durable than the original, unbroken item. By enduring and embracing life's hardships, we too can gain much more value, strength, perspective, and beauty when we treasure rather than try to hide our brokenness, scars, and imperfections.

View Hardships as "Spiritual Muscle Builders"

Another way to think of life's inevitable hardships comes from NDEr Dr. Joyce Brown who calls them "Spiritual Muscle Builders." Just as workouts in the weight room help build our physical muscles, so too do the hardships of life help build our spiritual muscles. Think about it . . . Athletes purposely go the weight room to lift heavy weights multiple times, taxing their muscles to the maximum. While they feel tremendous physical discomfort and even outright bodily pain during their strenuous workouts, they know it is all for the important purpose of building their muscles. They willingly endure the physical pain because they understand the phrase "no pain, no gain." They consciously and eagerly strain and pain themselves to break down their muscles because they know their bodies will build them back up again at a much stronger level.

Similarly, the hardships we face in life build our spiritual muscles. The problems we experience are often extremely painful as they break us down emotionally. We spiritually struggle through the difficult crisis much like we physically struggle to move the heavy weights, wondering if we will ever make it through the ordeal. However, just like consistent weight room workouts eventually build physical muscles, so too do life's hardships build our spiritual muscles. The unpleasant and sometimes searing pain we suffer through helps us grow stronger spiritually and gain more insight, humility, love, and appreciation than we would have without the trials.

> "I realized that living in the world and accepting the tests throughout life builds character for eternity. Life is somewhat like a game—only the score is actually kept more on the Other Side than on earth. When my life review showed that there were difficult tests in my life I had passed, I was filled with joy. As knowledge filled my mind, I knew that each of my adversities carried with it a seed of opportunity for growth and improvement. But I needed faith to recognize and continue with patience until the growth was realized. That was the challenge—to persist and look for the good . . . Also, I learned that problems can refine the spirit . . . they are spiritual muscle builders. I realized that there are all kinds of coping techniques available on earth if only we open our minds and hearts to them." Dr. Joyce Brown

Why Bad Things Happen to Good People

The suffering we endure breaks us down to build us up—better, stronger, wiser, and kinder—if we choose to grow from it. Hardships force us to dig deeper, prioritize what really matters, and get to know who we actually are at our core—marvelous and miraculous Spiritual Beings having a soul-refining human experience. Like the raging forest fire that devastates the landscape only to clear out the dead wood and make way for the new, vibrant, and heartier growth that often lies dormant underneath, the horrendous hardships we face in earthly life often eventually do the same for us—as they first seemingly ravage us, then, if we choose to let them, lovingly restore and revitalize our soul.

In fact, as an excellent analogy, the Lodgepole Pine has cones that are so tightly sealed with resin that the only way they can open is by being exposed to the intense heat of a forest fire. Only by being subjected to the extreme heat, the Lodgepole Pine cone cracks open and is finally allowed to sprout and grow. So too are we sometimes only able to grow after surviving the searing heat of life's hardships and cracking open to a spiritually bigger life. Ultimately, the hardships we experience aren't here to destroy us but rather to develop us. This is obviously tough to see, feel, and believe while experiencing the scorching heat and stifling smoke of the blaze itself.

"Sometimes we face many difficult roads on our journey before we attain the full stature of a spiritual human being. I learned a very important lesson from my transcendent experience. Each one of us is purified by the darkness the mystics call the dark night of the soul, a feeling God has deserted us. Our pain and suffering, the failures of our endeavors, the betrayals we experience are actually blessings in disguise. The moments of crisis or darkness are actually the beginning of a deeper intimate experience with our Creator calling us to grow beyond where we are at that particular time of our spiritual growth . . . We may not be able to understand why bad things happen to good people . . . As we make our passage through life, our experiences, the good and the bad, are ultimately, the growth of soul." Nancy Clark

"I always get the question: 'Why do bad things happen to good people?' I can tell people, based on my experience of what I learned, that we come here on a soul mission to learn. We are here to love and we are here to learn lessons to evolve to ascend our soul." Heidi Craig

"I learned why bad things happen to good people. If nothing bad ever happened to us, we would all basically be the same. It is like metal in a forge. You have to heat it and strike it repeatedly to make a useful tool from it." Henry W.

"When something bad happens you have three choices. You can either let it define you, let it destroy you, or you can let it strengthen you."

DR. SEUSS

"What is to give light must endure burning."
Viktor Frankl, Author of *Man's Search for Meaning*

Suffering Sets Up Soul Growth and Development

According to NDErs, the primary purpose of suffering human hardships is that they ultimately set us up for tremendous spiritual growth and development. Though we all wish there were more pleasant options, it seems our earthly struggles are the best shapers of our soul. Pain (physical, mental, emotional) seems to be built into the human experience in hopes that we respond lovingly, process the lessons, and transform the pain into powerful perspective and growth.

> "I was told why we are here and why we suffer. I was told we all have to live out lessons on earth for our souls to grow—like children learning new things. We suffer in order to learn how to cope with things and to develop our souls." Charmaine M.

> "Our souls are here to learn lessons and we learn them through the difficulties in this life. By embracing those difficulties and seeing them as learning opportunities, realizing that by manifesting that love and compassion in this imperfect realm, that that is how we progress in that higher spiritual realm." Dr. Eben Alexander

Interestingly, when NDEr Richard L. asked if he could stay longer in heaven after being told he was being sent back to earth, the angels told him, "We don't think you will want to stay long, you never do. You love your lessons, especially the hard ones." The angels seem to suggest that despite the pain we often experience from our earthly lessons, especially the hard ones, we actually value them once we view them from a heavenly vantage point because of what they teach us and the tremendous soul growth we can experience through them.

While most people are familiar with the concept of post-traumatic stress (PTS), psychologists also say there is an equally powerful condition called post-traumatic growth (PTG), defined as when a person experiences a positive change as the result of struggling with a major life crisis or tragic event. The struggle becomes the catalyst for significant growth that would not have occurred otherwise.

"Hardships prepare ordinary people for an extraordinary life."
C.S. Lewis, Author

7 WAYS TO PROCESS THE PAIN AND PURPOSE OF LIFE'S HARDSHIPS

Based on what they're told during their time in heaven, NDErs come back with some very helpful suggestions for the rest of us on how to best make sense of and process the seemingly inexplicable hardships we endure on earth. They encourage us to somehow find purpose and even value in the truly horrible on a human level, yet helpful on a soul level experience. Here are seven ways NDErs suggest we process our hardships and heartaches.

1. Experiencing hardships is normal, inevitable, and universal.

In addition to the many joys in life, we also should expect life to be difficult. When our soul jumps in a human body and comes to earth, we knowingly enter a dualistic world with both positives and negatives: pleasure and pain, fun and fear, happiness and hardships. Put bluntly: "stuff" happens to us and those we love. It is part of the deal. Hardships are a necessary part of the curriculum we all signed up for when God lovingly enrolled our courageous souls in this challenging Earth School. Problems, adversities, tragedies, and catastrophes come with the territory and are intentionally built into the lesson plan for us to learn and grow from them. Everyone experiences them to some degree—some obviously much more so and more intensely than others.

> "The Buddha was right: life is about suffering. While alive we are captors, chained by the pains and pleasures of our neurons. As long as we pursue sensory pleasure, we must endure pain." Ron K.

> "We came here for one thing. And that was to learn about ourselves. That's it . . . So we are not down here to prove anything to God. We're not down here to earn His love. We're not down here to do certain things to make ourselves righteous in His eyes. All those things are great, all those things are awesome, but that's not why we came down here. We came down here to experience opposition. We came down here to feel the opposite. For example, you would never know what great health felt like if you'd never been sick. You would never know what a wonderful day in Hawaii would be like if you didn't live in a winter environment. You'd go to Hawaii in the middle of the winter and you're going 'Yeah, this is awesome!' and the guy on the beach that's local is like 'What's your big deal, man? It's this way every day.' So it's the opposition that defines us. It's the space between these things that creates form. All of these things need each other. We need opposition to even know who we are." Ryan Rampton

"Earth is one of the stages for drama in which we play our part. What would drama be like without villains? In our theaters and TV shows, don't we enjoy the conflicts between the villains and the heroes? How flat life would be without marches for peace, caring for the ill and dying, building houses for the poor, entering the political arena for a cause, etc. Every stage is the evolution of man offered challenges. As I see it, this is the nature of the Divine plan. I believe that God not only enjoys the drama of exploding stars and colliding galaxies but also enjoys the dramatic evolution of life and human society." Eunice Brock

"We came into this world to have trouble and to learn from it. Unfortunately many people don't realize this and complain about their bad luck and spend their lives chasing pleasure, fame, and money. Then they die without making any spiritual progress." Arthur Yensen

---

"The lotus is the most beautiful flower, whose petals open one by one. But it will only grow in the mud. In order to grow and gain wisdom, first you must have the mud—the obstacles of life and its suffering . . . The mud speaks of the common ground that humans share, no matter what our stations in life . . . Whether we have it all or we have nothing, we are all faced with the same obstacles: sadness, loss, illness, dying and death. If we are to strive as human beings to gain more wisdom, more kindness and more compassion, we must have the intention to grow as a lotus and open each petal one by one."

Goldie Hawn, Actress

---

2. Try Not to Fear or Resist Your Growth-Promoting Hardships

NDErs also tell us not to fear the challenges that are ultimately designed to help us grow. While we very likely are going to hate them from a human perspective, especially in the moment, we are still challenged to accept and, if possible, eventually embrace them from a spiritual perspective for the soul growth they will eventually produce.

As those in the military often say, "Embrace the Suck." We too are encouraged to accept and embrace the hardships we experience—always keeping in mind the growth opportunities they provide us. Ellen Debenport, author of *Hell in the Hallway, Light at the Door* reminds us, "We are not on earth to transcend our humanity but to experience it fully. We came into human form because we could learn something here we couldn't learn otherwise."

"What you resist, persists. I resisted personal and spiritual growth, and the universe persisted in its efforts to teach me in spite of myself . . . It is imperative that we do not fear the challenges we have attracted to promote our growth. Armed with gratitude and good cheer, there is no mountain we cannot climb in order to reach the pinnacle of our spiritual power. Every obstacle we encounter is an opportunity for spiritual evolution." Dannion Brinkley

"We need to change our thoughts about suffering and learn to turn it around so then we can embrace it. Running away from suffering only prolongs it. I learned we should face the difficulty, look at it deeply and clearly, so we can rise above the problem. As we come to new understandings of our troubles they no longer give the same pain . . . We can use our difficulties and problems to awaken the heart and make it stronger." David Bennett

As Dannion says, "What you resist, persists." If you don't face the challenge and learn how to deal with it effectively, it will likely continue to rear its ugly head again in your life at some time in the future. Rather than continually fighting the hardship, learn how to make peace with it and effectively overcome it. Make it your friend instead of your foe. You can do this by simply asking yourself, "What am I to learn from this situation?" It is the best way to learn from and move past it so it doesn't continue to derail and dominate your life.

3. Hardships Come and Go—This Too Shall Pass and "It Gets Better"

NDErs remind us that the pains we experience throughout life seldom are permanent. Just as the ocean tides roll in and out—tough times ebb and flow in our lives in different phases.

"Life comes in phases, I realized, and each phase seems to stretch out in earth years feeling as if it will last forever—but it never does. Earth time is not forever. Situations come and go, and trials pass. I thought again of the young woman and the teenage boy who had committed suicide. If they had waited, things may have improved for them. It was tragic that by not realizing this, they had both taken actions that had forever stopped their earthly growth and regrettably stifled their spiritual life." Dr. Joyce Brown

"Whatever pain we experience, whether physical or emotional, will only last for a certain time. And when you compare time to eternity—that feeling of eternity I felt in that mesmerizing light—everything suddenly feels very, very trivial, including suffering and especially suffering. I know now that all the painful moments I experience here will all vanish in an instant when my soul leaves my body and is replaced with a type of well-being we can't even begin to imagine, but this time for eternity." Marion Rome

As your parents and grandparents probably told you when you were discouraged, "This too shall pass." The fears and struggles we have in one stage of our life often fade away and give rise to new and different struggles in later years. Of course these challenges are balanced by happy things as well.

The It Gets Better Project (www.itgetsbetter.org) is a terrific reminder to LGBTQ young people who might suffer from bullying and persecution that their challenges will almost always improve with time. This concept can be adopted by all of us, no matter what kind of struggles we might face. Given time, perspective, growth, and healing, things do get better.

4. Hardship = Opportunity

Our best bet in handling the hardships of life is to view and use them as opportunities. Opportunities for what you say? Let's see what the NDErs have to say . . .

> "Even the most terrible circumstances and events can stimulate great change in individuals and societies. Without observing cruelty, we would not be moved to compassion. Without personal trials, we would not develop patience or faithfulness . . . Have you ever really changed or experienced personal growth during times of comfort and complacency? The acceptance that change rarely comes without difficulty and challenge can truly free a person . . ." Dr. Mary Neal

> "We all choose the path we are on for the potential of growth and evolvement. We all have access to God's light and love, we just need to stop, listen, and be open to it, and finally that we all have obstacles and experiences that we must overcome and learn from so that we can evolve and grow. God hasn't abandoned us when things seem tough. It is necessary to experience what we perceive as good and bad in order to grow." Didier

> "Rich rewards and priceless joy await humble people on earth who valiantly suffer through their trials and tribulations . . . I learned that adversities are opportunities for personal growth and development and come with built-in benefits that can be enjoyed endlessly. I discovered that justice during earth life is usually found only in the dictionary . . . I recognized how important mercy is and how much more it can be received when it is freely given." Dr. Joyce Brown

> "It's not that this accident happened to me, it's something that happened for me. And I believe that the universe put that near-death experience, me

drowning in the water, my body being recovered in the lake that night, in order for me to get my life together so that I could live a better life, a more abundant life, a more focused life, and a happy life. And I'm grateful that that happened." James Nowlin

Finding the opportunity in the hardship means trusting the adage, "When one door closes, another one opens." Instead of lamenting the closed door that we clearly see behind us, we need to refocus our time and energies on finding the open door that this new opportunity presents us. It seems crazy, but try to see the hardship as something that happens for you, rather than to you.

"You never know how strong you are until being strong is your only choice."

Bob Marley, Singer

Helping Parents Heal

Elizabeth Boisson lost her beloved 20-year-old son Morgan from a severe case of altitude sickness at the base camp of Mt. Everest when he was a college student. Of course, Elizabeth and her family were initially devastated by Morgan's death; but Elizabeth knew in her heart that Morgan's soul lived on and said she could feel that he wanted them to move forward with their lives. She started looking for grief groups to help her process the pain of losing her son, however, all of the support groups weren't willing to talk about or accept the possibility of the soul living on. Undeterred, Elizabeth started her own Facebook group and held meetings in her Phoenix home for parents who had lost children but felt their spirits survived. She combined her efforts with Mark Ireland, who also had lost his son, to create Helping Parents Heal, a nonprofit support group for parents who have lost children but believe their souls live on. Since 2009, the initial group has mushroomed to 60 different support groups helping parents all across the United States as well as in Canada, Australia, and the United Kingdom. Despite suffering one of the most difficult hardships imaginable, Elizabeth transformed the heartache of losing her son into a worldwide movement that now heals and provides hope to over 10,000 parents. Elizabeth says, "I truly believe that it is possible to heal from the passing of a child. It is not something I wish on anyone, but the harder the thing we are going through, the more we are learning."

"I love when people that have been through hell walk out of the flames carrying buckets of water for those still consumed by the fire."

Stephanie Sparkles, Entrepreneur

5. Hardships are Purposeful, There is a Reason for Them

As difficult as things may seem, NDErs encourage us to believe there is some underlying purpose for suffering life's hardships; that everything happens for a reason.

> "When we think everything is falling apart, it is actually falling into place. Things happen for a reason. There are no accidents." Jeff Olsen

> "I came to understand that there is a higher purpose to life than to just live for a life of comfort. Life was about learning and evolving into a higher consciousness of morality and acquiring virtues. Most of these virtues are gained by enduring difficult challenges and overcoming problems. I realized that our trials and tribulations are the means to bring about the challenges that we need to go through to learn and evolve into our higher consciousness." Sandy B.

> "We are all courageously traveling this earthly road, a road filled with pain, loneliness, and confusion, even for the luckiest among us. We will all have to suffer to some extent, see loved ones die, have hopes and dreams shatter, and eventually die ourselves. Yet most of us put on a brave smile each morning and do our best to find meaning in the day. We should love ourselves for our courage. The most difficult question I had to find an answer to during my deep searching was why we have to suffer here on earth. I now think that it is a part of the lesson we need to learn. To learn love, sacrifice, feeling pain, and loss are part of the journey of life." Jessica

> "Suddenly, I began to understand things. I understood why I had cancer and how it was so very important for me to have cancer. In fact, it was so important that I realized I would not have it any other way." Arthur B.

NDErs come to realize that even devastating diseases like cancer and the inexplicable death of a child seem to have some kind of greater purpose for the person experiencing them as well as family and friends around them. As Nietzsche once said, "To live is to suffer, to survive is to find some meaning in the suffering."

"When the string of the violin was being tuned it felt the pain of being stretched, but once it was tuned then it knew why it was stretched."

RABINDRANATH TAGORE

"From time to time in the years to come, I hope you will be treated unfairly, so that you will come to know the value of justice. I hope that you will suffer betrayal because that will teach you the importance of loyalty. Sorry to say, but I hope you will be lonely from time to time so that you don't take friends for granted. I wish you bad luck, again, from time to time so that you will be conscious of the role of chance in life and understand that your success is not completely deserved and that the failure of others is not completely deserved either . . . I hope you'll be ignored so you know the importance of listening to others, and I hope you will have just enough pain to learn compassion. Whether I wish these things or not, they're going to happen. And whether you benefit from them or not will depend upon your ability to see the message in your misfortunes."

John Roberts, Supreme Court Chief Justice

6. Hardships May Be Customized to You

A radical concept for some people, many NDErs also believe the challenges we experience are not random, but are actually chosen by God (and possibly us) before coming to earth and are consciously customized to our own unique situations. Yes, this may sound far-fetched and absolutely ridiculous to some but hear them out and consider it with an open mind:

> "I now realized my problems were my own personal, educational building blocks, tailored just for me. Learning from my problems—the cause and effect from my choices, and my parents', and their parents' choices could help me overcome undesired social, cultural, or unwanted family traditions. Suddenly I knew I would not want to trade places with anyone else. I needed to grow and develop in my own way, which was different than any other person's way. Someone else's life experiences would not help me to become the individual that I needed to be. I needed my own individualized training. I now knew that facing challenges builds the 'muscles and strengths' of spirit and mind. Only through such exercises could I have developed as I needed to . . . To develop the 'muscles' of mind and spirit, we have the chance to solve problems, grow wise through them, and gain skills, knowledge, and talents that remain with us forever." Dr. Joyce Brown

> "Each person's hardships are directly related to the lesson that person must learn. It is our choice whether we accept the challenge or not.

Regardless of what path I choose, it seems as though I'm destined to learn these lessons. I might choose the time, place, or even circumstances, yet the lessons still remain the same. Those lessons come differently for everyone. I feel the lessons are about LOVE, such as how to give, receive, share, spread the love." William C.

Based on these insights, it seems as if the Universe chooses life courses for us that allow us to work on the areas where we can experience the most growth. In essence, the course (path we take in life) of our life is also the course (lesson we need to learn) of our life, and vice versa.

"I was shown how one can never assume either, that if someone lives a life of suffering that this is because of 'evil' deeds. Many may choose a life of suffering because of what it awakens in them, or because of how they can touch others from that position, etc. We can NEVER EVER assume that we can be accurate in guessing why each being lives the life they live." Amy Call

---

The Confederate Soldier's Prayer:
"I asked for strength that I might achieve;
I was made weak that I might learn humbly to obey.
I asked for health that I might do greater things;
I was given infirmity that I might do better things.
I asked for riches that I might be happy;
I was given poverty that I might be wise.
I asked for power that I might have the praise of men;
I was given weakness that I might feel the need of God.
I asked for all things that I might enjoy life;
I was given life that I might enjoy all things.
I got nothing that I had asked for,
but everything that I had hoped for.
Almost despite myself my unspoken prayers were answered;
I am, among all men, most richly blessed."

---

7. Seek to See the Hardship from Heaven's Higher Perspective
NDErs basically tell us that when sh*t happens, hopefully a shift happens. They encourage us to shift our thinking from a limited human view of the situation to a higher, heavenly perspective of the situation. They challenge us to see how we might learn and grow from the

extremely difficult situation. Obviously, this is MUCH easier said than done when we've lost a child, been fired from a job, put in jail, received a cancer diagnosis, and we are in the throes of crisis and chaos.

"Prior to being on the Other Side, I had not understood reasons for burdens and adversities. It seemed unfair that so many trials and problems brought so much grief during earth life. I wondered why some people have such dreadful lives of hardship and others seem to have relatively few problems. I learned that the answers could not be seen by viewing a short period of time in one's life on earth. But from the perspective of the Other Side, which included everyone's feelings and viewpoint—even the Creator's—everything fits together. Rich rewards and priceless joy await humble people who valiantly suffer through their trials and tribulations . . . During the first few weeks after my return I was grateful for each problem awaiting me, because I knew of the benefits I could receive when I overcame them. By understanding problems in their proper eternal perspective, I realized that each difficult experience, well lived with sincere intentions, was like a jewel on a crown. Its message would sparkle with rewards for having triumphed and passed through a refiner's fire. I knew that progressing through life would be enormously easier if I remember to evaluate events from the eternal perspective. The attitude I took in any given situation was my choice! With my new eternal outlook at that time, I was able to see life's experiences in a different way. Trials were blessings, and I wanted to make it through them with the right attitude." Dr. Joyce Brown

"Dear Divine,
I have been angry with You . . . Why did I have to suffer from cancer, from so many surgeries and their complications like incontinence and impotency? Why did I have to suffer depression, addiction, and chronic pain? Why did I have to lose money by gambling in the stock market? Why did I have to endure abuse in my childhood? Now I understand Your love for me. All of what is mentioned above, and other things were preparing me for a higher cause so I could serve humanity, especially people suffering from pain, depression, anger, and addictions. It was to make me stronger, a pillar for others. I am grateful for all I had to go through, especially my NDE, where I experienced true unconditional, supreme love . . . Now I understand that this grief represents an opportunity. Now that I have experienced the bad I can now understand it and spread your message of "forgiveness, love, and healing" to millions. I ask for forgiveness and seek Your blessings so I can be a more strong, passionate messenger.
With deep humble respects, Rajiv"
Dr. Rajiv Parti

"In the fifth grade, my charmed world came crashing down all around me. At that time, I met a teacher who was a real life changer—in a negative way, or so it seemed at the time. I remember her as a self-righteous, frustrated woman who thought the way to motivate children, little boys in particular, was to shame them into better performance. Her favorite form of motivation used on children struggling to write legibly was to hold the offending work up for the class to ridicule. 40 years later, I would realize that my hated fifth-grade teacher prepared me well . . . Looking back on it now from a metaphysical viewpoint, what was happening to me at the time was necessary and perfect, preparing me for a role I was preparing for later on. But, of course, I couldn't see it at the time." Duane Smith

In examining my own life, I can easily see this principle at work now, but obviously struggled to at the time when I was laid off from my job early in my career. My wife and I had a two year-old son at the time and another child on the way, due in the next three months. Talk about a potential financial crisis! However, after lots of soul searching, I forced myself to look at the situation as an opportunity to go out and start my own business. While the situation was scary and uncertain with another child arriving just months away, no steady income, and no insurance, the layoff that catalyzed the start of my own business was the best thing that could have happened for our family from a financial and freedom standpoint. What felt like a terrible crisis at the time ended up being one of the best things for all of us looking back on it.

Seeing situations from a higher, heavenly perspective is much like a traffic reporter viewing a traffic jam from high above in a helicopter. While you are in your car on the ground moving at a snail's pace, it is easy to get frustrated with the situation, experience the stress, and feel like you are going nowhere. However, from a higher vantage point, the person in the helicopter can see the entire situation from a much different perspective. They can see the extent of the traffic jam, the main issue that caused it, and the best routes that will help the drivers get out of the mess. Rather than being the agitated person in the car who impatiently honks the horn, incessantly changes lanes, and continually curses the situation, we need to rise above it and be more like the traffic reporter in the helicopter and see the hardship from a higher perspective.

"God changes caterpillars into butterflies, sand into pearls, and coal into diamonds using time and pressure.
He's working on you, too."
Pastor Rick Warren, Author of *The Purpose-Driven Life*

What We Learn from Hardships

Bottom line, NDErs say we must Learn Continuously, each and every day of our lives, no matter what happens. Every situation we face offers us a learning opportunity, if we choose to view it as such.

> "All situations and challenges, I saw, can be learning experiences. I could have reaped benefits if, when faced with a challenge, I had asked myself, 'What can I learn from this situation?' Also, I discovered that it had been a waste of time trying to wish away my challenges, problems, and trials; they were my 'spiritual muscle builders.'" Dr. Joyce Brown

> "Sometimes you have to go through things in your life (suffering, pain, all kinds of things) but in the end, there's always something that is wrapped up in that as a gift. There always is a lesson . . . All that I have been through has taught me compassion, has taught me love for others. It's taught me respect for God, respect for life, respect for other people." Bill McDonald

> "Try to feel some level of gratitude for the negatives in our lives as well as the positives. This can be difficult, especially if the negatives involve the illness or death of someone we love or some other terrible misfortune in our lives. But those negatives are a part of living. The negatives can teach us a lot about life, the world, spirituality, and ourselves . . . Try to pull some kernel of learning or gratitude out of each negative event . . . While we don't want to experience difficulties, it's best to try not to hate or fear them. How we handle the experience, and what we take away from it is often more important than the event itself." Nancy Rynes

In the end, it seems that the many millions of situations we face throughout our lifetime, especially the hardships, are all designed to help us learn our spiritual lessons. It is up to us how we want to view them, choose to handle them, and hopefully grow from them. We get to decide whether they are good for us or bad for us; whether they destroy us or develop us.

"Pain is inevitable—suffering is optional."
The Buddha

The Parable of the Chinese Farmer

We'll finish this chapter with the parable of the Chinese Farmer because it is a great way to summarize the impact of various hardships we face throughout life and how we choose to view them. The story goes like this:

A Chinese farmer had only one horse. One day, his horse ran away.

His neighbors said, "I'm so sorry. This is such bad news. You must be so upset."

The man just said, "We'll see."

A few days later, his horse came back with twenty wild horses following. The man and his son corralled all 21 horses.

His neighbors said, "Congratulations! This is such good news. You must be so happy!"

The man just said, "We'll see."

One of the wild horses kicked the man's only son, breaking both his legs.

His neighbors said, "I'm so sorry. This is such bad news. You must be so upset."

The man just said, "We'll see."

The country went to war, and every able-bodied young man was drafted to fight. The war was terrible and killed every young man, but the farmer's son was spared, since his broken legs prevented him from being drafted.

His neighbors said, "Congratulations! This is such good news. You must be so happy!"

The man just said, "We'll see."

The moral of the story: Various events will happen to each of us throughout our lifetime. It is up to us how we want to view and handle them. If we take an earthly perspective, it is easy to see the events as difficult and disastrous hardships to endure. Or, if we take the higher, heavenly perspective, they might just be the perfect opportunities for personal and spiritual growth. They might actually be happening for us rather than to us. It is up to us how we want to respond to them. As the farmer said, "We'll see . . ."

"Interpreting something that happens as being inherently 'good' or 'bad' is entirely a matter of perspective." Dr. Mary Neal

"Every experience we have is a stepping stone towards our greatest good and our ultimate spiritual growth. Yes, even the tragic experiences." Nancy Clark

LEARN CONTINUOUSLY | MAJOR LESSONS

- We come here to learn lessons experientially—you can't ride a bike by studying a textbook

- There are no mistakes or punishments—just lessons of what does and doesn't work

- Assess the situation, learn from the situation, try a different (loving) choice, and avoid repeating it

- What you resist will persist, so try to learn the lesson the first time around

- Hardships arise and may even be planned to teach us specific areas we want to improve

- Our worst experience in life can actually be our best experience in life

- When things seem like they are falling apart, they are actually falling into place

- Hardships cause us to appreciate more, dig deeper, love more, learn patience, be humble

- Accept the challenge and look for the lesson—it won't be self-evident and may show up later

- Pain is mandatory—suffering is optional

- Challenges help us understand, empathize, and better serve others

7.
SERVE SELFLESSLY

"Not all of us can do great things.
But we can do small things with great love."

Mother Teresa

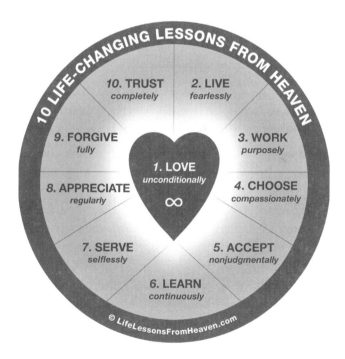

NDEr FEATURE

RaNelle Wallace: Plane Crash and Burn Victim Survivor

Burned over 75% of her face and body from a fiery plane crash into a remote mountain, RaNelle Wallace and her husband Terry somehow survived the horrific ordeal. During her NDE, RaNelle reunited with her deceased grandmother who shared numerous profound insights with her. Wanting desperately to stay in heaven with the horrendous burns she suffered as well as the horrible disfiguration to her virtually melted off face, RaNelle miraculously met her yet-to-be-born son Nathaniel and knew she had to return to earth to serve as his mother. After enduring months of surgeries and rehab, RaNelle dedicated her life to serving burn victim survivors. She also saved the lives of a neighbor and her family when she fought her fears by entering their burning house to rescue them. Her inspiring story is available in her book, *The Burning Within*.

Self-Serving Ego

As humans, we all have big egos to deal with—our own and others. Ego is our human sense of self that desperately wants to be right, loved, liked, important, in control, powerful, safe, secure, etc. The ego's primary motives are self-promotion and self-preservation. Ego continually looks to puff itself up, look good, be noticed, get ahead, and be number one. Simultaneously, ego also operates from a paranoid, fear-based mentality. As author John O'Donahue said, "The ego is the false self born out of fear and defensiveness." Ego takes everything personally and often feels persecuted. So whenever it feels threatened, which is often, ego will use force, denial, guilt, shame, blame, lies, and other human defense mechanisms to defend its precious and often fragile self-image. Ego selfishly and erroneously thinks the world revolves around itself—and has a hard time noticing, understanding, or empathizing with others.

> "I was also taught by my Great Teacher that ego is self-serving. Ego wants to be top-dog at any cost. Ego wants to elevate itself to a superior position over someone else, and ego will find all sorts of ways to trick self and others into believing this is fine. Ego will always try to pull one away from God, because its interest is serving self first and foremost . . . Ego wants

to shine. It wants to puff itself up by claiming to know more than others . . . Ego wants praise and attention from others. My Great Teacher felt this ego stuff was very important for me to learn and to then tell others about, since our culture is so wrapped up in it . . ." Nancy Clark

If left unchecked, which ego often is for many people, it drives many of our negative and unloving behaviors. While it can be helpful in some ways as we navigate our earthly world, many times we let our egos run amok and control our thoughts, feelings, actions, and reactions. Here's what the NDErs learned about the necessity of curbing the human ego during their time in heaven:

"All my life I thought that hard work was what counted. My life was devoted to building a monument to my ego. My family, my sculptures, my painting, my house, my gardens, my little fame, my illusions of power, were all an extension of my ego. All of those things were gone now, and what did they matter? All those things that I had lived for were lost to me, and they didn't mean a thing . . . The rugged individualism that I had learned from my father, my schooling, and my American culture was my religion . . . Life is every man for himself. The one who dies with the most toys wins. Compassion is for the weak. If you don't take care of yourself, no one else will." Howard Storm

"Prior to my NDE, one of the tenants I loosely subscribed to was one that was commonly held by many American males: 'He who has the most toys when he dies wins.' According to that, I had been doing pretty well. But now, I realized that none of that mattered at all, and most of the things I had accumulated meant nothing. Along with that belief went my standing and place within the crazy world in which I was now living." Duane Smith

"The Holy One showed me that throughout my entire life, my ego had occupied the center-stage of my life. I had lived solely for gratifying myself. I was motivated by self-interest in everything that I did; though, I had never consciously thought about this before. The foundation of my life was myself and all of my actions were performed to obtain some type of reward for myself; either tangible or intangible. Either I wanted money, sex, a pat on the back, a wink, a smile, someone to think well of me, etc. Thus, all of my acts had been polluted by selfish motives in varying degrees." Daniel Rosenblit

Leggo My Ego

A big part of spiritual development then is moving from letting our self-centered human ego run our life to letting go and allowing our spiritual Essence to guide our lives. NDEr Juliet Nightingale describes the difference she noticed in heaven:

"There's no such thing as 'putting on airs' and no need to hide on the Other Side. No one is there to hurt you in any way—not in the least—because there is no sense of lack . . . or the need to 'steal' someone else's power or energy. You are operating as a soul, not centered in ego or personality."
Juliet Nightingale

Part of the reason God gives us an earthly ego is because She wants us to develop spiritually by transcending our personal ego and focus more on serving others. We are continually offered choices where we can either honor our spiritual Essence and serve humanity or succumb to the selfishness and vanity of the human ego. Our challenge is to feed our soul and not our own ego. Letting go of our earthly ego is especially hard though given how our society defines success.

"The first half of life is devoted to forming a healthy ego,
the second half is going inward and letting go of it."

Carl Jung, Psychologist

Societal Success vs. Spiritual Significance

What society deems as successful and what Spirit considers significant are unfortunately two very different things. Society constantly conditions us to believe that success is all about money and status. It directly targets and preys upon our fragile and easily-influenced egos by telling us we need to make lots of money, climb the career ladder, earn the corner office, always look our best, drive the luxury car, be the best dressed, build the big house, marry the best-looking spouse, raise the perfect kids, etc., or we will not be successful. But NDErs tell us this is light years away from how heaven defines success. The real measure of success and significance in our lives according to NDErs is much more about meaning and service.

"I was undoubtedly superficial, even though I had never considered myself as such before my NDE. Yet, having lots of money and everything that goes with it was my life's 'goal.' Just like most people in the world we live in, I was in a jail called materialism. Don't get me wrong, being materialistic in the 21st century is almost unavoidable, and being resentful at whatever wrongdoing you may have been the victim of is only human. However, it no longer makes sense when you die. The regrets of people reaching their earthly lives are genuine. Perhaps they start seeing the light at the end of the tunnel—literally—and they realize that ultimately the only thing that matters is love." Marion Rome

"It's all about people; it's all about love. It's not about things. You don't take any of that with you. It doesn't matter how big your bank account or how big of a house you have. When you go into the Light it's just how much love have you left behind. How much love have you left behind? I was so grateful I was shown what is real while I still have most of my life left to live it." Charmian Redwood

"Since the near-death experience, when I look around me, all I see are the walking dead, people who have no clue as to what is important here. Some get it, but many don't. They base their self-worth on the number of diplomas hanging on the wall, the car in the garage, the house, or their career status; sadly, they judge others based on those things as well." Sherry Goodman

The Materialistic Marketing Machine of Madison Avenue

Madison Avenue marketers constantly bombard us with fearful messages carefully crafted especially for our ego that tell us we need to buy the latest and greatest of whatever it is they're selling (cars, clothes, TVs, jewelry, drugs, plastic surgery, etc.) or people will not want to be seen with us, be friends with us, date us, or marry us. From an early age on, kids are repeatedly taught and basically brainwashed by the omnipresent media and marketers what society sees as successful—so it is no wonder that materialism and superficiality rule the day.

Further, materialism can quickly become an unhealthy and out-of-control addiction we incessantly feed as we try to keep up with the Joneses. NDEr Dr. Rajiv Parti says, "I have learned that materialism is an addiction that takes our focus away from selfless service to others." In his book, *Dying to Wake Up*, Dr. Parti admits he mindlessly ran the rat race of a materialistic life prior to his NDE to afford a 10,000 square foot mansion on a golf course and drive a Hummer so he could appear successful to others and satisfy his bulging ego. "My religion became extreme materialism and my God became the almighty dollar," he said.

If we don't catch ourselves, it is easy to become a slave to materialism, trying desperately to fill our bank accounts as we simultaneously bankrupt our soul. Eventually, many of us discover that living this way doesn't fill us up, it only serves to fill the pocketbooks of the Madison Avenue marketers who selfishly sell us this superficial bill of goods.

As we look at our lives, we all need to really evaluate whether we are more motivated by and focused on Societal Success or Spiritual Significance. Check out the next table to see which side you are more likely to fall on.

"*People may spend their whole lives climbing the ladder of success only to find, once they reach the top, that the ladder is leaning against the wrong wall.*"

THOMAS MERTON

SOCIETAL SUCCESS	SPIRITUAL SIGNIFICANCE
Materialism	Meaning
Big House	Big Heart
Superficial	Substantive
Selfishness	Service
Soulless	Soulful
Getting	Giving
Outer Facades	Inner Fulfillment
Compensation	Compassion
Impressing People	Inspiring People
Me	We
Spiritually Asleep	Spiritually Awake
Fancy Vacation	Fulfilling Vocation
Ego	Essence
Hubris	Humility
High Powered Career	Higher Powered Calling
Temporary	Timeless
Self-centered	Spirit-centered
Fortune-focused	Family-focused
Gluttony	Generosity
Greed	Gratitude
Jealousy	Joy

After a lifetime of pursuing material wealth, many people regrettably learn that professional success and a big bank account are not what it is all about in the heavenly realm. They've spent decades climbing the career ladder to professional success only to find the ladder was up against the wrong wall. Their earthly accomplishments such as getting degrees from prestigious colleges, moving up the corporate ladder, gaining professional status, owning a mansion on the golf course, and driving fancy, expensive cars mean virtually nothing to God. They are not necessarily bad or evil; it's just that acquiring material riches doesn't count for anything in heaven.

Rather than acquiring earthly riches that we can't take with us to the Afterlife, NDErs say God is infinitely more concerned with how we have used our precious life to help and serve others.

"I now understood the things in life that mattered most to God. It wasn't material things, or money, or degrees, or even titles I had garnered. God deems those things insignificant, unimportant. They were the loving things I did from the goodness of my heart that were most important. Until God revealed those to me, I had been completely unaware of them. I saw myself helping an elderly person with their groceries, comforting a friend in need, saying something kind when others were mean, standing up for the unwanted, advocating for those who couldn't find their voice, and being a patient listener to those who desperately needed to be heard. It was giving the homeless money when I didn't have money to give, and putting others, often complete strangers, first over my own needs because my heart told me it was the right thing to do. It was having a huge heart for all animals, giving love to them, rescuing and caring for them in times of need. I felt the immediate effect of my words, thoughts, and actions on others. A great majority of these things I did not remember I had done because they were mostly things I did when no one was looking. But God was looking. I understood in that moment, that these things were displays of love, kindness, and compassion. They were the only things that mattered in God's eyes. They all required love. Love was the answer to everything!" Erica McKenzie, RN

"Most of what we think is important when we're on earth—getting ahead, being successful, making it big in business or politics or in a profession, making a lot of money, achieving high rank—are just chaff that the wind blows away. What really counts is what you did for others—how much you loved beyond yourself—how much you really loved and how well!" Dave

"I realized I had led a very selfish life, rarely reaching out to help anyone. Almost never had I smiled as an act of brotherly love or just handed somebody a dollar because he was down and needed a boost. No, my life had been for me and me alone. I hadn't given a damn about my fellow humans." Dannion Brinkley

To put it bluntly: Have you given more of a damn about yourself (your career, house, car, status, bank account) or your fellow human beings? Has your life been all about "building a monument to your own ego" as Howard Storm lamented during his NDE? That's ultimately what we will need to account for when we arrive in heaven. Unfortunately, many people don't realize this until it's too late—until they experience their intensive and revealing Life Review, see and feel the many times they withheld love, and wish they had made many more choices to serve others rather than just themselves. As a Turkish proverb wisely states: "No matter how far you've gone down the wrong road, turn back."

Mother Teresa sums up the importance of Spiritual Significance over Societal Success when she says, "We must know that we have been created for greater things, not just to be a number in the world, not just to go for diplomas and degrees, this work and that work. We have been created in order to love and be loved."

Selfless Service

Albert Einstein once said, "Only a life lived for others is a life worthwhile." NDErs remind us that life is indeed about service over selfishness. Not service because you feel you "have to" but genuine service because you sincerely want to; service out of the pure goodness of your heart. The term "Seva" means "selfless service" or work performed without any thought of reward or repayment. In ancient India, Seva was believed to help one's spiritual growth and at the same time contribute to the improvement of the community. The concept of Seva still holds true today.

> "Seva is not just any kind of service, but service performed with a sense of gratitude . . . It is service infused with kindness and respect for the ones served, and gives rise to peace and love. Seva is not about taking a few hours out of our busy week to help others. Seva is about designing our lives in such a way that we consistently serve others selflessly, especially those less fortunate than us." Dr. Rajiv Parti

> "I used to give service because I felt 'I should' and because it was the 'right' thing to do. That kind of service comes from the head, not from the heart. It comes from a feeling of obligation or a sense of duty, and it can drain our energy if we keep bowing to the pressure of continuing to serve in this way . . . True service comes from the heart and it comes naturally to us when we allow ourselves to just be who we really are, so there's no feeling of obligation. That's when we start to be of service, instead of performing a service. At that point, service stops being a heavy burden. Instead, it feels light and fun, and it then becomes a joy that uplifts us as well as the people who benefit . . . True service is a natural consequence of unconditional love." Anita Moorjani

> "I was shown that pure love was serving God and others without any self-centered motives. Even if one was motivated to perform a good deed in order to feel good about one's own self or to attain future treasures in heaven, this would be considered to be a tainted act; totally unacceptable to God. I was shown that God only accepts selfless acts of love . . . It means that your actions are not motivated by desires of any personal reward." Daniel Rosenblit

"Everybody can be great, because everybody can serve. You don't have to have a college degree to serve. You don't have to make your subject and your verb agree to serve . . . You only need a heart full of grace, a soul generated by love."

DR. MARTIN LUTHER KING, JR.

Some people engage in service out of a sense of obligation. They might grudgingly sign up for a service project because they feel pressure to do so from their spouse, church, or workplace. They do it because they feel they have to, not because they truly want to. Others might engage in service more because they think it makes them look good. They do it to be seen with the "right" group of people or it is an excellent photo op to promote themselves, their career, or their business. Remember, God knows what is in our hearts; He knows our motives. Service should never be an obligation or a photo opportunity. True service, or Seva, is a selfless and generous gift of your time, talent, and treasure from your heart.

> "Most of the great things I thought I had done were almost irrelevant. I had done them for myself. I had served people when it served me to do so. I had founded my charity on conditions of repayment, even if the repayment was merely a stroke to my ego." RaNelle Wallace

Service Is about Small, Simple, Random Acts of Kindness

Some people might think God only desires and values big acts of service; that somehow God wants each of us to create a large non-profit organization that serves thousands of people in all corners of the world. Of course, God appreciates the amazing non-profit organizations like Habitat for Humanity, Heifer International, A New Way of Life, and DC Central Kitchen, but He doesn't require everyone to start or even work for a nonprofit. However, NDErs tell us that God seems to get most excited when we recognize and take advantage of the small, simple, random acts of kindness that present themselves on a daily basis.

> "Random acts of kindness really do mean a lot, especially to God, and are priceless to those receiving them. Reviewing my random acts of kindness gave me the most joy because I was able to feel the difference I made in someone's life that I hadn't realized at the time—and I didn't even know them. I was shown it is not the big things we do in life that make the difference. All the little things we do each day make the difference. Little acts of kindness mean so much to God." Mary Beth Willi

> "During my life review with the Light, I was flabbergasted to understand that even the simplest act of kindness that one would overlook as insignificant was a major act of our spiritual selves. Our holiness and perfection despite our human faults appears during those moments when we forget ourselves, and whenever we place the needs of others before our own. That is why those small acts of kindness are so momentous. We think they are so insignificant that we tend not to remember them. But that is

precisely when we are at our spiritually best selves. When our ego has no awareness for the need to act lovingly but instead, spontaneously reacts lovingly, we are living holy lives. I beg of you, don't underestimate the value of what you might consider a tiny fragment of a loving response and choose not to act upon that response because it isn't 'big enough.' We do not see the larger picture as Spirit sees it in order that we may see the significance of our actions. But I can promise you, even the smallest act of kindness and compassion, in thought, word, or deed is just as great as the greatest act." Nancy Clark

Kindness Counts: Examples of Small, Simple, Random Acts of Kindness

Being kind is not complicated, time-consuming, or taxing. It's remarkably easy. Opportunities to demonstrate small, simple, random acts of kindness are available 24 hours a day, 7 days a week, 52 weeks a year. You don't have to plan them weeks in advance, dress up for them, spend any money, or even travel far to do them. They are in your own home, neighborhood, and community as well as on the other side of the world. Here are some examples.

> "Our simple, spontaneous acts of kindness make the greatest impression on Spirit. A smile given to a stranger, a pat on the back for a discouraged friend, or a meal prepared for someone who is ailing—these are the true marks of compassion in action. Learning to live and love from this place of innocent virtue is a goal we must all set for ourselves . . . I advise you to consciously seek opportunities to extend your love and share your laughter." Dannion Brinkley

> "Doing big deeds in service to Spirit, our fellow humans, and the Earth is great. Great can also be shoveling our elderly neighbor's sidewalk free of snow when no one is looking. It can be entering a profession that heals the sick because we know deep down inside that is our calling." Nancy Rynes

> "I knew that anything we do to show love is worthwhile: a smile, a word of encouragement, a small act of sacrifice. We grow by these actions." Betty Eadie

While I bet you can think of numerous Small, Simple, Random Acts of Kindness you can do, here are some more to get you started. Of course the key is not just listing them—it is ACTING ON THEM!

- Open the door for someone

- Pay for the drive-thru order for someone behind you

- Call a high school or college friend you haven't connected with in a long time

- Bake brownies for your neighborhood firefighters or police like my wife does every 9/11

- Look someone in the eyes and tell them "THANK YOU"

- Give your kids a BIG hug and remind them you love them

- Kiss your spouse

- Offer to babysit for a young couple who could really use a "Date Night"

- Offer to rebound for a kid shooting hoops alone in his driveway or at the park

- Buy a meal for a homeless person and sit and eat it with them

- Say "Hello" and "How are you?" to people as they walk by— and mean it

- Give an extra big tip to a waiter

- Secretly fill up your spouse's car with gas

- Share some vegetables out of your garden with a neighbor

Check out *The Kindness Diaries* by Leon Leonitis. The book and video series show Leon's travels around the whole world. He relies on people's acts of kindness to feed him, pay for the gas in his motorcycle, and house him as he brings no money along with him. However, Leon returns the acts of kindness by doing something kind for the dozens of people who help him on his inspiring and enlightening journey.

As we learned with the Ripple Effect of the Life Review, your small, simple, random acts of kindness cause a wave of positivity that impacts dozens of people, most you will never see—until realizing it later in your Life Review.

"God loves to see in me, not his servant, but himself who serves all."

Rabindranath Tagore, Bengali Poet

Mentoring the Next Generation

Finally, one of the best examples of Serving Selflessly is developing a mentoring relationship with someone who could use your help. Whether it is a formal mentorship like Big Brothers/Big Sisters or an informal one, dedicating your time to share your life and/or career lessons with someone else is a most generous gift.

> "I strongly recommend you give freely of your time, love, and tenderness to someone who has absolutely nothing to give you in return. I am also a staunch advocate of mentorship . . . I urge you to help mentor a child. Share your talents and the wisdom of your heart with a child who will become a more confident, optimistic person because of it." Dannion Brinkley

My mom was the school board president of our hometown where I grew up in Wisconsin. Her position and choices allowed her to impact the lives of many children across the community for over 20 years. While she had a big impact on many students and teachers, even helping to get a brand new elementary school built that still serves children in the district today, one of the things I admire most about her was the one-on-one mentoring she did with at-risk students. She met regularly with her mentees and dedicated her time and personal resources to help and inspire kids who didn't have much support at home. This simple act of selfless service is what God calls each of us to do, in our own unique way. We don't need to be the school board president in our community, just extend ourselves to one child, teenager, or adult who could use our help.

I guarantee there is at least one person in your community who could really benefit from your mentoring. Whether you go through an established mentoring organization in your area like Big Brothers/Big Sisters, the Boy's and Girl's Club, or take it upon yourself, your time and attention will make a difference for someone for now and for generations to come.

There is also very likely someone who is looking for guidance and mentoring in your profession. Offer your assistance. Not only will it be of tremendous help for your mentee as they look to develop professionally, but you will get a great feeling out of developing the next generation as well.

> "I realized that God was pleased when one of His children helps another one. Precious feelings of joy flooded over me and I knew that all compassionate acts of charity and kindness, even small ones, reap joy and great

rewards. I knew God had set the example for us by loving every one of us unconditionally." Dr. Joyce Brown

"Today's society, I feel, has conditioned us to think that one must do big, wonderful, or grandiose endeavors for it to count or be of any value. Yet I came to realize that it is not what we accomplish here on earth that promotes us to greatness, rather that greatness abides in any act we do, no matter how trivial, if done with deliberate love. There is no better greatness than this." Deidre DeWitt-Maltby

Serving Selflessly is likely one of the easiest of the 10 Life-Changing Lessons from Heaven and one you can implement this week—or even today. We'll now shift our focus with our next chapter on appreciating those people who have served you in an effort to thank and appreciate them.

SERVE SELFLESSLY | MAJOR LESSONS

- Societal success is measured in materialism—it takes our focus away from others and on to ourselves

- Materialism can quickly become an insatiable addiction we mindlessly feed, it consumes us and becomes a rat race where we feel we need to keep up with the Joneses

- Self-serving human ego thinks life is all about us

- We often define ourselves by our jobs, our toys, our cars, our homes

- Earthly standards and ego standards of success are different than spiritual standards

- Spiritual success is measured in simple, spontaneous, selfless service

- The little, simple acts of kindness count the most in heaven

- Random Acts of Kindness show compassion and love in action

- Mentoring others is a great example of serving selflessly

- Service must be genuine and come from the heart—not done out of guilt or to look good

8.
APPRECIATE
REGULARLY

"I cried because I had no shoes, until I met a man who had no feet."
Helen Keller, Author and Activist

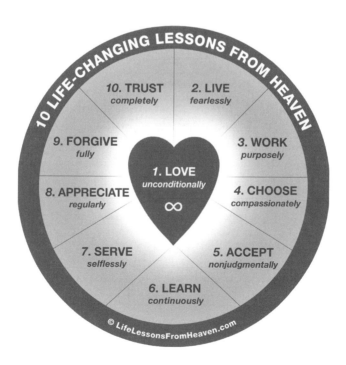

169

NDEr FEATURE

Dr. Joyce Brown: Life is One of God's Greatest Gifts

Joyce Brown had given up on life after suffering through a serious, prolonged illness. She was lonely, in severe pain, and prayed to God to end her misery. With her condition rapidly deteriorating, Joyce left her body and encountered a Being radiating brilliant white light. During her Life Review, she realized that we are all given life as an opportunity to grow and that our hardships provide us with the best opportunity to strengthen our souls. After reviewing her life, Joyce realized that she had wasted it and begged God to return to take full advantage of the life she had been given. She said, "I was overjoyed to have returned. Only a short time before I was wishing for release from my earthly existence, now I was ecstatic to have returned to life." She learned that life is one of God's greatest gifts to us and now works to help people overcome their stress and is a strong advocate for suicide prevention. For more information about Dr. Brown and her excellent book *Heavenly Answers for Earthly Challenges*, visit www.griefreliefnow.org

Start with a Sense of Perspective

NDErs tell us that living our lives with a healthy dose of perspective is one of the best ways to Appreciate Regularly. We often fail to see the many good things in our lives because we focus instead on the hassles and annoyances. To illustrate this point, let's look at what many people call "First World Problems."

First World Problems

- I don't have the newest iPhone model

- My first-class seat wouldn't recline all the way

- The wifi was slow in my hotel room

- I didn't get very many likes on my social media post

- The store didn't have my favorite brand of bottled water

- My filet mignon was under-seasoned and overcooked

- My shower water took over a minute to get hot

- I need a vacation from my luxury vacation

- The remote control for my home theatre system is on the other side of the room

- The card reader at the gas pump was broken, so I had to walk in to pay

- My double shot, three-pump caramel macchiato wasn't hot enough

First World Problems are the extremely minor inconveniences relatively privileged people get upset about, complain to their friends, or indignantly yell at customer service reps about when they don't meet their exacting expectations. While the list of First World Problems is meant to be somewhat humorous, it's also sad that many of us, myself included, have likely gotten at least frustrated by, if not totally freaked out about these minor misfortunes.

One of the best quotes that captures how people in the Western world tend to create faux-crises where there really aren't any comes from Jason Elliott, author of *An Unexpected Light: Travels in Afghanistan*, who writes, "What an extraordinary place of liberties the West really is . . . exempt from many of the relentless physical and social obligations necessary for a traditional life for survival, they become spoiled and fragile like over bred dogs; neurotic and prone to a host of emotional crises elsewhere."

Compare the trivial and even laughable "issues" of First World Problems to the deadly-serious situations that people in Developing Countries (Third World) must courageously face like war, starvation, disease, poverty, lack of clean water, illiteracy, maniacal dictators and corrupt governments, human trafficking, etc. First World Problems obviously pale in comparison to these life-threatening crises. It all comes down to a matter of perspective.

NDErs come back with a transformed perspective of what really constitutes a problem or crisis. They realize that most things people get their undies in a bundle about are really not that big of a deal. Despite having cancer and going through treatment, NDEr David Bennett was still able to adopt the healthy and positive perspective that he had much to be grateful for and could still pray for those who had it tougher than he did.

> "My friends and family members couldn't understand how I could be grateful while I was going through all this pain. What was there to be grateful for, they wondered . . . As bad as my health and pain was, I always met someone in the treatment areas who was going through even tougher times. So I made sure to include those less fortunate in my prayers." David Bennett

The next time we feel ourselves becoming upset over a situation, we should stop and ask ourselves, *Is this a First World Problem?* Honestly evaluate whether the issue we're stressed or annoyed about would be one that someone in a Developing Country would be the least bit bothered about. Odds are it's not. It's likely a minor inconvenience instead of a major tragedy. After gaining some much-needed perspective on the situation, we can better appreciate what we do have.

TWO WAYS TO SHOW APPRECIATION AND GRATITUDE

NDErs encourage us to Appreciate Regularly and express our gratitude to God and others for all that is good in our lives.

> "Two of the best ways to express gratitude, you already know. One is to stop and smell roses, which means to consciously slow down and open ourselves to what we are experiencing in each moment. The world's wonders are more apparent to us if we calm the chatter in our minds. The second is to count our blessings, which means to meditate on what we can be thankful for in our lives." Dr. Rajiv Parti

Based on Dr. Parti's suggestions, here are two ways we can Appreciate Regularly:

1. Count Our Blessings Rather Than Curse Our Burdens

2. See the Magic and Miracles in Our Midst

1. Count Our Blessings Rather Than Curse Our Burdens

When we take an honest and objective look at our lives, we really have so much going for us and should invest our time, focus, and energy on counting our blessings rather than cursing our burdens.

Think about it . . . How do you typically respond when someone asks, "How's it going?" More often than not, people quickly launch into a litany of lamentations, complaints, and problems. They might start by complaining about the weather, move on to the challenges they have been having at work, talk about the things they can't stand about their spouse, and end up talking about the annoying pains they've been having and the long wait to be seen at the doctor's office. It is so easy to curse all the burdens and hassles in our lives. We all have problems to some degree or another but constantly bemoaning them really does little good and drags others down with us. Behind it all, it's likely that our ego is looking for some attention and sympathy and trying to make it seem like we have it worse than others.

> "Repeatedly, I realized that things in my life could have been much worse than they had been. When I was caught up in what went wrong, I overlooked the things that went right and the many blessings I had received. One fact became clear: I found what I looked for. I learned it is better to look for and find things that have gone right—the many blessings received. I saw that by acknowledging and expressing gratitude for blessings received, even more would be given." Dr. Joyce Brown

Conversely, we all know positive people that no matter how bad their lives are going, they are still able to count their blessings.

> "True gratitude is a deep feeling of love and appreciation for what we do have. For what we have been given, and for what we experience every day of our lives no matter how small or insignificant." Nancy Rynes

They thank God for the blessings they do have like their family, friends, health, roof over their head, food to eat, and a beautiful world to play in. When we look at the many blessings in our lives, we have so much to be thankful for!

"I'M THANKFUL FOR:

- *the mess to clean up for after a party because it means I have been surrounded by friends.*

- *the taxes I pay because it means that I am employed.*

- *all the complaining I hear about our government because it means I have freedom of speech.*

- *that lady behind me in church who sings off key because it means I can hear.*

- *lawn that needs mowing, windows that need cleaning, and gutters that need fixing because it means I have a home.*

8. Appreciate Regularly

*"If the only prayer you ever
say is thank you,
it is enough."*

MEISTER ECKHART

- *weariness and aching muscles at the end of the day because it means that I have been productive.*

- *the alarm that goes off in the early morning hours because it means that I am alive."*

Nancy J. Carmody

---

2. See the Magic and Miracles in Our Midst

The other way NDErs tell us we can Appreciate Regularly is to notice the magic and miracles in our midst. Albert Einstein once said, "There are only two ways to live your life. One is as though nothing were a miracle. The other is as though everything is." Unfortunately, so many of us become numbed and jaded toward our own lives. We miss the many miracles going on all around us. We get locked into a monotonous routine like the movie *Groundhog's Day* starring Bill Murray—where everything seems to be the same old, same old day after day after day after day . . .

> "I felt that people had lost the ability to see the magic of life. They didn't share my wonder or enthusiasm for my surroundings—and just being alive. They seemed caught up in routine, and their minds were on the next thing they had to do. It was exactly what I used to do before my NDE. Everyone was so caught up with doing that they'd forgotten how to just be in the moment." Anita Moorjani

Rather than living a boring and anesthetized life on autopilot, NDErs come back with a whole new appreciation for human life and the amazing planet we live on. They are so much better able to notice the magic and miracles in their midst. NDErs encourage us to break out of the rut we often find ourselves in and view the world with fresh eyes. They want us to really notice and be absolutely awed by the many miracles all around us—truly see, experience, savor, and appreciate them for what they are.

> "I saw the world with a fresh pair of eyes. Everything was so new, so different. I looked forward to each and every minute of the day . . . It was like I never really experienced the beauty of each moment before, and now I couldn't get enough! I was constantly in awe of what was before me. Magic seemed to be everywhere and my heart was in a constant state of gratitude. Simple things, such as glistening frosty windowpanes, became glorious in their own right, and I relished living moment-to-moment, excited to see what would transpire." Deidre DeWitt-Maltby

Here are some examples of miracles in our midst we often take for granted. I have included some links showing mind-blowing time-lapse videos of these. Invest the time to watch the videos and reconnect with the absolute magic of these events we often take for granted.

- Gestation and birth of a baby—https://www.youtube.com/watch?v=ysyGGa5It9Q

- Flowers blooming—https://www.youtube.com/watch?v=LjCzPp-MK48

- Beautiful sunsets—https://www.youtube.com/watch?v=Tp6HQCb70yM

- A summer thunderstorm—https://www.stormlapse.com/

- Spider weaving a web—https://www.youtube.com/watch?v=2WBln5lD42Y&spfreload=10

- Monarch butterfly metamorphosis—https://www.youtube.com/watch?v=ocWgSgMGxOc

- A flock of starlings flying in sync through the air—https://www.youtube.com/watch?v=eakKfY5aHmY

- Earth as seen from space—https://www.youtube.com/watch?v=FG0fTKAqZ5g

- The smell and taste of warm, gooey, chocolate chip cookies—bake some and share them with your family and a neighbor!

- The comfort and compassion of a hug from a family member or friend—give a big one!

Unfortunately, all of these things might seem mundane at first glance but they are actually mighty miracles and gifts from God. Getting to experience them through our senses is a big part of what makes life as a human being so special.

"We tend to forget that happiness doesn't come as a result of getting something we don't have, but rather of recognizing and appreciating what we do have."

Frederick Keonig, German Inventor

The Miraculous Human Body

In fact, NDErs also remind us to value and appreciate our miraculous bodies as well and to stop taking all the amazing things they can do for granted. It's easy to become frustrated by the things our bodies can't do (or do as well) as we age like seeing, hearing, running, or jumping. However, simply watch some videos linked below of people who get to hear for the first time, or see for the first time, or see color for the first time, or walk for the first time following a devastating accident. The priceless expressions on their faces and sheer joy and thankfulness in their eyes shows how much they appreciate the ability to more fully use their senses and bodies—and remind us how remarkable and precious our human body truly is.

- People hear for the first time: https://www.youtube.com/watch?v=cVVwiHRLLxY

- Man sees color for first time: https://www.youtube.com/watch?v=XSD7-TgUmUY

- Paralyzed teen walking across stage: https://www.youtube.com/watch?v=bByAok5_P0Q

"Life in general seems more intricate and amazing than ever before. I feel that our bodies are the greatest gift of all, and I find that most people take them for granted. Most people do not stop to realize how lucky we are to be alive. I know that I have been given a second chance in life, and every day is so much more precious to me. Words cannot describe the feeling I get when I wake up in the morning and the sun is shining in through the window, and it is the beginning of a new day with all sorts of opportunities to experience new things, and to learn from them." Neev

"I came to understand that earthly life is a gift precious beyond belief. The body is a truly miraculous gift of the Creator. With my new understanding of what I could have been, life, with all of its trials and challenges, became an exciting adventure with almost limitless opportunities. I realized that life and each day had been a gift—if only I had noticed." Dr. Joyce Brown

NDErs challenge us to savor our senses, enjoy our bodies, and make life an adventure again! We should break out of our seemingly hum drum life and live and experience each day to its fullest! While doing so, we should pause to appreciate the little things that make it all worthwhile.

"I have learned to treasure the simple things, like holding my child's hand, or watching my wife as she sleeps . . . I've learned that choosing joy in every situation brings gratitude, not because the actual events are joyful, but because of what the events might teach me. What happens to us is not important, but the wisdom we gain is. I am thankful for every lesson I have learned and for every sacred choice." Jeff Olsen

---

"When I was a younger woman, I took my body so for granted. In midlife, I feel so grateful to it for working, and to God for giving it to me. There's something about having less of something—less energy, less time, less whatever—that creates a poignant shift in our sense of its value. The body is a miracle, after all."

Marianne Williamson, Author of *The Age of Miracles*

Be Careful Not to Take Your Life and Loved Ones for Granted

Finally, it's so easy to take our lives and our loved ones for granted. Keep in mind that things can change in an instant. Unfortunately it often takes a tragedy or near tragedy to remind us how precious the people in our lives truly are. I was reminded of how miraculous our lives and the people in them are in my own life when our teenage daughter fell 45-feet in an indoor climbing accident and broke her back in four places. In essence, she had a near-death experience, not in the spiritual sense as we have been talking about, but in the physical sense because many people do not survive the significant trauma caused by falling from this dangerous height.

I remember receiving the terrifying call telling me that Jillian had a really bad fall from high up and I should come immediately. I had no idea whether she would survive, or if she did, whether she would be a quadriplegic or paraplegic for the rest of her life. After rushing to the hospital, I met her in the ambulance where she was conscious but in a tremendous amount of pain. Despite falling four and a half stories and suffering three broken vertebrae and a broken scapula, miraculously Jillian's spinal cord was intact and unharmed. The doctors performed intricate back surgery to repair and fuse the broken bones and ensure they didn't cut into her spine. Jillian's pain, fear, and uncertainty throughout the ordeal was intense, but mercifully she was still alive. We came so frighteningly close to losing her. If she would have fallen at just a slightly different angle, things could have been irreparably and unthinkably different.

With limited mobility and ongoing pain during the recovery process, our job as parents was to provide Jillian with powerful pain pills at all hours of the day and night, strap on a stiff and cumbersome back brace to support her every time she sat up, carefully guide her in all of her movements around the house, and continually be there for her as she recovered mentally and physically from the nearly fatal fall. Of course we did all of these tough tasks cheerfully because we knew we were lucky to have her alive. While we loved her tremendously before the fall, the tragedy re-reminded us *how truly precious and miraculous our children are in our lives.*

Unfortunately, we shouldn't wait for a tragedy to take away or almost take away what matters the most to us. We all need to more fully appreciate the gifts we have been given whether it is the lives of our loved ones or even our own lives. As our daughter's freak and nearly fatal accident showed us, things can and do change in an instant so we need to fully appreciate what we do have each and every moment.

> "I learned that life is so precious and fleeting. We may not always have tomorrow so I resolved to do what must be done today. Don't put off writing that letter, having that conversation, or granting that forgiveness. You or your loved one might not be here tomorrow, so do it today." Jeff Olsen

---

"Let's say you're living life without the thought of death, and the Angel of Death comes to you and says, 'Come, it's time to go.' You say, "But no, you're supposed to give me a warning so I can decide what I want to do with my last week. I'm supposed to get one more week.' Do you know what Death with say to you? He'll say, "My God! I gave you fifty-two weeks this past year alone. And look at all the other weeks I've given you. Why would you need one more? What did you do with all of those?' If asked that, what are you going to say? How will you answer? 'I wasn't paying attention . . . I didn't think it mattered.' That's a pretty amazing thing to say about your life . . . You have to be willing to look at what it would be like if death was staring you in the face. Then you have to come to peace within yourself so that it doesn't make any difference whether it is or not. There is a story of a great yogi who said that every moment of his life he felt as though a sword were suspended above his head

by a spider web. He lived his life with the awareness that he was
that close to death. You are that close to death."
Michael A. Singer, Author of *The Untethered Soul*

Don't Cry Because It's Over, Smile Because It Happened

A final way to appreciate the blessings we've been given even after the fact is to adopt the mindset credited to the Dr. Seuss quote: "Don't cry because it's over, smile because it happened." Many of the relationships, jobs, and friendships we experience throughout our lifetime will change, morph, and come to an end for a variety of reasons. We will obviously physically lose people who are near and dear to us either through a long-distance move or death.

Rather than only lamenting the loss of these people, we can also broaden our perspective and appreciate the true blessing that we got to know, spend time with, and learn from these people in the first place. Instead of crying because the relationship seems over, we can also smile because it happened. When a beloved parent, grandparent, friend, spouse, or even child transitions, we can and should certainly grieve their physical loss but also eventually smile and remember the remarkable privilege it was to learn from them and be loved by them. We can reflect on, savor, and give thanks for the precious time we did have together, the fun we had, the lessons we learned, and the overwhelming difference they made in our lives.

As an example, Brian and Tywana Smith's beautiful daughter Shayna shockingly passed away in her sleep at the tender age of 15. Of course they were initially devasted and still miss her dearly. However, despite the immense emotional pain they suffered with her passing, Tywana says she would not trade one day of the 15 years they did have with Shayna despite the crushing loss. She says, "The 15 years with Shayna provided us with so many things to be grateful for. Shayna really loved life and lived in the moment. I have so many great memories. I would not trade any of that time." Brian and Ty have shed many tears through the years since Shayna passed, but they have also come to smile again because they are truly grateful for the special 15 years they did get to spend with their daughter.

Based on what NDErs tell us, we too can smile and rejoice in knowing that our loved ones who have passed on are being loved unconditionally in heaven by God and all of our deceased family and friends—and we will eventually see them again when it is our time.

We now transition from one of the easiest 10 Life-Changing Lessons from Heaven to understand and apply in Appreciating Regularly to what most people consider the absolute toughest: Forgive Fully . . .

APPRECIATE REGULARLY | MAJOR LESSONS

- Know the difference between First World Problems and Third World Problems

- Notice and appreciate the everyday miracles

- Treasure the simple things

- Count the many blessings in your life

- Appreciate the challenges that help you grow

- Express your appreciation to self, others, God

- Don't just cry because it is over, remember to smile because it happened

9.

FORGIVE FULLY

"Be the flower that gives its fragrance to even the hand that crushes it."
Ali ibn Abi Talib, Islamic Leader

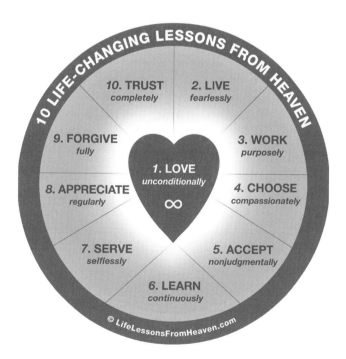

NDEr FEATURE

Dr. Rajiv Parti: From Hummer to Hybrid

A wealthy, self-centered, chief anesthesiologist at a California hospital who admittedly cared little about his patients before his NDE, Dr. Rajiv Parti thought life was all about making money in the stock market, living in a mansion, and driving a Hummer. During his NDE as part of a surgery gone wrong, he visited with his deceased father and discovered all the reasons why his father had been abusive to him as a child. Dr. Parti learned the importance of forgiving his father, himself, and even God for all the challenges he experienced in life. Since his NDE, he massively transformed his life from materialism to meaning as evidenced by trading in his gas-guzzling Hummer for a hybrid, significantly downsizing his house, and the loving and attentive way he treats his family and others. Dr. Parti's life is now devoted to teaching people how to forgive, love, and heal themselves when dealing with the diseases of the soul like addiction, depression, chronic pain, and cancer. His remarkable NDE and life story are detailed in his book *Dying to Wake Up*. More info on Dr. Parti is available at dyingtowakeup.com

Forgive Fully: Life's Toughest Lesson

To help us understand the challenge of Forgiving Fully, we'll begin this chapter with some difficult questions regarding a horrible situation I hope you NEVER EVER have to face:

Imagine someone callously killed one of your family members:

- How would you react?

- What would you say to the killer who took the life of your family member?

Many will likely remember the terrible June day in Charleston, South Carolina when Dylann Roof, a white supremacist, walked into the Emanuel AME Church and murdered nine innocent people who had gathered as part of a Bible study. They had done absolutely nothing at all against Roof or his family. In fact, they actually welcomed him to join with them in conversation and prayer. However, Roof spewed racial epithets at them and then shot them one by one in cold blood, killing nine.

At the bond hearing two days later, the family members had the chance to address the killer, Dylann Roof. Shockingly, rather than expressing their hatred of him for his heinous act of killing their son or mother or sister or grandfather, which certainly they would have been humanly justified to do, some family members somehow found it in their hearts to extend their forgiveness. Here's what they said:

Nadine Collier, daughter of victim Ethel Lance:
"I forgive you. You took something very precious away from me. I will never get to talk to her ever again. I will never be able to hold her again, but I forgive you, and have mercy on your soul . . . You hurt me. You hurt a lot of people. If God forgives you, I forgive you."

Felicia Sanders, mother of Tywanza Sanders:
"We welcomed you Wednesday night in our Bible study with welcome arms. You have killed some of the most beautiful people that I know. Every fiber in my body hurts and I'll never be the same. Tywanza Sanders was my son. Tywanza was my hero . . . May God have mercy on you."

Sister of DePayne Middleton Doctor:
"That was my sister, and I'd like to thank you on behalf of my family for not allowing hate to win. For me, I'm a work in progress. And I acknowledge that I am very angry. But one thing that DePayne always enjoined in our family . . . she taught me that we are the family that love built. We have no room for hating, so we have to forgive. I pray God on your soul."

What a powerful and moving example of forgiveness the families of the Emanuel AME Church in Charleston shooting victims showed during their time of immense grief.

Forgiveness is obviously one of the toughest forms of love because we are asked to unconditionally love someone despite the extreme emotional, mental, and/or physical pain their behavior likely caused us. We are asked to let go of and even pardon the terrible wrong(s) we feel they have done to us. Rather than seek revenge and retribution, which human nature clamors for us to do considering an "eye for an eye and a tooth for a tooth," we offer them the immeasurable and sacred gift of our forgiveness.

"An eye for an eye only ends up making the whole world blind."
Mohandas Gandhi, Indian Leader and Activist

9. Forgive Fully

Why Forgiveness?

Listen to how powerful and beautiful forgiveness can be when we choose to offer it:

> "Of all the advanced instruction I downloaded throughout my second expedition to Heaven, the astounding beauty in the act of forgiveness stands alone as the greatest value and consequence—both here and in the Hereafter. Without forgiveness, there can be no ripening of the soul, no authentic way of measuring our spiritual evolution. Therefore, forgiveness is indisputably our passport to divine greatness while we're still engrossed in the experience of our humanity. By refusing to forgive ourselves, or someone else, we inadvertently deny ourselves access to the highest spheres of happiness as well as the deepest levels of our essential spiritual nature . . . I had really relished holding on to my grudges . . . Now, for the first time, I realized how harboring these grudges really bound my energies to the same people I resented. As a result, my life and theirs would become significantly intertwined until the day I made the decision to open my heart and forgive . . . Forgiveness truly takes great strength and mighty courage, yet the rewards are beyond imagining . . . Through the sacred act of forgiveness, we exponentially expand our ability to reflect more love and joy in the world." Dannion Brinkley

The ability to forgive someone who has hurt us is one of the best ways to gauge our spiritual evolution. While none of the 10 Life-Changing Lessons from Heaven are easy to abide by continually, compared to Forgiving Fully, it seems relatively easy to Work Purposely, Choose Compassionately, and Appreciate Regularly. How dare the NDErs (and God) suggest we Forgive Fully those who have deeply hurt us! That seems crazy and extreme! Do they realize how badly people have been hurt? Do they realize how much they have ruined people's psyches, relationships, careers, lives? The young boy who was physically and mentally abused by his father throughout his childhood is supposed to forgive him? The young girl who was repeatedly raped by her uncle is supposed to forgive him? The mother whose only son was killed by a drunk driver is supposed to forgive her? We're even supposed to forgive the terrorist who barbarically killed dozens of innocent people? The list goes on and on . . .

"Everyone thinks forgiveness is a lovely idea until
he has something to forgive."

C.S. Lewis, Author

In short, NDErs tell us that as tough as they know it is to humanly forgive others because of the seemingly unbearable brokenness and emptiness we feel, the answer is, "Yes," just as the Charleston families forgave Dylann Roof. Just as God forgives us . . .

Instead of plotting your revenge or harboring grudges, resentment, and hatred, NDErs inform us that God wants us to eventually get to the point where we can rise above the situation, be the more spiritually evolved and loving person, and extend forgiveness. He understands it is typically an excruciatingly hard thing to do—and why forgiveness is such a strong indicator of spiritual development—but it still is the loving choice He encourages us to make. As Jesus Himself said with nails piercing his body and a crown of thorns on His head as He was dying on the cross, "Father, forgive them, because they know not what they do." (Luke 23:34)

Forgiveness is Often a Process

Rarely is forgiveness something we can extend immediately to the person who hurt us but rather is much more of a process that we work through over time. At first, most of us are understandably upset, irate, wounded, and bitter when we feel someone wrongs us. We often seek revenge and want the person to hurt as badly as we do or even more so for their crime against us. As time goes on, our anger typically softens but we still find it difficult or impossible to forgive. As we continue to process the situation and gain distance from it, we may eventually realize that stewing over the situation and continually rehashing it only brings us down and keeps us stuck in the misery of the past. At this point we might decide to internally let go of the hurt and move on from it. A significant step is actually offering forgiveness to the person who has hurt us either verbally or in writing. And finally, some can even get to the point of unconditionally loving and accepting the person who hurt them as you'll see in this next amazing story.

Forgiving the Seemingly Unforgivable

On Mother's Day Weekend 2002, Renee Napier got the soul-crushing call no parent wants to get informing her that a drunk driver, Eric Smallridge, driving at two and half times the legal limit, killed her 20-year-old daughter Meagan and best friend Lisa Dickson. Renee understandably calls it "the absolutely most devastating day of my life.

It felt like somebody had reached inside of me and pulled out all my insides and just left me as an empty shell of a person."

A year later, the state of Florida convicted the 24-year-old Smallridge of felony manslaughter and sentenced him to 22 years in prison. "Prison is like hell on earth; it's a really dark place," said Smallridge. "When it got down to it, that wasn't even the worst part. The worst part was the guilt I had to live with for the rest of my life."

Even though Eric was the person behind the bars, Renee said she felt like the prisoner because she had so much bitterness built up toward him for his deathly act. However, rather than letting the hatred fester as she had every reason to do, over time Renee somehow found it in her heart to forgive Eric saying, "At his sentencing I felt his pain for the first time. I was moved to tears when I saw him in chains. He is a young man in agony. Me hating Eric forever is not going to bring Meagan and Lisa back. It was healing for me and hopefully healing for him to tell him face to face I forgive him."

Not only did Renee and her family forgive Eric, but a few years later they actually went back to the judge and pleaded with him to reduce Eric's 22-year prison sentence. They had already seen two lives cut drastically short and they didn't want to watch a third life destroyed in the already difficult situation. Both the judge and prosecutor were dumbfounded because they had never heard of such an unusual and unprecedented request being brought forth by the victims of the crime. After hearing from the Napiers, the Dicksons, as well as Eric, the judge cut Smallridge's sentence in half to 11 years and Eric was eventually released in November of 2012.

Even more amazing than that, Renee and Eric now travel the country together as the most unlikely partners to deliver a powerful message to schools, churches, and other organizations about the dangers of drunk driving and the importance of forgiveness. Rather than letting the situation cause her to become bitter toward the world and Smallridge, Renee has actually teamed up with Eric, the very man who killed her daughter, to collectively impact and save lives. Eric too has learned to forgive himself for his selfish and murderous choice to drive under the influence and has committed his life to preventing similar tragedies in the future.

Renee says, "My experience has taught me that once we forgive those who have hurt us, healing begins, it frees us so that we can move forward unencumbered. It's the most freeing thing you can do. It's indescribable—the peace to say, 'I forgive you' and mean it."

4 NDEr INSIGHTS THAT MAKE IT EASIER TO FORGIVE

Because forgiving people is so hard for many of us to do, here are some insights NDErs learned while in heaven that made it easier for them to forgive. Notice how I didn't say "easy to forgive" but "easier to forgive." Forgiveness is rarely easy.

1. Realize that "Hurt People" Hurt People

One of the primary reasons people hurt others is because they hurt inside themselves. People who feel good about themselves rarely harm others. Think about it. When you feel good about yourself and your life there is no need to hurt or bring down others. Only "hurt people" hurt people. While in heaven, NDErs gained some revealing, in-depth insights about the pain the people who hurt them felt, which made it easier to forgive them.

> "When I had my NDE, it had been exactly seven years since I had spoken to my mother . . . I hated her with a passion. I could not spend even one minute in the same room as her. Yet, in that amazing world, I felt instant forgiveness for all the horrendous things she had done to me. I know now why she had caused me so much pain and torment. She herself was a very tortured and suffering soul and, in the ego-centered physical world, inflicting pain on others was the way she could feel her own [pain] to a lesser degree. I could feel her pain, enormous distress, her fears, and I knew that it was all of that that led her to treat me so badly, just like her dad treated her poorly in her childhood . . . My way of responding to her aggressive behavior has now completely changed. I used to fight back, return her insults, retaliate . . . I now simply couldn't fight back anymore. Not after the eternal and real forgiveness I experienced and felt for her in that magical world, without my ego in the way preventing me from doing so . . . Without my NDE, I would probably have had to see a therapist for a lifetime in order to figure out her abusive behavior. I now don't do any form of psychotherapy. I have all the answers I need." Marion Rome

> "In that other realm the picture was finally complete. I got all the answers, or remembered all the answers. And, yes, there was significant insight into others who I was in relationship with at the time, in particular, my step-moth-er. I was shown, or could see, her whole life, her struggles, her fears, and all that had made her into who she was. And I could finally see her abusiveness was not about me being a 'bad' kid. It was ALL because of her fears, her earthly amnesia, and her struggles, insecurity, etc. I saw that she had been abused growing up. And in the end, I could only feel great compassion and admiration for her . . . We are all blind and scared while we are here. We do our best, and it's all understood and our mistakes are forgiven once we have our expanded spiritual awareness back." Amphianda Baskett

"It's not that I don't see how people behave inappropriately at times, it's just that I know they have pain inside their souls and they don't know any other way to behave." Lee

After witnessing the pain behind the abuse, the NDErs better understood where the person was coming from and likely why they treated them so poorly. They realized the mistreatment they experienced had its origins in fear and trauma long before because the abuser never was able to process and release all the pain they felt. It doesn't make the pain they perpetuated on others right, but it does help explain why the pattern of unloving behavior continued. When we understand the situation from this higher, more expanded perspective, (the helicopter pilot view of the traffic jam as we discussed earlier), it is easier to forgive others.

NDEr Amy Call says it was much easier to forgive and actually love one of her "life's sworn enemies" when she understood the pain behind the bad behavior.

"I was able to explore the mind or energetic pattern of one of my life's sworn enemies, someone I couldn't imagine forgiving for what I'd witnessed. And yet, coming back from my NDE, I could feel nothing more than such a flood of Love for this woman. I dived in at the chance to write her a letter and tell her how much I loved her, and to ask for forgiveness for the energetic weight I might have held over her from my own dark thoughts and anger. She could have been my own firstborn. That is how much I adored her at that time. Because I was able to feel the Divine Love for her that the Essence of who God is, feels toward her, I too, couldn't help but Love her in a similar way, as that Higher Love moved through me. It was such a surprisingly marvelous feeling to relinquish the burden of my own anger and judgments, much of which I hadn't even carried consciously, most of my years." Amy Call

NDEr Robert Kopecky says pain and ego are often at the root of the tormentor's problem.

"Recognize that when someone has done something hurtful to you, it's usually a sign that they're suffering themselves. If you stay invested in other people's pain, you'll carry it around with you as if it were really yours— when, of course, it isn't. Take the opportunity to transcend the petty, destructive, and unconscious things that we humans can sometimes do, usually in an effort to enhance or 'protect' ourselves, and instead try to see them as opportunities to deal with someone's pain (maybe your own?) with generosity and compassion." Robert Kopecky

Mike Dooley, author of *10 Things Dead People Want to Tell You,* believes we are often not the actual reason people do unloving things to us—it is more because of the tormentor's own internal pain.

> "Your tormentors, past, present, and future, are lost in their own confusion and anguish. They didn't set out to hurt you, but to make some sense of a world that was hurting them . . . Loving them doesn't mean you have to stay with them, heal them, or even give them the time of day. It may mean reporting them to the police, meeting them in court, or becoming their teacher, whether from a distance or through others. It means remembering that they, like you, are doing their best and that the two of you are just learning what works and what does not." Mike Dooley

---

"If we could read the secret history of our enemies, we should find in each man's life sorrow and suffering enough to disarm all hostility."
Henry Wadsworth Longfellow, Poet

---

2. Forgiveness Doesn't Mean Excusing Bad Behavior

Mike Dooley also makes a great point in saying that we should forgive bad behavior but certainly not excuse it. As he says, there are certainly times when we need to remove ourselves from the relationship, hold people accountable for their actions, call the police, take them to court, etc. We can still love people and forgive them but it doesn't mean we need to continually subject ourselves to their ongoing abuse and bad behavior. NDEr Howard Storm concurs:

> "What does it mean to love someone? Sometimes to love someone means you need to incarcerate them. And that's not a lot of fun. Sometimes loving someone means you have to put as much distance between them and you as possible and tell them never to call you. And that's not a lot of fun. Loving people sounds so simple but it's very difficult." Howard Storm

3. Forgiveness Doesn't Mean Forgetting—It Means Letting Go of Resentments

Forgiveness also doesn't mean you have to completely forget about the wrongs that have been done to you. Some hurts cut so deeply they leave an indelible scar on our bodies, hearts, and minds. However, while you might not be able to forget the wrong, you still can learn to forgive it and allow yourself to heal from the hurt.

> "Most of us think that we have been wronged somewhere in our life. Whether it's a mother who was mean, a father who was abusive, a job

we didn't get because of some wrongdoing, or a sense that God didn't deliver what we prayed for. No matter what the case, these wrongs fester in our mind, taking up brain power that could be used for more positive things . . . Forgiveness does not mean forgetting. Some trespasses cannot be forgotten. But when you practice forgiveness you allow the physical body, the heart, and the soul to heal . . . I have seen people heal when they confront their emotions and let past fear and resentments go . . . Forgiving isn't the same as forgetting. We don't want to pretend that the things that once hurt us never happened. We want to be able to recall them without them causing us any more hurt. It also won't mean that we rush to social-ize or engage with those whom we are forgiving. We can forgive effectively within our heart without ever needing to meet someone again to make the healing complete. The purpose of the forgiveness is to release ourselves from the past. Not to renew or remake our chains to it." Dr. Rajiv Parti

4. Forgiveness Pardons Them and Releases You

Keep in mind that oftentimes forgiveness is something we do for our-selves as well, not just the offending person. When we hold grudges and withhold forgiveness, we unwittingly and continually tie ourselves to the person who hurt us. Actually, the Greek word for "forgive" means to "untie the knot." If we don't untie the knot that binds us to those who have hurt us, we get stuck in the past, dredge up the pain, and can't move forward with our lives.

"I was to forgive others unconditionally and treat others as I would want to be treated, not just for their sake, but for mine, because of how I would feel about myself and my actions. Forgiving, forgetting, and letting go of grudges brings benefits for all concerned, whether offenders apologize and ask for forgiveness or not. Knowing that the sooner I rid myself of feeling offended, the better off I would be. I saw that I could have gained peace of mind in the mortal world and had more peace in the Spiritual realm if I'd done this. I knew that anger at anyone hurt me mentally, physi-cally, and especially spiritually." Dr. Joyce Brown

"Refusing to forgive may seem like an insignificant burden, but its emo-tional weight will slowly crush us if we fail to let it go. It keeps us in bond-age to our past. It gives past events the power to define us, often limiting where we go, what we do, and the space available for love." Dr. Mary Neal

In my own life, I found Forgiving Fully to be one of the toughest lessons to apply. I had mentored a person for several years, provided her with numerous well-paying professional opportunities, wrote glowing recommendations for her, and even helped her get hired for a plum position where we would essentially be peers. However, once she had the new position, she turned on me and actively worked against me behind the scenes, doing everything in her power to get me fired so she could completely take over. After several years of what seemed like hell having to try to work with her, she eventually got her wish when a new boss came in by convincing the person not to renew my contract, costing me hundreds of thousands of dollars over the years. Naturally, my human side was bitter. I couldn't fathom how she could so callously stab me in the back after all I felt I had done for her. I held a grudge for a long time but eventually realized the adage that "resentment is like taking poison and waiting for the other person to die" as Malachy McCourt once said. I let go of the situation, forgave her internally, and chalked it up as a lesson learned. As time has gone on, I actually see the situation now as a valuable blessing because it not only helped me better understand this lesson having to struggle through it, but it allowed me to write this book and follow this more spiritually fulfilling path in life. Once again, what seemed like a terrible hardship at the time actually became a blessing in disguise.

The Two Monks and the River

There is a great story about two monks which illustrates the importance of letting go. As the story goes, two monks were traveling together when they came upon a river with a strong current that needed to be crossed. As the monks prepared to cross the river, they saw a very young and beautiful woman also attempting to cross. The young woman asked if they could help her cross to the other side. The two monks glanced at one another because they had taken vows not to touch a woman. Then, without a word, the older monk picked up the woman, carried her across the river, placed her gently on the other side, and carried on his journey. The younger monk couldn't believe what had just happened. After rejoining his companion, he was speechless, and an hour passed without a word between them. Two more hours passed, then three, finally the younger monk couldn't contain himself any longer and blurted out, "As monks, we are not permitted to touch a woman, how could you then carry that woman on your shoulders?" The older monk looked at him and replied, "Brother, I set her down on the other side of the river, why are you still carrying her?"

By not letting go and mentally moving on from the hurtful situation or ordeal, we stay psychologically connected to the people who abuse us and the pain they caused, which is usually the absolute last

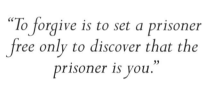

"To forgive is to set a prisoner free only to discover that the prisoner is you."

LEWIS SMEDES

thing we want to do. Instead, we want to mercifully release ourselves from the tormentor and the pain they caused. The only lasting way we can really achieve this is by releasing them through forgiveness. Like the young monk in the story, we don't want to continue carrying the problem and pain with us. Set yourself free from the perpetual pain you might experience and forgive what you might consider the unforgivable.

> "The Being of Light gave me the opportunity to forgive everyone who had ever crossed me. That meant that I was able to shake the hatred that I had built up against many people. I didn't want to forgive many of these people because I felt the things they had done to me were unforgivable. They had hurt me in business and in my personal life and made me feel nothing for them but anger and disdain. But the Being of Light told me I had to forgive them. If I didn't, he let me know, I would be stuck at the spiritual level I now occupied. What else could I do? Next to spiritual advancement, these earthly trespasses seemed trivial. Forgiveness flooded my heart, along with a strong sense of humility. It was only then that we began to move upward." Dannion Brinkley

As you've heard from the NDErs and know full well from your own experience, forgiving someone who hurt you is unbelievably difficult to do. Rarely is forgiveness something we can extend immediately but rather is much more of a process that we work through to arrive at. At first, most of us are angry and upset when we feel someone wrongs us and often seek revenge and retribution.

Yet, as mentioned earlier, forgiveness is a great way to ripen our soul and measure our spiritual evolution. So Forgiving Fully is something we sooner or later hopefully can bring ourselves to do, for our spiritual good and the spiritual good of the person who wronged us.

How to Extend Forgiveness

Arriving at the point where you are ready to forgive someone is a difficult process in its own right and can take days, weeks, months, years, decades, and sadly, sometimes a lifetime. But the journey to forgiveness doesn't end there because then you need to actually extend forgiveness to the person who you feel harmed you.

NDEr Dr. Rajiv Parti decided the best way to move on from the physical and emotional abuse his father had done to him was to write a letter to his father extending his forgiveness. This is a great option for those of us who know we would have such a hard time doing it face to face. Even though his father was deceased, Dr. Parti knew his father would be forgiven after seeing him in his NDE. The heart-felt forgiveness letter Dr. Parti wrote to his father is below:

"Dear Father,
When I saw you during my near-death experience, you revealed much to me about why you behaved so abusively toward me during my childhood. I had not known about your unhappy youth, but now I see and feel what you suffered as if I shared it with you. Harshness was your defense, your shield against unloving abusive parents . . . Your desire to hide your pain hardened your heart. You sometimes mocked and swore at me. If I cried, you would laugh at me and say that strong boys do not cry. I had to harden my own heart against you, often hating you as you hated your own father . . . I understand that you treated me as your father treated you because you knew of no other way to love me . . . I forgive you for every cruel word and every raised hand. I forgive you for the abuse and thank you for your love, unexpressed though it often was. You wisely told me during my NDE that anger was a choice. I now choose that the anger that plagued our family shall stop with me.
With Love and Forgiveness,
Rajiv"

Be the More Spiritually-Evolved Person and Forgive

No matter how hard it is, challenge yourself to be the more spiritually-evolved person and forgive others as quickly and completely as you can. You may not always see and feel the full benefits as a human, but NDErs tell us you will reap the rewards of being a forgiving person in heaven.

"Whenever anyone does anything to you that you perceive as (or truly that is) offensive or damaging to you—from stepping on your toe to stealing your wife; from stiffing you on a payment to sticking you with the check; from 'deeply disappointing' you to 'ruining your life'—forgive that person as immediately and as completely as you can . . ." Robert Kopecky

"I can't count the number of times I have accepted the unacceptable and forgiven the unforgivable from a human point of view. I often remained that loving person through the most horrible situations . . . Certainly, many times I have regretted giving my love to people who didn't deserve it in the human definition of being deserving. Now, however—and more than ever since my experience—I don't regret it anymore, and if I had to do it all over again, I would. I have become even more forgiving and so much more compassionate. My ability to forgive has now become considerably more genuine and stems from a deep sense of selflessness and altruism . . . What do I truly know about the real thoughts and feelings of others? What do I really know about their motives for treating me badly with care and love? I know nothing and, when in doubt, I will now always give love a chance. Always." Marion Rome

"I knew there were many benefits of being forgiving and that if I wanted to be forgiven for actions that I regretted, I would need to be forgiving of others during my earth life. I wanted to be able to forgive anyone and everyone who had offended me. I discovered that it was literally true that we earn what we receive on the Other Side by the choices we make while on the earth. As I experienced my life review and understood things in their proper perspective, I saw that each time I had wished justice on another I was determining the way I would judge myself." Dr. Joyce Brown

Make Amends While You Still Can

NDEr Mary Beth Willi encourages us to make amends with people we have hurt and who have hurt us while we still can. Taking a lifelong grudge to the grave with us might seem like a good idea while we are here on earth, but will be much tougher to view in our Life Review with God at our side in heaven.

"It is important that we take responsibility for our actions and make amends as we go along. As hard as it is to make amends here on earth, it is much harder to view and feel the hurt we caused others in God's loving presence when you can no longer do anything about it." Mary Beth Willi

"All the people that I had wronged and cheated in my life, I made it my mission to go and apologize to all of them. After doing so, I felt a heaviness lifted from my soul as if I had paid my karma. Now I have no more enemies or people that dislike me. I now try to see both sides of any argument and not pass judgment. I am not here to judge but to experience. I've become a better person with greater understanding and knowledge." Leonardo

Don't Forget to Forgive Yourself Too

Finally, don't forget to forgive yourself too. While it is difficult to forgive others, many of us find it just as challenging if not more so to forgive ourselves. We continually beat ourselves up over the mistakes we've made in our lives, especially if we tend to be perfectionists. We regret the hurtful things we've said to people, the times we might not have been there for others, or the unloving things we did. Like the monk mentally carrying the woman across the river, we too need to set down and let go of our own perceived shortcomings and the blame we heap on ourselves so we can carry on with our lives and focus on living purposefully without our problems continually weighing us down. We need to fully forgive ourselves just as much as we need to forgive others.

9 STRATEGIES TO FORGIVE YOURSELF

If you struggle to forgive yourself for whatever situation, be sure to try these strategies:

1. **Remember God loves us unconditionally**—As we learned in the Love Unconditionally chapter, God loves us unconditionally. Period. (Really, exclamation point!) There is absolutely NOTHING we can do, no matter how bad we think it might be, that would ever change God's unconditional and universal love for us. Go back and re-read some of the NDEr passages in chapter one if you ever doubt this.

2. **Remember God doesn't judge us**—Further, as we discussed in the Accept Nonjudgmentally chapter, God doesn't judge us. While others may judge us and we might harshly judge ourselves, God doesn't judge us in the least bit. God totally accepts and loves us for the perfectly imperfect people we are.

3. **What would you say to a friend?**—Consider what you might say to a friend who came to you with the situation you struggle to forgive yourself over. Odds are you would listen compassionately to their story, seek to understand their angst, and encourage them to forgive themselves, learn from it, and let it go. Whatever it is that you would say to a friend in a similar situation, you need to say to yourself.

4. **We did the best we could with what we knew at the time**—Whatever mistakes we've made, we need to realize that we did the best we could with where we were at that point in time. Whatever our beliefs and emotions were at that specific time led us to make the choices we made. Knowing what we know now, we might have made a different choice or we might not have, but hindsight is 20/20.

5. **Own the situation but don't be owned by it**—Accept 100% responsibility for the choice you made regarding the situation but don't let it dictate the rest of your life.

Remember that one choice out of the many millions you make in your life doesn't define who you are or determine who you can become moving forward. Own it but don't be owned by it.

6. **Learn a lesson from it**—Like God does, we need to view the "mistakes" we make in life as valuable lessons and simply resolve to make a different choice the next time we might be in a similar situation. Remember, NDErs tell us that life is a school where we continually learn lessons about what to do and what not to do when it comes to love.

7. **Transform your pain into someone else's gain**—Like Eric Smallridge did with his intense regret from his drunk driving crash that killed Meagan Napier and her friend, share your experience and the important lessons you learned with others to help them potentially avoid the situation themselves. Eric obviously can't bring back Meagan and Lisa but he can work purposely to help others avoid a drunk driving incident, saving numerous lives.

8. **Let it go ceremony**—You can use a physical trigger to help you let go of difficult situations. Some people write the situation on a piece of paper and burn it in a fire to symbolize letting it go. Others get a cord or rope and symbolically cut the cord that mentally and emotionally ties them to the situation. Some stuff heavy bricks in a backpack and carry it around with them for a day or longer to symbolize the emotional baggage they carry when they don't forgive themselves. Use a ceremonial trigger to shed the blame and shame you might feel and let it go from here on out.

9. **Seek professional help**—If you continue to struggle to move past an issue, seek a professional counselor who can help you process the situation and work through it.

Bottom Line: Life is too short to continually beat yourself up over something you did in the past. Learn from it, forgive yourself, let it go, and move on as a more loving and wiser person.

"Forgiveness. It's one of the greatest gifts you can give yourself, to forgive. Forgive everybody."

MAYA ANGELOU

Forgiving Fully is indeed hard and one of the best indicators of your spiritual growth. Use the insights the NDErs shared to help you better understand, even empathize with if possible, and extend forgiveness to those who have hurt you. Of course, it certainly won't be easy, but if Renee Napier was able to forgive Eric Smallridge and the families in Charleston found it in their hearts to forgive Dylann Roof, you too can forgive your tormentors, be that yourself or others.

"I'm sorry. Please forgive me. I love you. Thank you."
Ho'oponopono Prayer

FORGIVE FULLY | MAJOR LESSONS

- Likely the toughest form of love because someone has seriously wronged us in our minds, extending forgiveness is one of the highest forms of love

- Rise above the situation and try to see it from a higher more objective perspective

- We do the best we can with the current awareness we have

- "Hurt people" hurt people—only people who hurt inside feel the need to hurt others

- Forgiving doesn't have to mean forgetting

- Not forgiving people unnecessarily ties us to them and prolongs the problem/agony (we stay stuck in the situation and to the person)

- Forgiving is something we do as much for ourselves as for the other person, it releases the negative energy you have intertwined with them

- Forgiving may mean calling the police, incarcerating people, etc.—we can forgive but we still need to protect ourselves

- Forgiveness also means the ability to forgive yourself

9. Forgive Fully

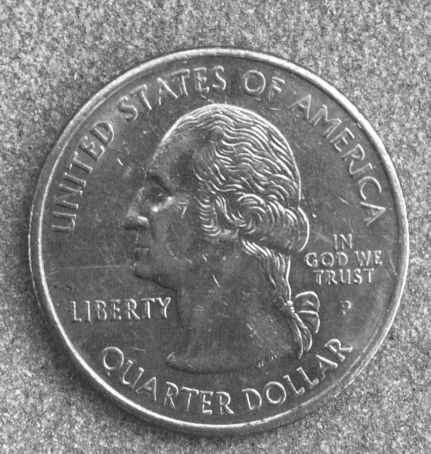

10.
TRUST COMPLETELY

"When God pushes you to the edge, trust Him fully, because only two things can happen. Either He will catch you when you fall, or He will teach you how to fly."

Anonymous

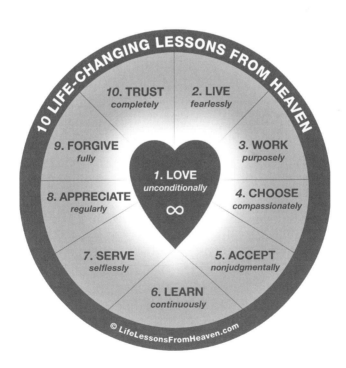

NDEr FEATURE

Dr. Mary Neal: Trusting Thy Will to Be Done

Orthopedic spine surgeon Dr. Mary Neal should have drowned after she and her kayak got pinned underwater for 30 minutes in a raging river in Chile. During her NDE, she experienced a joyous reunion with friends in heaven and spoke with Jesus. Shockingly, Jesus told her that one of her sons would die an early death (see the details in this chapter). One of Mary's main messages is that we need to trust God and His perfect plan for us, no matter what happens to us in life, even if it means losing a child. Jesus also challenged Mary to share her NDE story with others to provide them with a sense of hope when facing life's challenges and to see them as opportunities for spiritual growth. Her two *New York Times* best-selling books, *To Heaven and Back* and *7 Lessons from Heaven,* detail her visit to heaven and all she has learned since she returned. Learn more about Mary and her remarkable story at www.drmarynealbooks.com

In God We Trust—But Do We Really?

United States currency contains the phrase: In God We Trust. We claim to profess our undying trust in God and his Divine Plan but do we really? It's obviously easy to trust God's plan for us when things are going well; when we're happy, healthy, have a solid income, and at peace with friends and family. But do we really trust that God knows what He is doing when it seems like our own lives are spinning out of control and we experience things like disease, downsizing, divorce, death, and disaster? Do we really trust God when chaos reigns over portions of our planet with various wars and conflict? Do we really trust God when we, or people we love dearly, are diagnosed with a life-threatening illness?

It is so easy to say we trust in God and His Plan for our lives but so much tougher to sustain our faith when the "stuff" hits the fan in our world and especially in our own personal lives. Real faith and trust in God occurs not when everything is going great in our lives—but when it feels like we are going through hell on earth; when we must walk by faith and not by sight.

Trust that Beauty Can Come from All Things

NDEr Dr. Mary Neal was asked to display the ultimate form of trust when Jesus told her in her NDE that her oldest son Willie would be killed at an early age, though she was not told the specific date or method of how he would die. "Every day I wondered if that would be the day that he died. I woke up every day for 10 years wondering that," she said.

As unfathomably difficult as the news of her son's impending death must have been for Mary to learn, she said, "When the question of my son's death came up, I was taken back to my life review and shown the beauty that can come from every event. Our position is not to ask why and not to make that judgment. Our responsibility is to trust and to realize that beauty can come from all things." During her NDE, Mary was told part of her purpose in coming back to earth was to be a solid spiritual support for her family after her son's death and to share her story.

As Jesus foretold, roughly 10 years after her NDE, Willie was struck by a car and killed instantly. Mary said, "After my son died, I was as devastated as I could be. That boy and I had a very close and special relationship. And I loved him, and still love him, very intensely. But I absolutely will say that on my most sad day, I still have an absolute sense of joy. And that joy is based in that trust." Because she had witnessed the beauty of heaven, had been told by Jesus of Willie's death, and knew precisely where he was going, Mary trusted that her son was in heaven and his death would not be a tragedy but something beautiful because of the positive Ripple Effect it created. Sure enough, Mary Neal and her family created the Willie Neal Environmental Awareness Fund to support environmental programs and initiatives in Willie's honor.

Mary says, "In our life, we are going to face challenges, we are going to face setbacks, we are going to face loss. That is not only a given, but actually we should embrace it because those are the things that allow us to change and help us change. But the way you face those things with joy, is to have developed trust before them. And it's trusting that God's promises are true . . . Some of those promises include that there really is a God that has a plan for us that is one of hope and beauty. I have that trust because I experienced it—because I saw it. If you don't experience it and you don't see it, you have to work to develop that. But I absolutely believe that you don't need a near-death experience to develop it. What you have to do is look back at your life . . . When you go back and look at your life, you will see a clear handprint of God's presence, without a doubt. And I think it's seeing God's presence in your own life, that creates the transformation to trust."

Despite the horrific loss of her son and the terrible pain she felt, Mary trusted God that Willie was in heaven and that positive things could come from such a tragic event. In this chapter, NDErs assure us we can indeed completely trust God and His Divine Plan for us despite the seemingly devastating situations we face on our planet and in our individual lives.

6 REASONS NDErs TELL US WE CAN TRUST COMPLETELY

1. A Perfect Divine Plan is in Place

2. There is a Plan and Each of Us Plays a Role

3. The Plan is Not Predetermined

4. Everything Happens for a Reason

5. Even Evil Somehow Makes Sense in Heaven

6. We Will All End Up Where We Are Supposed to Be

1. A Perfect Divine Plan is in Place

Despite the chaos and craziness we often see and experience in the world and in our own personal lives, multiple NDErs assure us a perfect Divine Plan is in place for our universe, our planet, and even our own individual lives. We need to learn to surrender to it and accept it.

> "I could see that my life had 'perfect order' to it. In some way it was like watching a mathematical equation, or sum, that makes perfect sense. Such event and such event create this kind of result. It was a simple portrayal of natural cause and effect, with a gentle understanding. There was no judgment, only innocence. As I looked, I felt very peaceful. I could see how the last moment of my life was a result of everything that had ever happened to me before. I could see my life was a perfect manifestation of just what it was, who I was. There was complete acceptance, even of those moments that I remembered as less pleasant." Romy

> "My experience showed me purpose and order. I knew there was a master plan far greater than my limited earthly vision." Jeff Olsen

"I knew from the moment I felt the right front tire of my car go off the road that November day, and all that followed, was somehow planned and destined to be. The interaction with the doctors, my family, dealing with everything this unexpected experience put before us, all of it seemed to be unfolding in an orderly succession of miracles. It seemed as if God was directing it all and in a strange sort of way, all of it was perfect." Deidre DeWitt-Maltby

"The whole plan is perfect no matter what it looks like . . . It's all perfect. So I just rely on that knowing that God's got a perfect plan that's far more sophisticated and effective than I could ever come up with. So I just walk the path before me fearlessly. It's nice to know that you've got that much power at your back, that God's got your back, and nothing can go wrong." Tony Woody

Although God's Divine Plan may seem like an impossibly complicated and confusing equation our limited human mind has no earthly idea how to solve, NDErs tell us it is indeed solvable and there is an actual answer that we will come to know and completely understand once we see it from a heavenly perspective. Based on what NDErs have seen and come to know deep in their souls, they encourage us to trust that there is indeed an answer to the complex and seemingly impossible situations we face, but we won't likely fully comprehend it until we see it with our spiritual eyes and understanding on the Other Side.

"How wonderful! How wonderful!
All things are perfect exactly as they are!"
The Buddha

---

2. There is a Plan and Each of Us Plays a Role

NDErs remind us that not only does God have a plan for the world, but each of us has a key role in it. As we discussed in the Work Purposely chapter, each of us plays an important part in God's plan for the world, no matter what our job or role might be.

"There is a master plan and each and every one of us has a part in it. I am certain that each part of that plan is just as important as the next. Belief that position and status make your role more important than the lady who takes your money at the convenience store is nothing but egotistical nonsense. I know, I used to think that way too." Sammy

No matter what your role or station in life, you are an important piece to the puzzle of God's Plan. Your life matters and has a distinct and important purpose in the grand scheme of things.

3. The Plan is Not Predetermined—We Have Choice through Free Will

Further, NDErs tell us that the world is not predetermined but we get to choose how we want to be and respond to events in our own lives and around the world. Paradoxically, even though God has an over-arching, master plan in place, we still have the complete freedom to make free will choices within it.

> "In my conversation with Jesus and the angels, they told me . . . God knows everything that will happen and, more important, God knows everything that could happen. From one moment to the next, God is aware of every possible variable of every event and each outcome. God doesn't control or dictate the outcome of every event, which would be a violation of God's creation . . . Every living creature has its own will that must be expressed . . . The outcome will always serve God's ultimate purpose, no matter how long or how impossible it appears to us." Howard Storm

> "One thing I learned from my NDE is that God's plan is PERFECT. Yes, we have free will but that's still part of the plan. The best way I can describe it is that it's like the 'make your own adventure' books that 70's and 80's kids grew up with. You make a choice, go to another page. Make a different choice, go to another page. But you always come to the end of the book." Dana Roach Jones

> "Although everything is well planned, we have a choice as to how we use the information. Everyone whose path we cross, for example, crosses our path for a reason. We have the choice to disregard the individual and the experience, and we have the choice to be open to the possibilities offered with the interaction." Cara

Our NDEr friends tell us that our lives seem to have a general blue-print, overall template, and likely probabilities of things we will experience designed to aid our spiritual growth, but it is ultimately up to us to exercise our free will and decide our path in life.

Life is Like a Dot to Dot Picture

It's as if the path of our life is like a Dot to Dot picture for us to complete based on our own free will and choices. There is a general theme and direction to our life based on the spiritual principles we and God would like us to cultivate, yet we still have free will to decide whether we want to draw a straight line between the various dots or take a squiggly, indirect route to them through our choices. Further, we have the choice and complete latitude to take the high road and live lovingly between the dots and events of our lives by courageously choosing to live with love, kindness, generosity, forgiveness, patience, peace, and joy—or take the low road and choose fear, callousness, greed, resentment, impatience, hate, and jealousy as we frightfully navigate our way to the next dot. As we mentioned earlier, our choices and the roads we take not only determine our lives, but their Ripple Effects directly and indirectly influence the lives of countless others as well.

4. Everything Happens for a Reason—There are No Coincidences

You have no doubt heard the phrase, "Everything happens for a reason—there are no coincidences." NDErs confirm this trite phrase is indeed true for all of us.

> "There are no coincidences—everything happens for a reason whether we understand it at the time or not . . . Everyone is here for a reason and that is why we are all so different. If everything was wonderful and everyone was the same, we wouldn't learn anything. We only see part of the big picture—God knows the whole picture." Mary Beth Willi

> "I saw purpose in every event of my entire life. I saw how every circumstance had been divinely provided for my learning and development. I had the realization that I had actually taken part in creating every experience of my life. I knew I had come to this Earth for only one reason, which was to learn, and that everything that had ever happened to me had been a loving step in that process of my progression. Every person, every circumstance, and every incident was custom created for me. It was as if the entire universe existed for my higher good and development. I felt so loved, so cherished, so honored . . . I knew that there are not accidents in this life. That everything happens for a reason. Yet we always get to choose how we will experience what happens to us here . . . Everything suddenly made sense. Everything had Divine order." Jeff Olsen

> "I had a sense of all knowing—a knowledge of the past, present, and future, 'the big picture'—universal order and purpose. I know that everything is very well choreographed. Nothing is by chance. There are no coincidences." Cara

> "There were three messages that I received over and over again and those were that we are unconditionally loved, that everything is always how it is supposed to be, and that everything will always be alright. And I knew instantly that if I didn't go back to my husband, my family, my friends, my three beautiful little babies, I knew that they'd be okay . . . I just had this

"Someday everything will make perfect sense. So for now, laugh at the confusion, smile through the tears, and keep reminding yourself that everything happens for a reason."

JOHN MAYER

knowing. And I knew and I understood why everything happened. I understood that going forward in the future, there is a higher purpose and there is a reason for everything, good and bad." Heidi Craig

Despite the sometimes randomness, craziness, and meaninglessness of life, NDErs assure us that there is indeed an underlying and trustworthy method to the madness that is nearly impossible to see from our human perspective. Instead of viewing situations from our limited, earthly, ego-based perspective, we are asked to see things from a higher, heavenly, and soul-stretching perspective.

Trusting completely doesn't mean our lives are automatically going to be "successful" from an earthly standpoint, in fact, it is often quite the contrary. We will experience numerous hardships over the course of our lifetime; losing loved ones, jobs, relationships, and our health. NDErs tell us that Trusting Completely means that no matter what happens to us here on earth, we should consider that everything happens for an underlying, though often unseen and unclear reason, and to trust God that some greater good eventually comes from it for ourselves and/or others.

"Everything happens for a reason. Sometimes good things fall apart so better things can come together."
Marilyn Monroe, Actress

We need to believe and ideally trust that we live in a benevolent Universe that ultimately wants what is best for us, though it may seem absolutely brutal and barbaric at times. Each experience, whether we perceive it as good or bad from a human perspective, is meant to help us spiritually to learn, grow, and stretch ourselves in some meaningful and valuable way, although we rarely understand its full value until later on in life or by re-experiencing it in our Life Review. As pastor Leon Brown says, "Everything happens for a reason, for experience or a lesson. Nothing is ever wasted because the soul is always gaining insight." Just as we tell our children that they need to trust us when we make a difficult decision they totally disagree with because we know it will help them later on in life, so too do we need to trust God completely that the situations we experience on earth will be in some way valuable for our spiritual development and/or serve some greater good for others.

10. Trust Completely

5. Even Evil Somehow Makes Sense in Heaven

NDErs tell us that in heaven, absolutely everything somehow makes perfect sense, even all the bad things that happen in the world like wars, murder, floods, famine, discrimination, etc. NDErs are able to see these "evils" through spiritual eyes and omnisciently understand how they fit in to the bigger picture of life. They encourage us to try to do the same when we face our own evils.

"I remember I knew that everything, everywhere in the universe was OK, that the plan was perfect. That whatever was happening—the wars, famine, whatever—was OK. Everything was perfect. Somehow it was all a part of the perfection, that we didn't have to be concerned about it at all . . . And love and safety and security and knowing that nothing could happen to you and you're home forever. That you're safe forever. And that everybody else was." Jayne

"I was allowed to see all the social injustices, the wars, the murders, the chaos, and disorder. Although this will sound bizarre, I felt there was indeed order. Not mankind's order but Divine order among the chaos. I was observing without condemnation, judgment, anger, or hatred of the thieves, the drunkards, the diseased. The Light was exuding unconditional love for everyone, and everything below, and my own consciousness reflected the same. I understood at my soul level that everything was working out the way it was supposed to. Yes, even the worst kind of tragedy. I cannot articulate this in any way to prevent anyone from regarding this as ludicrous and sheer nonsense. We live in a world that conditions us to respond to negative situations in a negative way. We have not yet learned to live lives of unconditional love, a love that says, 'I will love you no matter what!' This does not mean that you love the behavior if it is bad. It does mean that you still love the pure, innocent core of the person's being. I understood that everything was working out the way it was supposed to, ultimately to fit some larger plan." Nancy Clark

"In His presence I absolutely understand that in every way God's plan is perfect. Sheer, utter perfection. Does that mean I can now explain how a child being murdered fits into God's plan? No. I understand it in heaven, but we aren't meant to have that kind of understanding here on Earth. All I can tell you is that I know God's plan is perfect. In His radiance, it all makes perfect, perfect sense." Crystal McVea

"Everything is perfect! Nothing is 'wrong.' Even the greatest 'evil' to us in our limited thinking is the way it is meant to be. I tried hard to remember what I was supposed to do, but knew it was ok, it would all happen, unfold." Tory

Despite the unfathomable atrocities we hear about and witness as human beings on the earthly plane, NDErs assure us that from a spiritual perspective they all make sense.

6. We Will All End Up Where We Are Supposed to Be

Finally, and most assuredly, NDErs calm our fears by letting us know that everything will be okay. We will all end up where we are supposed to be in this life and in the Afterlife.

> "Let me assure you that every one of us will wind up exactly where we are supposed to be at the end of our lives, no matter what. The Divine Plan has made allowances for every unforeseen contingency we could throw at it. The universe is wise enough to know that without having full knowledge of why we are here, we will probably screw up along the way. However, the good news is, unfolding universal perfection is an absolute given. Everything is going to turn out just the way Spirit has planned it. So we can act up and be resistant all we want; the will of Spirit will be done, regardless of what we decide to do." Dannion Brinkley

> "What occurred on the Other Side, for me, was a special opportunity to experience and know—with total certainty—that everything was evolving exactly the way it should and that the ultimate destiny for every living being is to return to the Source, The Light . . . Pure Love." Juliet Nightingale

> "God said, 'In the way that I love you now, I've always loved you. And I love every single human being in that way—eternally, forever. Only they don't know it because they can't see it because they're on the earth and they've got this veil that they can't see through. But when they die, all will be well for them as well because my love is eternal and unending and all-fulfilling . . . Because of my love, all is well, all has been well, and all will be well.'" Peter Panagore

> "All is well. Let me assure you that all is well." Dr. Eben Alexander

NDErs assure us that both here and the Hereafter, everything is as it should be. Almost all of them believe that when we die we will end up back with God in heaven, back with the unconditionally loving Source from which we all came.

"My soul is from elsewhere,
I'm sure of that, and I intend to end up there."

Rumi, Sufi Poet

---

*"Who you are cannot be touched
by time; water cannot wet it;
wind cannot dry it; weapons
cannot shatter it, fire cannot
burn it. It's ancient, it's unborn,
and it does not know death."*

BHAGAVAD GITA

WHAT ABOUT HELL?

Many religions talk about the existence of hell and threaten people that they will end up there for all eternity if they sin and don't obey God's commandments and laws. Interestingly, over 95% of all NDE accounts are of visits to heaven rather than hell. Regardless of whether a person takes their own life, doesn't believe in God, robs a bank, etc., the overwhelming majority of NDErs believe we will all end up back home with God in heaven. In fact, most NDErs don't believe in the existence of hell because of two primary reasons: they didn't encounter one in their experience and they can't fathom how such an unconditionally and universally loving God would ever create such a horrible place let alone banish someone there for eternity.

> "There is not the eternal damnation that is pictured in the kind of classic Christianity and the reason for that is that this God is so perfect and so loving and so all-powerful that there is no way that part of that creation would be in eternal damnation." Dr. Eben Alexander

> "When I reached the point of light I found myself in a world of light. Everything in this place was made of, and radiated light. It was beautiful and radiant beyond expression. 'Heaven' would be an adequate description, but I had no religious feeling, and knew there was no such thing as a 'hell.' I knew, without knowing how and why I knew this, that this was the place where everyone eventually got when they died, regardless of who they were and what they had done during their lives." Lisa M.

However, in full disclosure and all honesty, there have been a very small minority of NDErs (one to five percent), including Dr. Rajiv Parti and Reverend Howard Storm quoted in this book, who report a temporary hellish experience as part of their NDEs, or what NDE researchers call Distressing NDEs. Currently, there seem to be a few viable explanations for these rare instances of momentarily experiencing a realm that might be considered hell or purgatory by some.

The Void is Interpreted as Hell

One explanation for a Distressing NDE is that some people experience a silent, black void, sometimes referred to as "the bardo" by Buddhists, right after leaving their physical body but before seeing the overwhelmingly loving Light. This black void transitional realm can understandably unnerve some experiencers and be interpreted as hell by some. If their NDE is extremely short and shallow, they may return to their body before seeing the Light and believe the Afterlife is just a dark void of nothingness, which can be interpreted as hell.

> "In my experience there was nothing resembling hell. Although, the first part of my experience, where I was in the void, and I was getting confused, and scared, and ramping up and getting very frightened. If I had been revived at that point, I would have called that a hellish experience; it was that scary. Maybe that's part of the explanation for it." Raymond Kinman

> "The first thing I remember about my near-death experience is that I discovered myself in a realm of total darkness. I had no physical pain; I was still somehow aware of my existence as George, and all about me there was darkness, utter and complete darkness—the greatest darkness ever, darker than any dark, blacker than any black. This was what surrounded me and pressed upon me. I was horrified!" George Rodonaia

> "Something only reported in 5 percent of NDEs. I went to 'the void'. Total darkness, total silence, total nothingness. Zero. Zip. Zilch . . . Even a 'negative' NDE . . . can have its positive outcomes . . . Those who have a negative one often return and reform." Gigi Strehler

The Life Review Feels Like Hell

Other NDErs say the "hell" they experience is during their Life Review when they see and feel all of the unloving things they said or did to others throughout their lifetime. Having to relive and experience all the hurt and pain their own words and actions caused others is like going through hell for them, even though God doesn't judge them for it. The self-judgment can be hellish enough in its own right.

> "The hell I suffered was to see, hear, feel, understand, and embody all of the pain I had ever caused during my earthly life to anyone I had known, from their point of view. I had carried their pain with me and brought their pain with me into the afterlife. How unexpected. It was a record, a file, a folder, a book of life somehow written and recorded in my soul. God had not done this to me. God had not caused my hell. I saw that immediately. I had done it to myself. I had woven it on my own. I had burned each wrong action on to my own DVD, and yet it was also clear to me that my brokenness was simply a part of being a human being." Peter Panagore

> "For those who hand out mayhem and pain and agony to others, they end up reaping what they sow because in the Life Review, when they leave this body and go through their Life Review, they end up living that pain and agony that they dished out in every single instance as the recipient. And it's much worse in that pure spiritual realm to feel the agony of that pain

that they've caused others. So in that sense, you could say there is a hell."
Dr. Eben Alexander

---

*"My definition of hell is one day God showing me everything
I could have accomplished had I only tried."*
Wes Moore, Author

Hell is a Rare, Temporary, Self-Imposed Period of Reflection

A small number of NDErs who experience a Distressing NDE believed they lived a "bad" life and expected to go to hell for all of their bad choices. These people initially did experience a dark, hellish realm but were eventually able to find and move towards the Light and enter heaven after a period of reflection. It's almost as if their own expectation mentally manifested a self-fulfilling hellish realm they briefly experienced until they looked for the Light. These NDErs would do best to remember Winston Churchill's famous quote, "If you're going through hell, keep going" and look for the Light.

"I had a descent into what you might call hell, and it was very surprising. I did not see Satan or evil. My descent into hell was a descent into each person's customized human misery, ignorance, and darkness of not-knowing. It seemed like a miserable eternity. But each of the millions of souls around me had a little star of light always available. But no one seemed to pay attention to it. They were so consumed with their own grief, trauma, and misery. But, after what seemed an eternity, I started calling out to that light, like a child calling to a parent for help. Then the light opened up and formed a tunnel that came right to me and insulated me from all that fear and pain. That is what hell really is." Mellen-Thomas Benedict

"When I open my eyes there is total blackness. I perceive what lies before, behind, above, and beneath me is a deep and endless void . . . All alone in this place, it's as though no one else has ever existed . . . It's not Hell, of that I'm certain, but knowing that doesn't diminish my hopelessness . . . Lamenting my situation, it dawns on me, the void isn't a real place! It's symbolic! The realization that I'd built this prison around myself caused the void to shatter with a thunderous boom! A bright light shown before me, and pushed the darkness back, until it was behind and beneath me. I felt myself being pulled, as if by a magnet, into the arms of a glorious spirit." Penny Wilson

Thus, in the extremely unlikely event that a negative or Distressing NDE occurs, most believe the hellish experience, while highly impactful, is a temporary, self-imposed, instructive, purifying phase a person goes through before entering the Light, as opposed to hell being a permanent realm that God intentionally created and unmercifully and sadistically sentences people to for eternity to punish them forever for their misdeeds.

Dr. Jeffrey Long, author of *Evidence of the Afterlife* and the cofounder of the Near-Death Experience Research Foundation that has documented over 4,500 NDEs and found only 2% of them mentioned a hellish realm, says, "Very importantly, there is no near-death researcher that I am aware of that believes that there is a permanent, involuntary hell. I think that's an important point." Further, NDE researcher Kevin Williams says, "These hell realms are not for judgment nor punishment, nor are they eternal. They are states of mind, which act as a 'time out' condition for reflection, education, and purification of negative thought patterns. The way out of these hellish realms is to have a willingness to see the Light."

"When our souls leave our bodies, the only judgment we endure is that which we pass on ourselves. We evaluate all we've said and done from a place of fear, rather than from a place of love. In a religious context, this would be thought of as our period in Hell; I prefer to call it a period of reflection. The length and pain associated with our period of reflection depends on how we lived our lives. We are simply here to love and learn, and each of us is at a different level in terms of our spiritual growth and development." Kelly Walsh

"Hell is a state of being. It is a state of being separated from the loving grace of God by our choices. His love is constant. His grace is constant. But we choose. If we want to be separated from that, that's our choice. He doesn't put us in hell, we put ourselves there . . . It can be a pretty dark place, but it's not a permanent place and we can get out of it. All we need to do is ask and that Light will be right there." Sharon Milliman

"The Less-Than-Positive Experience (LTP) is a spiritual wake-up call, causing the person to stop, look back, and review past choices. It can help him or her understand the consequences of those choices, reevaluate thought patterns and 'glitches' in thinking or reasoning, and then make necessary changes where indicated. The LTP becomes the nexus point of that individual's path, causing him or her to change their walk and direction. Not only do I believe that it is the person who causes the LTP to happen, but he or she is also responsible for the type of imagery that occurs in the experience and the total content of it. In the LTP, we see what we need to see, hear what we need to hear, and feel what we need to feel in order to do those re-evaluations." Dr. Barbara Rommer

Much like Ebenezer Scrooge changed his miserly ways after the Ghosts of Christmas Past, Present, and Future visited him in Charles Dickens' *A Christmas Carol,* so too may a very small minority of NDErs have a brief yet unforgettable hellish experience in an effort to help them reflect upon the unloving choices made in their life, see their negative Ripple Effect on others, change their ways, and be much more loving when they return to earth.

Finally, when it comes to the existence of hell, keep in mind what NDErs emphatically told us in the very first chapter: God's love is unconditional. We don't need to earn it, beg for it, or act in certain prescribed ways to be worthy of receiving it. We are loved for simply existing. Period.

> "I was shown how much all people are loved. It was overwhelmingly evident that the Light loved everyone equally without any conditions. I really want to stress this because it made me so happy to know we didn't have to believe or do certain things to be loved. WE ALREADY WERE AND ARE, NO MATTER WHAT.'" Peggy P.

If God loves us so completely and unconditionally, would God judge us and intentionally and eternally banish us to hell for the unloving choices we made as perfectly imperfect humans? Or would God lovingly help us learn and grow from our choices by fully feeling and understanding their consequences in our Life Review?

Bottom Line: Don't let the extremely small percentage of Distressing NDEs frighten or torment you. While they may be initially confusing and upsetting, the rare person who may temporarily find themselves in a dark, hellish realm eventually sees the Light, both literally and figuratively. Ultimately, based on what thousands of NDErs and dozens of respected NDE researchers tell us, you can trust God that you too will return home to the Source from which you came and go to heaven to be with Him and your loved ones, even if a small handful of you have to temporarily go through a distressing layover in hell to get there.

Thy Will or My Will Be Done?

When we trust God and His Divine Plan completely, it is easier for us to let go and let God. When we trust God completely, it is easier to live our lives out of love rather than fear. When we trust God completely, it is easier for us to know the hardships we face aren't happening *to* us but *for* us. When we trust God completely, we can focus more on allowing Thy Will to be done and flowing with the Divine undercurrent of life rather than forcing my will to be done.

Ultimately, NDErs assure us we can indeed live our lives by the phrase: In God We Trust. They provide us with strong assurance and great comfort in knowing there is a greater plan, we have an important role within it, that everything happens for a reason even though we may not comprehend it from an earthly vantage point, that all is well, and that we will end up exactly where we need to be, both on earth and in the Afterlife.

"Changing what we base our life on—from hope and beliefs, to an unshakable trust in the truth of God's promises transforms almost everything about daily life, yet most people avoid doing so. Every person is capable of making this transformational change—and thankfully, it doesn't require a traumatic experience like mine! The wonderful news is that the promises of heaven are meant for everyone, and they're intended to transform how we live now in very practical ways: how we listen for God during the course of our day; how we welcome success and overcome defeat; how we make decisions; how we face challenges like the death of a loved one; how we approach our work, raise our children, interact with people around us, and pursue our dreams." Dr. Mary Neal

"We feel alienated, alone, disconnected and frightened almost all the time on earth . . . But during an NDE you see how large and heavy the load of fear was that you carried. Everyone carries far more than they think they do. I saw that everything is truly OKAY. That we are loved beyond what we can fathom. That we are never gonna die. That there is a purpose. And that there is not EVER . . . Ever ever ever . . . any reason to be afraid. We can never be harmed!" Amphianda Baskett

TRUST COMPLETELY | MAJOR LESSONS

- Trust that God has a Divine Plan for our universe, our world, our lives

- Everything happens for a reason—there are no accidents or coincidences

- While events may not make any sense from an earthly view, believe they do from a heavenly view

- Accept life's events as they come along—it doesn't mean you will like them but learn to accept them for what they are and know they are a part of the plan

- Everyone has an important part and valuable role in this drama called life

- No matter what happens to us on earth, realize it will all work out in the end and we will all eventually end up in heaven

BRING HEAVEN
TO EARTH

"We're in this world to bring heaven down to earth."

Bo Sanchez, Preacher and Author

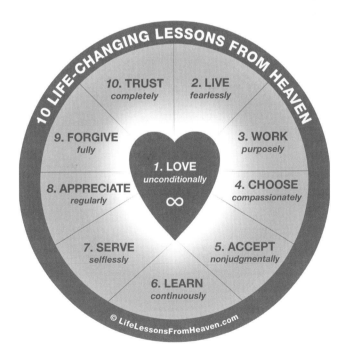

NDEr FEATURE

David Bennett: Reliving the Past and Seeing Future Possibilities

David Bennett was the chief engineer of an ocean research vessel and experienced his NDE when the boat he was in capsized in rough seas, causing David to drown. In heaven, David met his soul family and said the love and sense of family he experienced from them was more than he had ever felt before. In addition to having a Life Review of his life to that point, David also saw the potentials and likelihoods for his future including getting cancer but surviving it—which he eventually did. God told David that he needed to come back to earth because he had a distinct purpose, which he feels he fulfills through delivering his NDE message of hope and love. "In my NDE I'd seen I was going to have cancer and I also saw I would survive it. I recognize that healing from cancer was also part of my greater purpose, so that I can now help end-stage cancer patients . . ." David shares his NDE in his terrific book *Voyage of Purpose* and his website is www.dharma-talks.com

Imagine if more of us could live and love in these 10 ways . . .

1. LOVE unconditionally

2. LIVE fearlessly

3. WORK purposely

4. CHOOSE compassionately

5. ACCEPT nonjudgmentally

6. LEARN continuously

7. SERVE selflessly

8. APPRECIATE regularly

9. FORGIVE fully

10. TRUST completely

"I now live for love, joy, and happiness and I don't fear anything anymore, let alone 'death.' After such an experience I know that no such thing as death exists—quite the opposite. You reach such a level of awareness and consciousness that you actually feel a million times more alive. So much so that I believe the term near-death experience should be renamed Real-Life Experience. One thing that has changed since my NDE is that I now try to direct that love more wisely. In our ego-based earthly life, conflicts are inevitable, just as much as hatred. However, we have a choice between love and hatred. I choose love, genuine love. Love is now my ultimate goal in life. It really feels like I have brought back a little bit of that amazing loving light's energy with me to earth. I value love in a way I didn't before." Marion Rome

"I've learned that true joy comes through the simple things in life—the way my wife's toes touch my leg under the covers in the morning, feeling the laughter of my sons, buying a twelve-dollar hummingbird feeder and watching the birds gather to it. Looking for happiness in big things usually leaves me empty, while embracing life's beautiful, little miracles fills my heart with joy and gratitude . . . Each moment is sacred. Each moment is a gift. Life is not a test. Life is a gift . . . Being open to that divine gift in each and every moment is what brings life profound meaning. Recognize it. Feel it. Embrace it. Know it." Jeff Olsen

That's one of the primary goals of this book: To change our perspective and paradigm of life to help all of us recognize and value the importance of being, giving, and receiving love in a way that maybe we didn't before. To do our lives differently: with more love, compassion, gratitude, and forgiveness. To help us all live life more fully, less fearfully, noticing the miracles in our midst, and bringing a bit of heaven into our earthly lives. By understanding and applying these 10 simple yet profound principles shared by near-death experiencers into our daily lives, we are able to bring a little piece of heaven down to earth and make our world a much better place!

How to Live Moving Forward

Hopefully, as you complete this book, you are now much more conscious of the powerful and sacred choices you have each and every day and the positive or negative Ripple Effect they have on others. You recognize that there is a different and more loving way of living your life.

"It became clear that a higher way of living could be accomplished on earth. It required constant choices to avoid condemning, gossiping, criticizing, and judging others." Dr. Joyce Brown

"In one of my visits with the Light I was told that the near-death experience would become more and more popular and it would have an effect on the entire world when a critical mass was hit and all these people have died and come back and are telling you that there is a lot more going on than we think." Mellen-Thomas Benedict

Consider yourself an important piece of this critical mass of people who now realize the positive effect you can have on the entire world by living and loving according to the 10 Lessons.

NDE Stories Influence and Impact Lives

NDE researcher Dr. Ken Ring found that people who read and listened to NDE stories and learned their lessons were positively influenced and impacted by them. The stories touched their hearts and souls and their lives too were transformed without having to suffer the trauma.

"Persons who are exposed to the stories and views of NDErs—as long as they are open to such matters—become influenced by them and begin to express beliefs and attitudes about death that are very similar to NDErs themselves . . . They have not had the experience, but 'they get the message,' and it, in turn, becomes theirs . . . The near-death experience isn't given just to those who have the experience, it's given to all of us to learn from because all of us can profit from the lessons that near-death experiencers learn in the course of a life review or other aspects of their experience. We can grow from these lessons. We can apply these lessons in our daily lives." Dr. Ken Ring

The whole purpose of this book is to share the amazing insights NDErs gain on their visits to heaven so that those of us who have not had an NDE can benefit from them and lovingly put them into practice in our own lives. We too, by doing life differently, can transform our lives and the lives of others in a much more positive way. My hope is that because you have been exposed to and ultimately applied the ideas in this book, you now think, speak, act, live, and love in ways that are more aligned with each of the 10 Life-Changing Lessons from Heaven. As Oliver Wendall Holmes once said, "The mind, once stretched by a new idea, never returns to its original dimensions." These 10 Lessons hopefully stretched your mind, heart, and soul to live and love in greater dimensions.

In fact, take a moment to assess yourself on how you might have grown and changed spiritually over the course of reading this book and applying its lessons. I actually encourage you to rate yourself twice using a one (low) to ten (high) rating on the 10 Life-Changing Lessons from Heaven Self Evaluation. First, knowing what you know now, put a box around where you would rate yourself right before you began reading the book. Next, put a circle around where you think you are presently after being more conscious of the principles and attempting to implement them into your life.

10 LIFE-CHANGING LESSONS FROM HEAVEN SELF EVALUATION

Honestly evaluate yourself on a 1-10 scale on how well you live and love by the 10 Lessons. Project back to the time right before you started reading the book and rate yourself for where you think you were, putting a square around the number. Then use a circle to rate yourself right now.

1. Love unconditionally—I love everyone (family, friends, coworkers, strangers) fully, universally, and unconditionally regardless of whom they are or what they can do for me.

    1   2   3   4   5   6   7   8   9   10

2. Live fearlessly—I live my life fearlessly and fully and don't let my fears limit me, worry about what others think of me, or let self-induced stress negatively impact me or my health.

    1   2   3   4   5   6   7   8   9   10

3. Work purposely—I work purposely and passionately because I have discovered my life's calling and use my unique gifts and talents to benefit others and our world.

    1   2   3   4   5   6   7   8   9   10

4. Choose compassionately—I consciously and compassionately choose my thoughts, words, and actions because I recognize the powerful Ripple Effect they have on others (and me).

    1   2   3   4   5   6   7   8   9   10

5. Accept nonjudgmentally—I accept everyone nonjudgmentally regardless of their race, religion, gender, sexual orientation, etc., because I realize they are all worthy children of God.

    1   2   3   4   5   6   7   8   9   10

6. Learn continuously—I learn continuously from my many life experiences, especially the hardships, and believe they do not happen to me but for me and my spiritual growth.

1   2   3   4   5   6   7   8   9   10

7. Serve selflessly—I selflessly, simply, and sincerely serve others without any thought for being praised or looking good because I genuinely want to help, not because I feel obligated to.

1   2   3   4   5   6   7   8   9   10

8. Appreciate regularly—I regularly count and appreciate the many blessings and positives I have in my life and recognize the miracles happening all around me, especially in nature.

1   2   3   4   5   6   7   8   9   10

9. Forgive fully—I am able to fully forgive others who have hurt me, realizing they likely acted from their own pain, and let go of grudges against them because it releases both them and me.

1   2   3   4   5   6   7   8   9   10

10. Trust completely—I completely trust God's Divine Plan for my life and our world and know that it unfolds exactly the way it should for my highest good and the highest good of all.

1   2   3   4   5   6   7   8   9   10

If you are like most people, you will notice at least a slight if not a significant improvement from where you were when you started the book to where you are now. As you look at the differences, which specific lessons did you improve the most in and why?

This improvement and spiritual growth and development is exactly what we all want and what God wants for us as we navigate our way through life's labyrinth; it's one of the primary reasons we came to earth—to grow, challenge, and develop our souls.

Is there still room for growth? Of course, that's exactly why we're still here on earth! We are here to continually evolve our souls so we should expect there are more ways we can develop. Which specific areas would you like to see greater growth and improvement in over the coming weeks?

While you may struggle in these areas, remember from God's unconditionally loving perspective there are no mistakes, only lessons. Redouble your commitment and efforts to improve in these areas and understand that "spiritual muscle building" is an ongoing process that takes time. It's important to realize that even our NDEr friends, although they received the VIP Pass to Heaven and know God's Final Exam questions, also struggle with applying these lessons on a daily basis.

NDErs Aren't Perfect—They're Human Too, Like Us

While we featured and focused on over 130 NDErs in this book, it is important to remember that they too are still perfectly imperfect humans, just like us. Just because they have gone to heaven and interacted with God doesn't automatically make them perfect people, enlightened sages, or canonize them for sainthood. Trust me, they still have struggles and make mistakes just like everyone else does. NDErs readily admit they don't have all the answers and are still trying to figure things out themselves.

> "Many people turn to those who have had NDEs because they sense we have the answers. But I know this is not true, at least not entirely. None of us will fully fathom the great truths of life until we finally unite with eternity at death. But occasionally we get glimpses of the answer here on Earth, and that alone is enough for me. I love to ask questions and to seek answers, but I know in the end I must live the questions and the answers. But that is okay, isn't it? So long as we love, love with all our heart and passion, it doesn't matter." George Rodonaia

> "Please remember something that should be obvious: NDErs, though they may have seen the Light, are still human and have human failings. Not they, but only the Light should be exalted. So do not let your enthusiasm for these teachings and for what the Light represents blind you to possible excesses in its name." Dr. Ken Ring

Don't Hope for an NDE—Do the Work

Further, hopefully you thoroughly understand that this book was not written to encourage you to seek out an NDE—that would be both ludicrous and dangerous. The point of examining these principles is to gain the life-changing insights without having to go through the life-threatening experience; transformation without the trauma as we mentioned at the beginning. The point of this book is to share the Life-Changing Lessons with you so they will assist you in doing the spiritual

"Life is too short to wake up in the morning with regrets. So, love the people who treat you right, forgive the ones who don't, and believe that everything happens for a reason. If you get a chance, take it. If it changes your life, let it. Nobody said it would be easy, they just promised it would be worth it."

HARVEY MACKAY

work we are all called to do. The book provides you with a practical framework and a program, but just like physical strength training requires the consistent work, so does spiritual strength training. It requires the daily, challenging, and unglamorous work mentioned by David Sunfellow in the quote below—and earth is the perfect training room for it.

"Don't waste your time pining for near-death experiences . . . Instead, do the daily, challenging, unglamorous work of becoming a better, kinder, healthier, more loving and compassionate person. Step-by-step, little by little. And let the spiritual experiences take care of themselves." David Sunfellow

NDEs powerfully and permanently change people's lives and awaken them to a much greater reality and spirituality than what we see with our human eyes. As we said in the beginning, NDErs come back transformed people.

"Since my NDE, my values have changed. My beliefs have changed. My personality has changed. What I will tolerate from others has changed. My attitude toward life is different. It took off in a completely different direction. I'm smarter, more adventurous, more open, more forgiving, more aware, more alive . . . I have no fear of death because I know we don't die. I had lived life unconsciously, waiting to be told what to do, what to think, who to be, where to go or not go, what is true and not. But in the light, I saw face to face and my spiritual nature was reawakened. I was no longer afraid, no longer alone, no longer incomplete or unsure of who I really am." Diane Goble

For the rest of us though, change most often occurs gradually over time. It takes a plan, hard work, patience, and persistence. Some NDErs admit they admire non-NDErs even more because of the work needed to implement these insights rather than them happening all at once.

"In many ways, the transformations that take a long time are to be more admired than the ones that take place in the blink of an eye. To change over time with no mystical event to inspire such change calls for a great deal of effort. After all, a near-death experience brings a person into a different consciousness almost immediately by giving him a glimpse of a spiritual world that replaces faith with fact. Transformation without mystical experience is the spadework of personal spirituality because it calls for the faith that a spiritual world will provide guidance." Dannion Brinkley

You too can make significant positive changes in your life but it will take a commitment, support, reflection, and time. It won't necessarily be easy, but it will be worth it.

Transforming Yourself and Your Life

So how do we do the work necessary to implement the change? Fortunately, since you have made it to the end of the book, you have a fantastic foundation already in place! You have learned the powerful and profound principles and understand how they can make a positive impact on your life, the lives of people you come in contact with, and the world at large. Now it is a matter of continuing to build them into your daily life and your spiritual practice. Ultimately, our goal is to respond to every situation we face with unconditional love, compassion, gratitude, and forgiveness—obviously much easier said than done in our challenging world.

As I mentioned at the beginning of the book, it is extremely helpful to develop a spiritual support group of people to continually discuss the lessons, share and evaluate how you apply them on a weekly basis, and lovingly hold you accountable. As spiritual teacher and author of *Be Here Now* Ram Dass once said, "We are all just walking each other home." After going through the book yourself or as a participant in a group, you may want to put together another group of people consisting of your friends, family, co-workers, church community, etc., where you facilitate them through the process. To get varied viewpoints, I would encourage you to create a diverse group of people with different religious, cultural, and racial backgrounds if at all possible.

To infuse the lessons into your life, I have found it best to continually revisit them at different points throughout the year. Early January is always a great time to go through the 10 Life-Changing Lessons as you start fresh with a new year. You could run a group January to March. You can also do a Summer Book Club and run it from May to July. Finally, as the kids go back to school, you can initiate a group in the fall and run it from September to November. Just like all worthwhile books, it is best to study, revisit, and review the material on a regular basis. Each time you read it, you will likely be at a different place in your life and at a different juncture on your spiritual journey so different lessons will resonate with you.

Thanks again for going on this journey and may you live and love with these 10 Life-Changing Lessons from Heaven in your mind, in your heart, and in your soul!

ADDITIONAL RESOURCES AND PROGRAMS

10 Life-Changing Lessons from Heaven Journal
We've found it is one thing to understand the *10 Life-Changing Lessons from Heaven* intellectually but it is sometimes another thing to practically and consistently implement them into your thinking and living. That's why we created the *10 Life-Changing Lessons from Heaven Journal.*

The *Journal* transforms the material from the book into your own personal, practical, and powerful Spiritual Development Program. It provides you with a special and sacred space to reflect and record your thoughts so you can put them into practice on a regular basis. It also includes several Practical Application Activities you can do to infuse the ideas into your life on a weekly basis. Plus, there are additional recommended readings. This next level resource allows you to customize each chapter's concepts and ideas to your own life and unique spiritual path.

For information on how you can get the *Journal* for yourself or your Book Club Discussion Group, visit www.LifeLessonsFromHeaven.com

Online Soul Peeps Discussion Groups
Looking to go even deeper? Join one of our online 10-week Soul Peeps Discussion Groups. You and a small group of fellow spiritual seekers will meet weekly via Zoom videoconference to learn more about the *10 Life-Changing Lessons from Heaven.* Led by author Jeff Janssen or one of his experienced team members, you'll go in-depth into each one of the ten lessons and learn how you can personalize and apply them to significantly improve, if not totally transform, your life. Many have told us that 10 weeks in a Soul Peeps Discussion Group made a bigger difference in their lives than years of therapy—and was much cheaper too.

You'll get your own *10 Life-Changing Lessons from Heaven Journal* to record your personal thoughts, feelings, transformations, and spiritual insights. There will also be a special, private Facebook Group to create an online community of support. Plus, you will interact with and learn from a NDEr and get to ask them your specific questions about life and death.

This interactive, ongoing, and immersive 10-week experience provides you with all the resources, insights, access, and support necessary to fully absorb and implement these powerful *10 Life-Changing Lessons from Heaven* into your own life.

The Groups are for people from all faiths, agnostics, and even atheists. The program is not designed to replace your current beliefs but to give you an opportunity to explore them and possibly expand them in light of what people who have been to heaven have learned.

What You'll Receive:

- 10 weekly Soul Peeps Discussion Group calls for an hour via Zoom

- A copy of the *10 Life-Changing Lessons from Heaven Journal* to track your growth

- Special access to a private Facebook Group to stay connected

- The chance to learn directly from a NDEr and ask your big questions

- Weekly emails and links to inspiring videos, articles, and resources

- A support group of like-minded spiritual seekers taking the journey with you

Visit www.LifeLessonsFromHeaven.com to see our schedule of Soul Peeps Discussion Groups to join as an individual or put together your own group of 8-15 people and contact us to create your own dedicated group.

APPRECIATIONS

So many people have inspired and supported me during the researching, writing, and piloting of this book and program and I am honored and humbled to thank them here.

First, thank you to my dear friends and Archangel Soul Peeps Tammy Shain and Cathy Shaw. We first met in college at Marquette and have deepened our friendship ever since. Your support of me and this book is truly heaven sent. I can't thank you enough for your unconditional love, support, and encouragement.

Thanks to my treasured Spiritual Mastermind Friends: Lynn Robinson, Nancy Rynes, Howard Falco, Christine Moriarty, and Amy Collette. Your patient and persistent support of me working through the process of finally having the courage and confidence to share these insights and truths with the world is so appreciated.

Thank you to the numerous Soul Peeps who shared their helpful feedback and suggestions to make this book so much better as we piloted the program: Michelle Gonzalez, Kim Mancuso, Beth Matkom, Cathy Shaw, Tammy Shain, Molly Monday Schmidt, Heidi Cotter, Janine Baudhuin, Beth Smits, Reverend James King, Reverend Tina Brown, Dave Vieweg, Linda Clark, Wayne Benenson, Brian and Tywana Smith (Shayna's parents), Courtney Dewar (Lucas' mom), Shannon Hache (Dominique's mom), Christiane Robbins (David's mom), Cathy Christensen (Dot's Mom), Brenda Oller (Ashley's mom), Sherry Matthews (Ethan's mom), Sharon Cavanaugh (Sarah's mom), Claire Arce, Susan Burton, Michael Towler, and many others. You have made this book and the Soul Peeps program 10 times better with your help!

Thank you to the amazing NDEr friends who have supported me on this journey, especially Nancy Rynes and Jeff Olsen. Thank you for sharing your wisdom and friendship with me.

Thank you to all the NDErs who have had the courage and conviction to share their stories, especially Eben Alexander, Mary Neal, Howard Storm, Marion Rome, David Bennett, RaNelle Wallace, Joyce Brown, Dannion Brinkley, Erica McKenzie, Rajiv Parti, Anita

Moorjani, and so many others. You will experience the Ripple Effects of your love and generosity in your next Life Review.

Thank you to respected NDE researchers Dr. Raymond Moody, Dr. Ken Ring, Dr. Bruce Greyson, John Audette, Dr. Michael Sabom, Dr. Jeffrey Long, Jody Long J.D., Dr. Penny Sartori, PMH Atwater, IANDS, and so many others who have studied this sacred phenomenon. I am privileged to learn from you and humbled to stand on your shoulders for the decades of work you have lovingly invested.

Thank you to all of the people who have significantly influenced my ongoing spiritual development with your inspiring books, talks, videos, and/or podcasts and encouraged me to Love Unconditionally, Live Fearlessly, Work Purposely, Serve Selflessly, and Trust Completely: Suzanne Giesemann, Rebecca Campbell, Kute Blackson, Lynn Robinson, Rick Archer, Debra Diamond, Sandra Champlain, Oprah Winfrey, Michael Singer, Ellen Debenport, Laura Lynne Jackson, George Anderson, Mike Dooley, Neale Donald Walsch, Marianne Williamson, Chas Hathaway, Gina Lake, Paul Ferrini, Mark Pitstick, Matthew McKay, Jeff O'Driscoll, Steve Nobel, Bob Goff, Brian Weiss, Wayne Dyer, Adyashanti, Tom Campbell, Frances Key, Sanaya Roman, Rasha, John Pavlovitz, Steven Pressfield, and Mark Anthony.

Thanks to Sherry Roberts for her graphic design work to bring these ideas to life. I always enjoy working with you and appreciate your patience as we get things just right.

Thanks to my parents, Tom and Mary Janssen, for always believing in me and encouraging me to make a difference in the world. It was my utmost privilege to be with you during your last days on this earth and watch you take your last breath as you transitioned to heaven. Thanks to my sister Jaclyn for your support of this new calling.

Saving the sacred souls closest to my heart for last—thanks to my unconditionally loving family for all of your support. Ryan and Jillian, I am most privileged to be your father and have learned (and continue to learn) so much from both of you about what love, compassion, kindness, patience, and forgiveness really mean. You have the most beautiful hearts and souls and many of my most cherished memories are the times when you extended your simple kindness to others. Kristi, through sickness and health, poorer and richer, sports and spirituality, climbs, falls, and recoveries, you have shared your unconditional love with me. Thank you for being the amazing wife, mother, person, and soul you are! I am honored to walk life with you.

ABOUT THE AUTHOR

After almost suffering a widowmaker heart attack at the relatively young age of 42, author Jeff Janssen sought answers to Life's Biggest Questions like: who am I, why are we here, and what happens to us when we die? His way too close brush with death put him on a serious quest to discover solid and soul-satisfying answers. Jeff's research led him to the stories of Near-Death Experiences (NDEs). After studying over 2,500 NDE accounts, Jeff synthesized their findings into the *10 Life-Changing Lessons from Heaven* so that he and others could benefit from their profound wisdom.

Jeff has shared these life-changing lessons with numerous groups including parents who have had children pass away as part of Helping Parents Heal, formerly incarcerated women as part of A New Way of Life, members of the International Association of Near-Death Studies (IANDS), and people from all religious backgrounds and faiths through his Soul Peeps Support Groups.

Jeff worked over 25 years in the sports world as a highly respected leadership and championship culture coach helping professional, college, and high school teams from all sports perform to their potential. He has consulted with Olympic gold medal winning athletes and helped over 30 teams win NCAA National Championships at colleges such as Arizona, Arkansas, Colorado, Illinois, Michigan, North Carolina, Notre Dame, South Carolina, and Stanford. A popular speaker and prolific writer, Jeff has spoken to and inspired tens of thousands of people across the world and written 15 books including *The Team Captain's Leadership Manual, How to Build and Sustain a Championship Culture*, and *What It Takes to Win Championships*.

Jeff lives in the Raleigh/Durham NC area with his lovely wife Kristi and their children Ryan and Jillian and dog Trey. They enjoy reading, traveling, nature walks, eating at great restaurants, and watching sports.

For additional info on Jeff and his programs and resources, visit www.LifeLessonsFromHeaven.com

RECOMMENDED READING

NDE Accounts

Awakenings from the Light—Nancy Rynes
Dying to Be Me—Anita Moorjani
What If This is Heaven?—Anita Moorjani
Proof of Heaven—Eben Alexander
The Map of Heaven—Eben Alexander, MD
Living in a Mindful Universe—Eben Alexander, MD
To Heaven and Back—Mary Neal, MD
7 Lessons from Heaven—Mary Neal, MD
Dying to Wake Up—Rajiv Parti, MD
Dying to Fit In—Erica McKenzie, RN
Voyage of Purpose—David Bennett
Secrets of the Light—Dannion Brinkley
Saved by the Light—Dannion Brinkley
At Peace in the Light—Dannion Brinkley
Beyond Sight—Marion Rome
Through the Light—Marion Rome
My Descent into Death—Howard Storm
The Burning Within—RaNelle Wallace
God's Heavenly Answers—Joyce Brown
I Knew Their Hearts—Jeff Olsen
Beyond Mile Marker 80—Jeff Olsen
Fast Lane to Heaven—Ned Dougherty
Embraced by the Light—Betty Eadie
Hear His Voice—Nancy Clark
Divine Moments—Nancy Clark
While I Was Out—Deirdre DeWitt-Maltby
Application of Impossible Things—Natalie Sudman
Heaven is Beautiful—Peter Panagore

Researchers on NDEs

Lessons from the Light—Ken Ring
Heading Toward Omega—Ken Ring
Life After Life—Raymond Moody
Evidence of the Afterlife—Jeffrey Long
God and the Afterlife—Jeffrey Long

The Transformative Power of Near Death Experiences—Penny Sartori and Kelly Walsh
The Wisdom of Near Death Experiences—Penny Sartori
Life After Near Death—Debra Diamond
Love the Person You're With—David Sunfellow
Revelations of Profound Love—Ann Ellis
The Big Book of Near Death Experiences—PMH Atwater

NOTES

Introduction

Gallup, G., & Proctor, W. (1982) *Adventures in immortality: a look beyond the threshold of death*. New York, NY: McGraw Hill.

Moody, R. (1975) *Life after life*: Harlan, IA: Guideposts.

Wallace, R. (1994). *The burning within*. Warren, MI: Gold Leaf Press.

Rynes, N. (2015). *Awakenings from the light: 12 life lessons from a near death experience*. Scotts Valley, CA: CreateSpace.

Alexander, E. (2014). *Map of heaven: how science, religion, and ordinary people are proving the afterlife*. New York, NY: Simon & Schuster.

Thomas, K. (2017, September 9). *We don't die radio show* [Audio podcast]. Retrieved from https://www.youtube.com/watch?v=QWgw1xAEolY

Alexander, E. (2014). *Map of heaven: how science, religion, and ordinary people are proving the afterlife*. New York, NY: Simon & Schuster.

Brinkley, D., & Brinkley, K. (2008). *Secrets of the light: lessons from heaven*. San Francisco: HarperOne.

Brown, J. (2014). *Heavenly answers for earthly challenges*. Mesquite, NV: Davidson Press.

Molinero, P. (2016). *Does mother exist? Is there life after birth?* Morrisville, NC: Lulu.

John Wintek quoted in Berman, P. (1998). *The journey home*. New York: NY: Simon & Schuster.

Linda Stewart quoted in Williams, K. (2016). *Linda Stewart's near-death experience*. Retrieved from http://www.near-death.com/experiences/notable/linda-stewart.html

Roland Webb quoted in Dominguez, H. (2016). *Consciousness continues: near-death experiences and the aftereffects*. p. 42.

McVea, C. (2013). *Waking up in heaven: a true story of brokenness, heaven, and life again*. Brentwood, TN: Howard Books.

Dr. Raymond Moody quoted in Parti, R. (2016). *Dying to wake up: a doctor's voyage into the afterlife and the wisdom he brought back*. New York, NY: Atria Books.

Neev quoted in Ring, K. (2006). *Lessons from the light: what we can learn from the near-death experience*. Needham, MA: Moment Point Press. p. 24.

Reinee Pasarow quoted in Williams, K. (2016). *Reinee Pasarow's near-death experience*.

Retrieved from https://www.near-death.com/experiences/notable/reinee-pasarow.html

Diamond, D. (2016). *Life after near death: miraculous stories of healing and transformation in the extraordinary lives of people with newfound powers.* Newburyport, MA: New Page Books. p. 74.

Dr. Melvin Morse quoted in Sunfellow, D. (2013). *Shadows: perceptions of near-death experiencers.* Retrieved from https://www.youtube.com/watch?v=HR0x57aMv-k

Clark, Nancy (2012). *Divine moments: ordinary people having spiritually transformative experiences.* Fairfield, IA: 1st World Publishing. p. 24-25.

Parti, R. (2016). *Dying to wake up: a doctor's voyage into the afterlife and the wisdom he brought back.* New York, NY: Atria Books. p. 179.

Griggs, L. (2012). *The gift of near death; Lewis Brown Griggs at TEDx american riviera 2012.* Retrieved by https://www.youtube.com/watch?v=bi_QsbnrTXo

Dr. Diane Morrissey quoted in Williams, K. (2016). *Dr. Diane Morrissey's near-death experience.* Retrieved from https://www.near-death.com/experiences/notable/dianne-morrissey.html

Rome, Marion (2014). *Beyond sight: the true story of a near-death experience.* Scotts Valley, CA: CreateSpace.

Juliet Nightingale quoted in Williams, K. (2016). *Juliet Nightingale's near-death experience.* Retrieved from https://www.near-death.com/experiences/notable/Juliet-nightingale.html

Daniela quoted in Ellis, A. (2012). *Revelations of profound love: new insights into the power of love from near-death experiences.* Tulsa, OK: Trail of Hope Publishing. p. 103.

Craig quoted in Ring, K. (2006). *Lessons from the light: what we can learn from the near-death experience.* Needham, MA: Moment Point Press.

Long, J. & Perry, P. (2010). *Evidence of the afterlife: the science of near-death experiences.* San Francisco, CA: HarperOne. p. 202.

Ring, K. (2006). *Lessons from the light: what we can learn from the near-death experience.* Needham, MA: Moment Point Press. p. 33 and 52.

Sartori, P. & Walsh, K. (2017). *The transformative power of near-death experiences: how the messages of ndes can positively impact the world.* London, UK: Watkins Publishing. p. 186.

Ring, K. (2006). *Lessons from the light: what we can learn from the near-death experience.* Needham, MA: Moment Point Press.

Chapter 1—Love Unconditionally

Kubler-Ross, E. (2018) *Elizabeth Kubler-Ross quotes.* Retrieved from https://www.goodreads.com/quotes/7202570-the-ultimate-lesson-all-of-us-have-to-learn-is

Nichole BD. *Nichole BD nde*. NDERF.org Retrieved from https://www.nderf.org/Experiences/1nichole_bd_nde.html

Carlos K. *Carlos K ste*. NDERF.org Retrieved from http://www.nderf.org/Experiences/1carlos_k_ste.html

Bobbi D. *Bobbi D nde*. NDERF.org Retrieved from http://www.nderf.org/Experiences/1bobbi_d_nde.html

Woody, T. (2014). *Former us navy flight engineer Tony Woody—his meeting with God!* Retrieved from https://www.youtube.com/watch?v=iiHvLn-xXg4

Moorjani, A. (2012). *Dying to be me: my journey from cancer, to near death, to true healing*. Carlsbad, CA: Hay House. p. 66.

Clark, Nancy (2012). *Divine moments: ordinary people having spiritually transformative experiences*. Fairfield, IA: 1st World Publishing. p. 35.

Tabitha quoted in Ellis, A. (2012). *Revelations of profound love: new insights into the power of love from near-death experiences*. Tulsa, OK: Trail of Hope Publishing. p. 68.

Bennett, D. (2011). *Voyage of purpose: spiritual wisdom from near death back to life*. Rochester, VT: Findhorn Press. p. 82.

Rome, Marion (2014). *Beyond sight: the true story of a near-death experience*. Scotts Valley, CA: CreateSpace.

Bennett, D. (2011). *Voyage of purpose: spiritual wisdom from near death back to life*. Rochester, VT: Findhorn Press. p. 122.

Peggy P. quoted in Ring, K. (2006). *Lessons from the light: what we can learn from the near-death experience*. Needham, MA: Moment Point Press. p. 188.

Alexander, E. (2012). *Proof of heaven: a neurosurgeon's journey into the afterlife*. New York, NY: Simon & Schuster. p. 71.

Tricia B. *Tricia B nde*. NDERF.org Retrieved from http://www.nderf.org/Experiences/1tricia_b_nde.html

Yvonne Kason quoted in Berman, P. (1998). *The journey home*. New York: NY: Simon & Schuster. p. 47.

Dr. Raymond Moody quoted in Pitstick, M. (2015). *The eleven questions: everything you wanted to know about life, death, afterlife*. Cardiff by the Sea, CA: Waterfront Press. p. 30.

Clark, Nancy (2012). *Hear his voice*. Fairfield, IA: 1st World Publishing. p. 101.

Rynes, N. (2015). *Awakenings from the light: 12 life lessons from a near death experience*. Scotts Valley, CA: CreateSpace. p. 54-55.

Rodonaia, G. (2011). *George Rodonaia's near death experience*. Retrieved from https://www.youtube.com/watch?v=jcEbQdy-BAM

Kennedy, R. (2019). *Dr. Ron Kennedy talks about his near-death experience*. Retrieved from https://bit.tube/play?hash=QmNTELA699gbWZmZUWdAAcDZJ6v5XY7sN4iw4hRFaArqxN&channel=222295

Brown, J. (2014). *Heavenly answers for earthly challenges.* Mesquite, NV: Davidson Press. p. 93-96.

Jean R. *Jean R nde.* NDERF.org Retrieved from http://www.nderf.org/Experiences/1jean_r_nde_6166.html

Mary Beth Willi. *Mary W nde.* NDERF.org Retrieved from http://www.nderf.org/Experiences/1mary_w_nde.html

Dougherty, N. (2002). *Fast lane to heaven: a life-after-death journey.* Newburyport, MA: Hampton Roads Publishing. p. 29.

Keith Keller quoted in Berman, P. (1998). *The journey home.* New York: NY: Simon & Schuster. p. 119.

Heather V. *Heather V nde.* NDERF.org Retrieved from http://www.nderf.org/Experiences/1heather_v_nde.html

Storm, H. (2005). *My descent into death: a second chance at life.* New York, NY: Harmony. p. 69.

Storm, H. (2005). *My descent into death: a second chance at life.* New York, NY: Harmony. p. 34-35.

Karen M. Karen M nde. NDERF.org Retrieved from http://www.nderf.org/Experiences/1karen_m_nde_8141.html

Lynnclaire Dennis quoted in Williams, K. (2016). *Lynnclaire Dennis' near-death experience.* Retrieved from http://www.near-death.com/experiences/notable/lynnclaire-dennis.html

Moorjani, A. (2016). *What if this is heaven?: how our cultural myths prevent us from experiencing heaven on earth.* Carlsbad, CA: Hay House. p. 19.

McVea, C. (2013). *Waking up in heaven: a true story of brokenness, heaven, and life again.* Brentwood, TN: Howard Books.

Weiler, D.S. (2007). *Dead is just a four letter word.* Retrieved from http://www.1way2see.com/thebook.html

Rynes, N. (2015). *Awakenings from the light: 12 life lessons from a near death experience.* Scotts Valley, CA: CreateSpace. p. 52-53.

Sharon M. Sharon M nde. NDERF.org Retrieved from https://www.nderf.org/Experiences/1sharon_m_nde_7925.html

Moorjani, A. (2012). *Dying to be me: my journey from cancer, to near death, to true healing.* Carlsbad, CA: Hay House. p. 135.

Sandy B. quoted in Clark, Nancy (2012). *Divine moments: ordinary people having spiritually transformative experiences.* Fairfield, IA: 1st World Publishing. p. 35. p. 105.

Rynes, N. (2015). *Awakenings from the light: 12 life lessons from a near death experience.* Scotts Valley, CA: CreateSpace. p. 62.

McKenzie, E. (2015). *Dying to fit in.* Erica McKenzie. p. 88-89.

Sharon M. Sharon M nde. NDERF.org Retrieved from https://www.nderf.org/Experiences/1sharon_m_nde_7925.html

Jobs, S. (2005). *Steve Jobs' 2005 Stanford commencement address.* Retrieved by https://www.youtube.com/watch?v=UF8uR6Z6KLc

Brinkley, D. & Perry, P. (1995). *At peace in the light: the further adventures of a reluctant psychic who reveals the secret of your spiritual powers.* New York, NY: HarperCollins. p. 138.

Dougherty, N. (2002). *Fast lane to heaven: a life-after-death journey.* Newburyport, MA: Hampton Roads Publishing. p. 35.

Ritchie, G. & Sherrill, E. (2006). *Return from tomorrow.* Ada. MI: Revell. p. 58-65.

Brown, J. (2014). *Heavenly answers for earthly challenges.* Mesquite, NV: Davidson Press. p. 87-88.

Mary Jo Rapini. *Mary Jo R* NDERF.org Retrieved from http://www.nderf.org/Experiences/1mary_jo_r_nde.html

Putnoki, T. (2016). *Tibor Putnoki my path to the light.* Retrieved from https://www.youtube.com/watch?v=S7-LOH8hVTE

Clark, Nancy (2012). *Divine moments: ordinary people having spiritually transformative experiences.* Fairfield, IA: 1st World Publishing. p. 38.

Rynes, N. (2015). *Awakenings from the light: 12 life lessons from a near death experience.* Scotts Valley, CA: CreateSpace. p. 64.

Ron K. *Ron K nde.* NDERF.org Retrieved from http://www.nderf.org/Experiences/1ron_k_nde.html

McVea, C. (2013). *Waking up in heaven: a true story of brokenness, heaven, and life again.* Brentwood, TN: Howard Books. p. 340.

Howard Storm quoted in Sunfellow, D. (2016.) *Love the person you're with: life-changing insights from the most compelling near-death experiences ever recorded.* Scotts Valley, CA: CreateSpace. p. 16.

Panagore, P. (2017). *Let's talk near death: Peter Panagore.* Retrieved from https://www.youtube.com/watch?v=B3dXE-nSyzY

Goff, B. (2018). *Everybody always: Becoming love in a world full of setbacks and difficult people.* Nashville: TN: Nelson Books. p. 223.

Chapter 2—Live Fearlessly

Schucman, H. (1975). *A course in miracles.* Mill Valley, CA: Foundation for Inner Peace.

Anita Moorjani quoted in Pitstick, M. (2015). *The eleven questions: everything you wanted to know about life, death, afterlife.* Cardiff by the Sea, CA: Waterfront Press. p. 58.

RaNelle Wallace quoted in Williams, K. (2016). *RaNelle Wallace's near-death experience.* Retrieved from http://www.near-death.com/experiences/notable/ranelle-wallace.html

Kopecky, R. (2014). *How to survive life (and death): a guide for happiness in this world and beyond.* Newburyport, MA: Conari Press. p. 70.

Rynes, N. (2015). *Awakenings from the light: 12 life lessons from a near death experience.* Scotts Valley, CA: CreateSpace. p. 130-131.

Chodron, P. (2016). *When things fall apart: heart advice for difficult times.* CO: Shambhala.

Rynes, N. (2015). *Awakenings from the light: 12 life lessons from a near death experience.* Scotts Valley, CA: CreateSpace. p. 166.

Moorjani, A. (2012). *Dying to be me: my journey from cancer, to near death, to true healing.* Carlsbad, CA: Hay House. p. 132.

Bennett, D. (2011). *Voyage of purpose: spiritual wisdom from near death back to life.* Rochester, VT: Findhorn Press. p. 71.

Dr. Raymond Moody quoted in Lundahl, C. & Widdison, H. (1997). *The eternal journey: how near-death experiences illuminate our earthly lives.* New York, NY: Grand Central Publishing. p. 260.

Sharkey, J. (2012). *Clinically dead: I've seen heaven and hell.* Scotts Valley, CA: CreateSpace.

Howes, L. (2017). *The mask of masculinity: how men can embrace vulnerability, create strong relationships, and live their fullest lives.* New York, NY: Rodale Books.

Moorjani, A. (2012). *Dying to be me: my journey from cancer, to near death, to true healing.* Carlsbad, CA: Hay House. p. 132.

Mary Beth Willi. *Mary W nde.* NDERF.org Retrieved from http://www.nderf.org/Experiences/1mary_w_nde.html

Chodron, P. (2016). *When things fall apart: heart advice for difficult times.* CO: Shambhala.

Anita Moorjani quoted in Pitstick, M. (2015). *The eleven questions: everything you wanted to know about life, death, afterlife.* Cardiff by the Sea, CA: Waterfront Press. p. 58.

Terri R. *Terri R nde.* NDERF.org Retrieved from http://www.nderf.org/Experiences/1teri_r_nde.html

DeWitt-Maltby, D. (2012). *While I was out . . .* Self Publish. p. 105.

Rynes, N. (2015). *Awakenings from the light: 12 life lessons from a near death experience.* Scotts Valley, CA: CreateSpace. p. 89.

Ellen Dye quoted in Sunfellow, D. (2016.) *Love the person you're with: life-changing insights from the most compelling near-death experiences ever recorded.* Scotts Valley, CA: CreateSpace. p. 67.

Mellon Thomas Benedict quoted in Sunfellow, D. (2016.) *Love the person you're with: life-changing insights from the most compelling near-death experiences ever recorded.* Scotts Valley, CA: CreateSpace. p. 96.

Hindu Legend Story Retrieved from http://www.hinduhumanrights.info/divinity-lies-within-us-all/

Mcdowell, E. Retrieved from https://www.facebook.com/105433989565465/posts/finding-yourself-is-not-really-how-it-works-you-arent-a-ten-dollar-bill-in-last-/1784152248360289/

Rynes, N. (2015). *Awakenings from the light: 12 life lessons from a near death experience.* Scotts Valley, CA: CreateSpace. p. 114.

Bennett, D. (2011). *Voyage of purpose: spiritual wisdom from near death back to life.* Rochester, VT: Findhorn Press. p. 132.

Schucman, H. (1975). *A course in miracles.* Mill Valley, CA: Foundation for Inner Peace.

Nel quoted in Ring, K. (2006). *Lessons from the light: what we can learn from the near-death experience.* Needham, MA: Moment Point Press. p. 191.

Rynes, N. (2015). *Awakenings from the light: 12 life lessons from a near death experience.* Scotts Valley, CA: CreateSpace. p. 164-165.

Umebinyuo, I. *Start now.* Retrieved from https://www.goodreads.com/quotes/3247698-start-now-start-where-you-are-start-with-fear-start

Moorjani, A. (2016). *What if this is heaven?: how our cultural myths prevent us from experiencing heaven on earth.* Carlsbad, CA: Hay House. p. 23.

Rynes, N. (2015). *Awakenings from the light: 12 life lessons from a near death experience.* Scotts Valley, CA: CreateSpace. p. 130-131.

Rynes, N. (2015). *Awakenings from the light: 12 life lessons from a near death experience.* Scotts Valley, CA: CreateSpace. p. 171-172.

Carrey, J. (2014). *Jim Carrey commencement speech.* Retrieved from https://www.mum.edu/whats-happening/graduation-2014/full-jim-carrey-address-video-and-transcript/

Brown, B. (2010). *The gifts of imperfection.* Center City, MN: Hazelden Publishing.

Chapter 3—Work Purposely

Brinkley, D., & Brinkley, K. (2008). *Secrets of the light: lessons from heaven.* San Francisco: HarperOne. p. 163-164.

RaNelle Wallace quoted in Williams, K. (2016). *RaNelle Wallace's near-death experience.* Retrieved from http://www.near-death.com/experiences/notable/ranelle-wallace.html

Winfrey, O. (2018, August 14) *India Arie why she walked away from music.* Super Soul Sunday. Retrieved from https://www.youtube.com/watch?v=IvEZRb9R0dw

Williamson. M. (1992). *Return to love: reflections on the principles of a course in miracles.* New York, NY: HarperCollins.

Brown, J. (2014). *Heavenly answers for earthly challenges.* Mesquite, NV: Davidson Press. p. 73-75, 89-90.

Robbins, J. (2012). *The man who planted trees: lost groves, champion trees, and an urgent plan to save the planet.* Jim Robbins.

RaNelle Wallace quoted in Williams, K. (2016). *RaNelle Wallace's near-death experience*. Retrieved from http://www.near-death.com/experiences/notable/ranelle-wallace.html

Karola quoted in Ellis, A. (2012). *Revelations of profound love: new insights into the power of love from near-death experiences*. Tulsa, OK: Trail of Hope Publishing. p. 103.

Mary Beth Willi. *Mary W nde*. NDERF.org Retrieved from http://www.nderf.org/Experiences/1mary_w_nde.html

Heather V. *Heather V nde*. NDERF.org Retrieved from http://www.nderf.org/Experiences/1heather_v_nde.html

Juliet Nightingale quoted in Williams, K. (2016). *Juliet Nightingale's near-death experience*. Retrieved from https://www.near-death.com/experiences/notable/Juliet-nightingale.html

Tolle, E. (1999). *The power of now: a guide to spiritual enlightenment*. Novato, CA: New World Library.

Lisa B. Lisa B nde. NDERF.org Retrieved from http://www.nderf.org/Experiences/1lisa_b_nde.html

Calvert, O. *Experiencer Oliver John Calvert*. Retrieved by http://lovethepersonyouarewith.com/references/experiencer-oliver-john-calvert/

Peggy P. quoted in Ring, K. (2006). *Lessons from the light: what we can learn from the near-death experience*. Needham, MA: Moment Point Press. p. 40.

Bennett, D. (2011). *Voyage of purpose: spiritual wisdom from near death back to life*. Rochester, VT: Findhorn Press. p. 24-25.

Betty Eadie quoted in Bailey, L. & Yates, J. (1996). *The near death experience: a reader*. Florence, KY: Routledge. p. 56.

Kinman, R. (2014). *Present! Raymond Kinman's near death experience*. Retrieved from https://www.youtube.com/watch?v=tgYHxrBn5Ao

Lisa M. *Lisa M nde*. NDERF.org Retrieved from http://www.nderf.org/Experiences/1lisa_m_nde.html

Mary Beth Willi. *Mary W nde*. NDERF.org Retrieved from http://www.nderf.org/Experiences/1mary_w_nde.html

Ring, K. (1980). *Life at death; a scientific investigation of the near death experience*. New York, NY: Coward-McCann. p. 68.

RaNelle Wallace quoted in Williams, K. (2016). *RaNelle Wallace's near-death experience*. Retrieved from http://www.near-death.com/experiences/notable/ranelle-wallace.html

McKenzie, E. (2015). *Dying to fit in*. Erica McKenzie. p. 78.

Neal, M. (2017). *7 lessons from heaven: how dying taught me to live a joy-filled life*. New York, NY: Convergent Books. p. 152-153.

Betty Eadie quoted in Bailey, L. & Yates, J. (1996). *The near death experience: a reader*. Florence, KY: Routledge. p. 56.

Ring, K. (2006). *Lessons from the light: what we can learn from the near-death experience.* Needham, MA: Moment Point Press. p. 51.

Neal, M. (2017). *7 lessons from heaven: how dying taught me to live a joy-filled life.* New York, NY: Convergent Books. p. 144.

Mary Beth Willi. *Mary W nde.* NDERF.org Retrieved from http://www.nderf.org/Experiences/1mary_w_nde.html

Gary Wood quoted in Roth, S. & Lane, L. (2016). *Heaven is beyond your wildest expectations.* Destiny Image Publishers. P. 146.

Chapter 4—Choose Compassionately

Kubler-Ross, E. *50 quotes by Dr. Elizabeth Kubler-Ross.* Retrieved from http://www.ekrfoundation.org/quotes/

McKenzie, E. (2015). *Dying to fit in.* Erica McKenzie. p. 76.

Rynes, N. (2015). *Awakenings from the light: 12 life lessons from a near death experience.* Scotts Valley, CA: CreateSpace. p. 151-152.

Betty Eadie quoted in Bailey, L. & Yates, J. (1996). *The near death experience: a reader.* Florence, KY: Routledge. p. 159.

Brown, J. (2014). *Heavenly answers for earthly challenges.* Mesquite, NV: Davidson Press. p. 192.

Olsen, J. (2018). Personal communication.

Olsen, J. (2012). *I knew their hearts: the amazing true story of a journey beyond the veil to learn the silent language of the heart.* Plain Sight Publications. p. 188.

Stout, Y. (2017). *Yolaine Stout a suicidal near death experience and what it taught me about life.* Retrieved from https://www.youtube.com/watch?v=BMfjM6TrkV8

Alexander, E. (2012). *Proof of heaven: a neurosurgeon's journey into the afterlife.* New York, NY: Simon & Schuster.

Oakford, D. (2018). *Soul bared: a metaphysical journey.* Maryland: Publish America.

RaNelle Wallace quoted in Williams, K. (2016). *RaNelle Wallace's near-death experience.* Retrieved from http://www.near-death.com/experiences/notable/ranelle-wallace.html

Reinee Pasarow quoted in Sunfellow, D. (2016.) *Love the person you're with: life-changing insights from the most compelling near-death experiences ever recorded.* Scotts Valley, CA: CreateSpace. p. 16.

Brinkley, D., & Brinkley, K. (2008). *Secrets of the light: lessons from heaven.* San Francisco: HarperOne. p. 114.

Brown, J. (2014). *Heavenly answers for earthly challenges.* Mesquite, NV: Davidson Press. p. 88-89.

RaNelle Wallace quoted in Williams, K. (2016). *RaNelle Wallace's near-death experience.* Retrieved from http://www.near-death.com/experiences/notable/ranelle-wallace.html

Whitfield, B. (2010). *The natural soul.* Muse House Press.

Daniel A. Daniel A nde. NDERF.org Retrieved from https://www.nderf.org/Experiences/1daniel_a_nde.html

Dougherty, N. (2002). *Fast lane to heaven: a life-after-death journey.* Newburyport, MA: Hampton Roads Publishing.

Andy Petro quoted in Sunfellow, D. (2016.) *Love the person you're with: life-changing insights from the most compelling near-death experiences ever recorded.* Scotts Valley, CA: CreateSpace. *http://lovethepersonyouarewith.com/videos/AndyPetro/*

Neal, M. (2017). *7 lessons from heaven: how dying taught me to live a joy-filled life.* New York, NY: Convergent Books. p. 24-25.

Ring, K. (1985). *Heading toward omega: in search of the meaning of the near-death experience.* New York, NY: Harper Perennial. p. 70.

Grace Bulbulka quoted in Williams, K. (2016). *Grace Bulbulka's near death experience.* http://www.near-death.com/experiences/notable/grace-bubulka.html

Neev quoted in Ring, K. (2006). *Lessons from the light: what we can learn from the near-death experience.* Needham, MA: Moment Point Press. p. 22.

Brown, J. (2014). *Heavenly answers for earthly challenges.* Mesquite, NV: Davidson Press. p. 86.

Storm, H. (2005). *My descent into death: a second chance at life.* New York, NY: Harmony.

Brinkley, D., & Brinkley, K. (2008). *Secrets of the light: lessons from heaven.* San Francisco: HarperOne. p. 190.

Farr, S., & Sawyer, T. (1993). *What Tom Sawyer learned from dying.* Newburyport, MA: Hampton Roads Publishing. p. 30.

Neev quoted in Ring, K. (2006). *Lessons from the light: what we can learn from the near-death experience.* Needham, MA: Moment Point Press. p. 22.

Whitfield, B. (2010). *The natural soul.* Muse House Press. p. xi-xii, 5.

David Bennett quoted in Sartori, P. & Walsh, K. (2017). *The transformative power of near-death experiences: how the messages of ndes can positively impact the world.* London, UK: Watkins Publishing. p. 73-74.

Call, A. *Amy Call nde.* NDERF.org Retrieved from http://www.nderf.org/Experiences/1amy_c_nde_4720.html

Beckman, D. (2012). Dr. Jeffrey Long—near death experiences. Retrieved from https://www.youtube.com/watch?v=LwyVFW9kT8k

Neev quoted in Ring, K. (2006). *Lessons from the light: what we can learn from the near-death experience.* Needham, MA: Moment Point Press. p. 22.

Webb, R. (2013). *Consciousness continues.* Retrieved from https://www.amazon.com/gp/video/detail/B01N59JX39?ie=UTF8&language=tr_TR

Tom Sawyer quoted in Ring, K. (2006). *Lessons from the light: what we can learn from the near-death experience*. Needham, MA: Moment Point Press. p. 175.

Rome, Marion (2014). *Beyond sight: the true story of a near-death experience*. Scotts Valley, CA: CreateSpace.

Mary Beth Willi. *Mary W nde*. NDERF.org Retrieved from http://www.nderf.org/Experiences/1mary_w_nde.html

Rome, Marion (2014). *Beyond sight: the true story of a near-death experience*. Scotts Valley, CA: CreateSpace.

Minette Crow quoted in Ring, K. (2006). *Lessons from the light: what we can learn from the near-death experience*. Needham, MA: Moment Point Press. p. 162.

Ring, K. (2006). *Lessons from the light: what we can learn from the near-death experience*. Needham, MA: Moment Point Press. p. 162.

Helen S. *Helen S nde*. NDERF.org Retrieved from https://www.nderf.org/Experiences/1helen_s_ste.html

Neal, M. (2014) *Mary Neal—the gift of life*. IANDS presentation. Newport, CA.

Rynes, N. (2015). *Awakenings from the light: 12 life lessons from a near death experience*. Scotts Valley, CA: CreateSpace. p. 152-153.

Anova, A. (2016). *Alon Anava—NDE, DNDE*. Retrieved from http://ndestories.org/alon-anava/

Anthony, P. (2017) *Peter Anthony—near death experience: back in a moment*. Retrieved from https://www.youtube.com/watch?v=LamlFhFnlLE

Jorgensen, R. (2017). *Chapter 7—near-death-like experiencer Rene Jorgensen—the full consequences of my actions*. Retrieved from http://lovethepersonyouarewith.com/videos/renejorgensen/

Fenimore, A. (2015). *Angie answers question, "what happens to people who commit suicide when they cross over?"*. Retrieved from https://www.youtube.com/watch?v=Mn_QZec5jK8

Pasarow, R. (2017). *Chapter 5—near-death experiencer Reinee Pasarow—the greatest of all actions*. Retrieved from http://lovethepersonyouarewith.com/videos/reineepasarow/

Brown, J. (2014). *Heavenly answers for earthly challenges*. Mesquite, NV: Davidson Press. p. 79.

Dannion Brinkley quoted in Bailey, L. & Yates, J. (1996). *The near death experience: a reader*. Florence, KY: Routledge. p. 69.

Sawyer, T. quoted in Williams, K. (2017). *Thomas Sawyer's near-death experience*. Retrieved from https://www.near-death.com/reincarnation/experiences/thomas-sawyer.html

Neev quoted in Ring, K. (2006). *Lessons from the light: what we can learn from the near-death experience*. Needham, MA: Moment Point Press. p. 177.

Neev quoted in Ring, K. (2006). *Lessons from the light: what we can learn from the near-death experience.* Needham, MA: Moment Point Press. p. 22.

Ring, K. (2006). *Lessons from the light: what we can learn from the near-death experience.* Needham, MA: Moment Point Press. p. 155.

Neal, M. (2017). *7 lessons from heaven: how dying taught me to live a joy-filled life.* New York, NY: Convergent Books. p. 26-27.

Dougherty, N. (2002). *Fast lane to heaven: a life-after-death journey.* Newburyport, MA: Hampton Roads Publishing. p. 34.

Jeff Olsen quoted in Sartori, P. & Walsh, K. (2017). *The transformative power of near-death experiences: how the messages of ndes can positively impact the world.* London, UK: Watkins Publishing. p. 108-109.

Thomas, K. (2018). *Near Death Experiences Facebook* Group. Retrieved from https://www.facebook.com/groups/returnfromdeath/

Olsen, J. (2019). *The near-death experience of Jeff Olsen.* Retrieved from https://www.youtube.com/watch?v=1FD5lReqe64

Meyler, L. (2019). *Near Death Experiences Facebook* Group. Retrieved from https://www.facebook.com/groups/returnfromdeath/

Leach, T. (2017). *Rev Tom Leach—feel the love that they have for you.* Retrieved from https://www.youtube.com/watch?v=nrwiTz7o-qY

Brinkley, D. & Perry, P. (1995). *At peace in the light: the further adventures of a reluctant psychic who reveals the secret of your spiritual powers.* New York, NY: HarperCollins. p. 136-137.

Chapter 5—Accept Nonjudgmentally

Storm, H. (2005). *My descent into death: a second chance at life.* New York, NY: Harmony. p. 41.

Horne, A. (2014). *The light bringers—near death experience—anne horne.* Retrieved from https://www.youtube.com/watch?v=Eu-9yx0BXok

Daniela quoted in Ellis, A. (2012). *Revelations of profound love: new insights into the power of love from near-death experiences.* Tulsa, OK: Trail of Hope Publishing. p. 70.

McKenzie, E. (2015). *Dying to fit in.* Erica McKenzie. p. 74.

Linda Stewart quoted in Williams, K. (2016). *Linda Stewart's near-death experience.* Retrieved from http://www.near-death.com/experiences/notable/linda-stewart.html

Lisa M. *Lisa M nde.* NDERF.org Retrieved from http://www.nderf.org/Experiences/1lisa_m_nde.html

McKenzie, E. (2015). *Dying to fit in.* Erica McKenzie. p. 89.

Mia quoted in Ring, K. (2006). *Lessons from the light: what we can learn from the near-death experience.* Needham, MA: Moment Point Press. p. 137.

Bennett, D. (2011). *Voyage of purpose: spiritual wisdom from near death back to life.* Rochester, VT: Findhorn Press. p. 34.

Olsen, J. (2012). *I knew their hearts: the amazing true story of a journey beyond the veil to learn the silent language of the heart.* Plain Sight Publications. p. 102.

Joyce Brown quoted in Allan, D. *Book report: heavenly answers for earthly challenges.* Retrieved from http://www.allanstime.com/Spiritual/BookReports/heavenly.htm

Willie Lyle quoted in Parrish, T. (2013). *Pastor goes undercover for 5 days as homeless man.* USA Today. Retrieved by https://www.usatoday.com/story/news/nation/2013/07/24/pastor-homeless-experience/2583241/

Kimberly Clark-Sharp quoted in Williams, K. (2016). *Kimberly Clark-Sharp's near death experience.* https://www.near-death.com/experiences/notable/kimberly-clark-sharp.html

Olsen, J. (2019). *The near-death experience of Jeff Olsen.* Retrieved from https://www.youtube.com/watch?v=1FD5lReqe64

Tonja B. Tonja B nde. NDERF.org Retrieved from http://www.nderf.org/Experiences/1tonja_bb_nde.html

Reinee Pasarow quoted in Williams, K. (2016). *Reinee Pasarow's near-death experience.* Retrieved from https://www.near-death.com/experiences/notable/reinee-pasarow.html

Neal, M. (2017). *7 lessons from heaven: how dying taught me to live a joy-filled life.* New York, NY: Convergent Books. p. 33.

Kubler-Ross, E. *50 quotes by Dr. Elizabeth Kubler-Ross.* Retrieved from http://www.ekrfoundation.org/quotes/

Clark, Nancy (2012). *Hear his voice.* Fairfield, IA: 1st World Publishing. p. 70.

McKenzie, E. (2015). *Dying to fit in.* Erica McKenzie. p. 98-99.

Juliana quoted in Rommer, B. (2000). *Blessing in disguise: another side of near death experience.* Woodbury, M: Llewellyn Publications. p. 113.

Betty Eadie quoted in Bailey, L. & Yates, J. (1996). *The near death experience: a reader.* Florence, KY: Routledge. p. 59.

Anthony, P. (2018). *The near-death experience of Peter Anthony.* Retrieved from https://www.youtube.com/watch?v=5XrA79_T_R0

Bartolome, B. (2016). *The near-death experience of Barbara Bartolome.* Retrieved from https://www.youtube.com/watch?v=zg3HnkSg38s

Rynes, N. (2015). *Awakenings from the light: 12 life lessons from a near death experience.* Scotts Valley, CA: CreateSpace. p. 101.

Carrey, J. (2014). *Jim Carrey commencement speech.* Retrieved from https://www.mum.edu/whats-happening/graduation-2014/full-jim-carrey-address-video-and-transcript/

Rynes, N. (2015). *Awakenings from the light: 12 life lessons from a near death experience.* Scotts Valley, CA: CreateSpace. p. 82-83.

Bennett, D. (2011). *Voyage of purpose: spiritual wisdom from near death back to life.* Rochester, VT: Findhorn Press. p. 56, 84.

Josiane Antonette quoted in Williams, K. (2016). *Josiane Antonette's near death experience.* Retrieved from http://www.near-death.com/experiences/notable/josiane-antonette.html

Olsen, J. (2012). *I knew their hearts: the amazing true story of a journey beyond the veil to learn the silent language of the heart.* Plain Sight Publications. p. 37.

Baker, K. (2018). *Near death experience—life review of an abusive father.* Retrieved from https://www.youtube.com/watch?v=l8Lun3xpVhk

Wilson, Penny quoted in Sartori, P. & Walsh, K. (2017). *The transformative power of near-death experiences: how the messages of ndes can positively impact the world.* London, UK: Watkins Publishing. p. 90.

Rynes, N. (2015). *Awakenings from the light: 12 life lessons from a near death experience.* Scotts Valley, CA: CreateSpace. p. 50-51.

Brown, J. (2014). *Heavenly answers for earthly challenges.* Mesquite, NV: Davidson Press. p. 115.

Bennett, D. (2011). *Voyage of purpose: spiritual wisdom from near death back to life.* Rochester, VT: Findhorn Press. p. 72.

Brinkley, D. & Perry, P. (1995). *At peace in the light: the further adventures of a reluctant psychic who reveals the secret of your spiritual powers.* New York, NY: HarperCollins. p. 137.

Aubier, Julie quoted in Sunfellow, D. (2018). *NDEs & the purpose of life.* Retrieved from http://the-formula.org/ndes-the-purpose-of-life/

Craig, H. (2018). *The near-death experience of Heidi Craig.* Retrieved from https://www.youtube.com/watch?v=YSa3El8VFOo

Dougherty, N. (2002). *Fast lane to heaven: a life-after-death journey.* Newburyport, MA: Hampton Roads Publishing. p. 34-35.

Ron K. *Ron K. nde.* NDERF.org Retrieved from https://www.nderf.org/Experiences/1ron_k_nde.html

Brian S. *Brian S. nde.* NDERF.org Retrieved from https://www.nderf.org/Experiences/1brian_s_nde.html

Chapter 6—Learn Continuously

Storm, H. (2005). *My descent into death: a second chance at life.* New York, NY: Harmony. p 80-81, 91.

Mary Beth Willi. *Mary W nde.* NDERF.org Retrieved from http://www.nderf.org/Experiences/1mary_w_nde.html

Longfellow, H. (1841). *The rainy day.*

Hemmingway, E. (1929). *A farewell to arms.*

William C. William C nde. NDERF.org Retrieved from http://www.nderf.org/Experiences/1william_c_nde.html

McKenzie, E. (2015). *Dying to fit in.* Erica McKenzie. p. vi.

Brown, J. (2014). *Heavenly answers for earthly challenges.* Mesquite, NV: Davidson Press. p. 101.

Clark, Nancy (2012). *Hear his voice.* Fairfield, IA: 1st World Publishing. p. 24.

Henry W. Henry W nde. NDERF.org Retrieved from https://www.nderf.org/Experiences/1henry_w_probable_nde.html

Frankl, V. (1984). *Man's search for meaning: an introduction to logotherapy.* New York: Simon & Schuster.

Charmaine M. *Charmaine M nde.* NDERF.org Retrieved from https://www.nderf.org/Experiences/1charmaine_m_ndes.html

Alexander, E. (2015, June 4). *Neurosurgeon's near death experience: doctor says heaven is real.* After Life TV with Bob Olson. Retrieved from https://www.afterlifetv.com/tag/dr-eben-alexander/

Richard L. *Richard L nde.* NDERF.org Retrieved from https://www.nderf.org/Experiences/1richard_l_nde.html

Ron K. *Ron K nde.* NDERF.org Retrieved from http://www.nderf.org/Experiences/1ron_k_nde.html

Ryan Rampton quoted in Sunfellow, D. (2016.) *Love the person you're with: life-changing insights from the most compelling near-death experiences ever recorded.* Scotts Valley, CA: CreateSpace. p. 70.

Kopecky, R. (2014). *How to survive life (and death): a guide for happiness in this world and beyond.* Newburyport, MA: Conari Press. p. 7.

Brock, E. quotes in Clark, Nancy (2012). *Divine moments: ordinary people having spiritually transformative experiences.* Fairfield, IA: 1st World Publishing. p. 112.

Yensen, A. quoted in quoted in Williams, K. (2017). *Arthur Yensen's near-death experience.* Retrieved from https://www.near-death.com/reincarnation/experiences/arthur-yensen.html

Hawn, G. (2005). *Goldie: a lotus grows in the mud.* New York, NY: Putnam Adult.

Debenport, E. (2015). *Hell in the hallway, light at the door: how to move gracefully through change into renewed and abundant life.* Carlsbad, CA: Balboa Press.

Brinkley, D., & Brinkley, K. (2008). *Secrets of the light: lessons from heaven.* San Francisco: HarperOne. p. 92, 198.

Bennett, D. (2011). *Voyage of purpose: spiritual wisdom from near death back to life.* Rochester, VT: Findhorn Press. p. 124.

Brown, J. (2014). *Heavenly answers for earthly challenges.* Mesquite, NV: Davidson Press. p. 98.

Rome, Marion (2014). *Beyond sight: the true story of a near-death experience.* Scotts Valley, CA: CreateSpace.

Neal, M. (2012). *To heaven and back: a doctor's extraordinary account of her death, heaven, angels, and life again: a true story.* NewYork, NY: WaterBrook. P. 100-101.

Didier quoted in Ellis, A. (2012). *Revelations of profound love: new insights into the power of love from near-death experiences.* Tulsa, OK: Trail of Hope Publishing. p. 127-128.

Brown, J. (2014). *Heavenly answers for earthly challenges.* Mesquite, NV: Davidson Press.

Nowlin. J. (2018). *The purposeful millionaire with James Nowlin, JD.* Retrieved from https://player.fm/series/moments-with-marianne/the-purposeful-millionaire-with-james-nowlin-jd-past-lives-for-beginners-with-douglas-delong

Boisson, E. (2018). Personal communication.

Olsen, J. (2017). *Choosing joy for a transformational life.* March 24, IANDS presentation, Durham, NC.

Sandy B. quoted in Clark, Nancy (2012). *Divine moments: ordinary people having spiritually transformative experiences.* Fairfield, IA: 1st World Publishing. p. 104.

Jessica quoted in Ellis, A. (2012). *Revelations of profound love: new insights into the power of love from near-death experiences.* Tulsa, OK: Trail of Hope Publishing. p. 121-122.

Arthur B. *Arthur B nde.* NDERF.org Retrieved from http://www.nderf.org/Experiences/1arthur_b_nde.html

Roberts, J. (2017). *Cardigan's commencement address by chief justice John G. Roberts, Jr.* Retrieved from https://www.youtube.com/watch?v=Gzu9S5FL-Ug

Brown, J. (2014). *Heavenly answers for earthly challenges.* Mesquite, NV: Davidson Press. p. 95.

William C. *William C nde.* NDERF.org Retrieved from http://www.nderf.org/Experiences/1william_c_nde.html

Amy Call. *Amy C nde.* NDERF.org Retrieved from NDERF.org Retrieved from *http://www.nderf.org/Experiences/1amy_c_nde_4720.html*

Brown, J. (2014). *Heavenly answers for earthly challenges.* Mesquite, NV: Davidson Press. p. 91, 182.

Parti, R. (2016). *Dying to wake up: a doctor's voyage into the afterlife and the wisdom he brought back.* New York, NY: Atria Books. p. 154.

Smith, D. (2014). *Dying to really live: memories of the afterlife; a non-believer returns to life after a surprising near death experience.* Ashland Press. p. 46-47.

Mary Beth Willi. *Mary W nde.* NDERF.org Retrieved from http://www.nderf.org/Experiences/1mary_w_nde.html

Warren, R. (2012). *The purpose driven life: what on earth am I here for?* Grand Rapids, MI: Zondervan.

Brown, J. (2014). *Heavenly answers for earthly challenges.* Mesquite, NV: Davidson Press. p. 108.

McDonald, B. (2017). *Near death experience: foretold future events for 50 years.* Retrieved from https://www.youtube.com/watch?v=lm9O3F_fSL8

Neal, M. (2015). *October 18, 2015: sunday forum: "to heaven and back" with guest dr. Mary Neal.* Retrieved from https://www.youtube.com/watch?v=QttkO6jgVZ8

Olsen, J. (2012). *I knew their hearts: the amazing true story of a journey beyond the veil to learn the silent language of the heart.* Plain Sight Publications. p. 88.

Rynes, N. (2015). *Awakenings from the light: 12 life lessons from a near death experience.* Scotts Valley, CA: CreateSpace. p. 181-182.

Neal, M. (2012). *To heaven and back: a doctor's extraordinary account of her death, heaven, angels, and life again: a true story.* NewYork, NY: WaterBrook. p. 103.

Clark, Nancy (2012). *Divine moments: ordinary people having spiritually transformative experiences.* Fairfield, IA: 1st World Publishing. p. 44.

Chapter 7—Serve Selflessly

Clark, Nancy (2012). *Divine moments: ordinary people having spiritually transformative experiences.* Fairfield, IA: 1st World Publishing. p. 47.

Storm, H. (2005). *My descent into death: a second chance at life.* New York, NY: Harmony. p. 21-23.

Smith, D. (2014). *Dying to really live: memories of the afterlife; a non-believer returns to life after a surprising near death experience.* Ashland Press. p. 79.

Rosenblit, D. quoted in Williams, K. (2016). *David Rosenblit's near-death experience.* Retrieved from https://www.near-death.com/experiences/notable/daniel-rosenblit.html

Juliet Nightingale quoted in Williams, K. (2016). *Juliet Nightingale's near-death experience.* Retrieved from https://www.near-death.com/experiences/notable/Juliet-nightingale.html

Rome, Marion (2014). *Beyond sight: the true story of a near-death experience.* Scotts Valley, CA: CreateSpace.

Redwood, Charmian (2012). *My near death experience.* Retrieved from https://www.youtube.com/watch?v=s5tqhN-nGVU

Goodman, Sherry. Retrieved from https://nhne-nde-network.org/forums/topic/462/sherry-goodman-s-near-death-experience

Parti, R. (2016). *Dying to wake up: a doctor's voyage into the afterlife and the wisdom he brought back.* New York, NY: Atria Books.

Merton, Thomas. Retrieved from https://www.azquotes.com/quote/856466

McKenzie, E. (2015). *Dying to fit in.* Erica McKenzie. p. 89.

Dave quoted in Lundahl, C. & Widdison, H. (1997). *The eternal journey: how near-death experiences illuminate our earthly lives.* New York, NY: Grand Central Publishing. p. 270.

Brinkley, D., & Perry, P. (1994). *Saved by the light: the true story of a man who died twice and the profound revelations he received*. New York: Villard. p. 20.

Teresa, Mother. Retreived from https://www.goodreads.com/quotes/295720-we-must-know-that-we-have-been-created-for-greater

Parti, R. (2016). *Dying to wake up: a doctor's voyage into the afterlife and the wisdom he brought back*. New York, NY: Atria Books. p. 215-216.

Moorjani, A. (2016). *What if this is heaven?: how our cultural myths prevent us from experiencing heaven on earth*. Carlsbad, CA: Hay House. p. 23 and 39.

Rosenblit, D. quoted in Williams, K. (2016). David Rosenblit's near-death experience. Retrieved from https://www.near-death.com/experiences/notable/daniel-rosenblit.html

RaNelle Wallace quoted in Williams, K. (2016). *RaNelle Wallace's near-death experience*. Retrieved from http://www.near-death.com/experiences/notable/ranelle-wallace.html

Mary Beth Willi. *Mary W nde*. NDERF.org Retrieved from http://www.nderf.org/Experiences/1mary_w_nde.html

Clark, Nancy (2012). *Hear his voice*. Fairfield, IA: 1st World Publishing. p. 161.

Brinkley, D., & Brinkley, K. (2008). *Secrets of the light: lessons from heaven*. San Francisco: HarperOne. p. 191-192.

Rynes, N. (2015). *Awakenings from the light: 12 life lessons from a near death experience*. Scotts Valley, CA: CreateSpace. p. 71.

Betty Eadie quoted in Bailey, L. & Yates, J. (1996). *The near death experience: a reader*. Florence, KY: Routledge. p. 60.

Brinkley, D., & Brinkley, K. (2008). *Secrets of the light: lessons from heaven*. San Francisco: HarperOne. p. 108.

Brown, J. (2014). *Heavenly answers for earthly challenges*. Mesquite, NV: Davidson Press. p. 114.

DeWitt-Maltby, D. (2012). *While I was out . . .* Self Publish. p. 121-122.

Chapter 8—Appreciate Regularly

Elliott, J. (2000). *An unexpected light: travels in Afghanistan*. London. Picador.

Bennett, D. (2011). *Voyage of purpose: spiritual wisdom from near death back to life*. Rochester, VT: Findhorn Press. p. 98-99.

Parti, R. (2016). *Dying to wake up: a doctor's voyage into the afterlife and the wisdom he brought back*. New York, NY: Atria Books. p. 179-180.

Brown, J. (2014). *Heavenly answers for earthly challenges*. Mesquite, NV: Davidson Press. p. 100.

Rynes, N. (2015). *Awakenings from the light: 12 life lessons from a near death experience*. Scotts Valley, CA: CreateSpace. p. 179.

Carmody, N. (November, 1999). *I'm thankful for*. Family Circle.

Moorjani, A. (2012). *Dying to be me: my journey from cancer, to near death, to true healing*. Carlsbad, CA: Hay House. p. 107.

DeWitt-Maltby, D. (2012). *While I was out . . .* Self Publish. p. 111-112.

Neev quoted in Ring, K. (2006). *Lessons from the light: what we can learn from the near-death experience*. Needham, MA: Moment Point Press. p. 18.

Brown, J. (2014). *Heavenly answers for earthly challenges*. Mesquite, NV: Davidson Press. p. 100.

Olsen, J. (2012). *I knew their hearts: the amazing true story of a journey beyond the veil to learn the silent language of the heart*. Plain Sight Publications. p. 102.

Williamson. M. (2009). *The age of miracles: embracing the new midlife*. Carlsbad, CA: Hay House.

Olsen, J. (2018). Personal communication.

Singer, M. (2007). *The untethered soul: the journey beyond yourself*. Oakland, CA: New Harbinger. p. 159.

Chapter 9—Forgive Fully

Izadi, E. (2015, June 19). The powerful words of forgiveness delivered to Dylann Roof by victims' relatives. *The Washington Post*. https://www.washingtonpost.com/news/post-nation/wp/2015/06/19/hate-wont-win-the-powerful-words-delivered-to-dylann-roof-by-victims-relatives/?tid=a_inl&utm_term=.3c6cd48e85dc

Brinkley, D., & Brinkley, K. (2008). *Secrets of the light: lessons from heaven*. San Francisco: HarperOne. p. 47.

Napier, R., & Smallridge, E. (2015). *Renee Napier and Eric Smallridge: an incredible story of grace, forgiveness and repentance in florida*. Retrieved from https://wonderingeagle.wordpress.com/2015/05/13/renee-napier-and-eric-smallridge-an-incredible-story-of-grace-forgiveness-and-repentance-in-florida/

Napier, R., & Smallridge, E. *Eric's story*. Retrieved from http://www.themeagannapier-foundation.com/story_eric.php

Rome, Marion (2014). *Beyond sight: the true story of a near-death experience*. Scotts Valley, CA: CreateSpace.

Amphianda Baskett quoted in Sunfellow, D. (2016). Love the person you're with: life-changing insights from the most compelling near-death experiences ever recorded. Scotts Valley, CA: CreateSpace. p. 144.

Lee quoted in Ellis, A. (2012). *Revelations of profound love: new insights into the power of love from near-death experiences*. Tulsa, OK: Trail of Hope Publishing. p. 103.

Call, A. *Amy Call nde*. NDERF.org Retrieved from http://www.nderf.org/Experiences/1amy_c_nde_4720.html

Kopecky, R. (2014). *How to survive life (and death): a guide for happiness in this world and beyond.* Newburyport, MA: Conari Press. p. 46.

Dooley, M. (2014). *The top ten things dead people want to tell you.* Carlsbad, CA: Hay House. p. 96.

Storm, H. (2017). *Howard Storm love the person you're with.* Retrieved from http://love-thepersonyouarewith.com/videos/howardstorm/

Parti, R. (2016). *Dying to wake up: a doctor's voyage into the afterlife and the wisdom he brought back.* New York, NY: Atria Books. p. 160-161, 198.

Brown, J. (2014). *Heavenly answers for earthly challenges.* Mesquite, NV: Davidson Press. p. 117.

Neal, M. (2017). *7 lessons from heaven: how dying taught me to live a joy-filled life.* New York, NY: Convergent Books. p. 52.

Smedes, L. (1996). *The art of forgiving.* New York, NY: Random House.

Brinkley, D., & Perry, P. (1994). *Saved by the light: the true story of a man who died twice and the profound revelations he received.* New York: Villard. p. 152.

Parti, R. (2016). *Dying to wake up: a doctor's voyage into the afterlife and the wisdom he brought back.* New York, NY: Atria Books. p. 155-157.

Kopecky, R. (2014). *How to survive life (and death): a guide for happiness in this world and beyond.* Newburyport, MA: Conari Press. p. 46.

Rome, Marion (2014). *Beyond sight: the true story of a near-death experience.* Scotts Valley, CA: CreateSpace.

Brown, J. (2014). *Heavenly answers for earthly challenges.* Mesquite, NV: Davidson Press. p. 117.

Mary Beth Willi. *Mary W nde.* NDERF.org Retrieved from http://www.nderf.org/Experiences/1mary_w_nde.html

Leonardo. *Leonardo probable NDE.* NDERF.org Retrieved from http://www.nderf.org/Experiences/1leonardo_probable_nde.html

Chapter 10—Trust Completely

Neal, M. (2017, May). *To heaven and back.* Presentation conducted at The Academy for Spiritual and Consciousness Studies. Chapel Hill, NC.

Romy. *Romy nde.* NDERF.org Retrieved from http://www.nderf.org/Experiences/1romy_nde.html

Olsen, J. (2012). *I knew their hearts: the amazing true story of a journey beyond the veil to learn the silent language of the heart.* Plain Sight Publications. p. 88.

DeWitt-Maltby, D. (2012). *While I was out . . .* Self Publish. p. 119.

Woody, T. (2017). *Episode 203 US vavy chief petty officer Tony Woody shares nde, spiritual journey and commitment.* Retrieved from https://www.youtube.com/watch?v=bCmGou_dGvk

Sammy. *Sammy NDE*. NDERF.org Retrieved from http://www.nderf.org/Experiences/1sammy_nde.html

Storm, H. (2005). *My descent into death: a second chance at life*. New York, NY: Harmony. p. 38.

Jones, D.R. (2018) Near Death Experiences Facebook group. March 5, 2018.

Cara. *Cara nde*. NDERF.org Retrieved from http://www.nderf.org/Experiences/1cara_nde.html

Mary Beth Willi. *Mary W nde*. NDERF.org Retrieved from http://www.nderf.org/Experiences/1mary_w_nde.html

Olsen, J. (2012). *I knew their hearts: the amazing true story of a journey beyond the veil to learn the silent language of the heart*. Plain Sight Publications.

Cara. *Cara nde*. NDERF.org Retrieved from http://www.nderf.org/Experiences/1cara_nde.html

Craig, H. (2018). *The near-death experience of Heidi Craig*. Retrieved from https://www.youtube.com/watch?v=YSa3El8VFOo

Jayne quoted in Ring, K. (2006). *Lessons from the light: what we can learn from the near-death experience*. Needham, MA: Moment Point Press. p. 274.

Clark, Nancy (2012). *Hear his voice*. Fairfield, IA: 1st World Publishing. p. 74.

McVea, C. (2013). *Waking up in heaven: a true story of brokenness, heaven, and life again*. Brentwood, TN: Howard Books. p. 340.

Tory quoted in Ellis, A. (2012). *Revelations of profound love: new insights into the power of love from near-death experiences*. Tulsa, OK: Trail of Hope Publishing. p. 103.

Brinkley, D., & Brinkley, K. (2008). *Secrets of the light: lessons from heaven*. San Francisco: HarperOne. p. 182.

Juliet Nightingale quoted in Williams, K. (2016). *Juliet Nightingale's near-death experience*. Retrieved from https://www.near-death.com/experiences/notable/Juliet-nightingale.html

Panagore, P. (2017). *Let's talk near death (near death experiences): Peter Panagore*. Retrieved from https://www.youtube.com/watch?v=B3dXE-nSyzY

Alexander, E. (2015). *Neurosurgeon's near-death experience—doctor says heaven is real!* Retrieved from https://www.youtube.com/watch?v=jFIF8K1fkg8

Lisa M. *Lisa M nde*. NDERF.org Retrieved from http://www.nderf.org/Experiences/1lisa_m_nde.html

Rodonaia, George. NDERF.org Retrieved from https://www.nderf.org/Experiences/1george_rodonaia_nde.html

GiGi Strehler quoted in Sartori, P. & Walsh, K. (2017). *The transformative power of near-death experiences: how the messages of ndes can positively impact the world*. London, UK: Watkins Publishing. p. 32-33.

Panagore, P. (2015). *Heaven is beautiful: how dying taught me that death is just the beginning.* Newburyport, MA: Hampton Roads Publishing. p. 86.

Alexander, E. (2015). *Neurosurgeon's near-death experience—doctor says heaven is real!* Retrieved from https://www.youtube.com/watch?v=jFIF8K1fkg8

Benedict, M. (2019). *NDEs and hell.* Retrieved from https://the-formula.org/ndes-hell/

Penny Wilson quoted in Sartori, P. & Walsh, K. (2017). *The transformative power of near-death experiences: how the messages of ndes can positively impact the world.* London, UK: Watkins Publishing. p. 82-85.

Williams, K. (2017). *Hell and the near-death experience.* Retrieved from https://www.near-death.com/science/research/hell.html

Sartori, P. & Walsh, K. (2017). *The transformative power of near-death experiences: how the messages of ndes can positively impact the world.* London, UK: Watkins Publishing. p. 15.

Milliman, S. (2017). *Let's talk near death: Sharon Milliman.* Retrieved from https://www.youtube.com/watch?v=Q5RlgozR0Hs

Rommer, B. (2000). *Blessing in disguise: another side of near death experience.* Woodbury, M: Llewellyn Publications.

Peggy P. quoted in Ring, K. (2006). *Lessons from the light: what we can learn from the near-death experience.* Needham, MA: Moment Point Press. p. 188.

Neal, M. (2017). *7 lessons from heaven: how dying taught me to live a joy-filled life.* New York, NY: Convergent Books. p. 193.

Baskett, A. (2019). *Near Death Experiences Facebook* Group. Retrieved from https://www.facebook.com/groups/returnfromdeath/

Bring Heaven to Earth

Bennett, D. (2011). *Voyage of purpose: spiritual wisdom from near death back to life.* Rochester, VT: Findhorn Press.

Rome, Marion (2014). *Beyond sight: the true story of a near-death experience.* Scotts Valley, CA: CreateSpace.

Olsen, J. (2018). *Knowing: memoirs of a journey beyond the veil and choosing joy after tragic loss.* Peoria, AZ: Envoy Publishing. p. 307-308.

Brown, J. (2014). *Heavenly answers for earthly challenges.* Mesquite, NV: Davidson Press. p. 114.

Mellon Thomas Benedict quoted in Sunfellow, D. (2016.) *Love the person you're with: life-changing insights from the most compelling near-death experiences ever recorded.* Scotts Valley, CA: CreateSpace. p. 131.

Dr. Ken Ring quoted in Sunfellow, D. (2016.) *Love the person you're with: life-changing insights from the most compelling near-death experiences ever recorded.* Scotts Valley, CA: CreateSpace. p. 24.

Rodonaia, G. (2017). *Some people were dead for several days.* Retrieved from https://www.near-death.com/science/evidence/some-people-were-dead-for-several-days.html

Ring, K. (2006). *Lessons from the light: what we can learn from the near-death experience.* Needham, MA: Moment Point Press. p. 303.

Sunfellow, D. (2016.) *Love the person you're with: life-changing insights from the most compelling near-death experiences ever recorded.* Scotts Valley, CA: CreateSpace. p. 144.

Diane Goble quoted in Sartori, P. & Walsh, K. (2017). *The transformative power of near-death experiences: how the messages of ndes can positively impact the world.* London, UK: Watkins Publishing. p. 125.

Brinkley, D. & Perry, P. (1995). *At peace in the light: the further adventures of a reluctant psychic who reveals the secret of your spiritual powers.* New York, NY: HarperCollins. p. 145.

Photo Credits

Cover—Image by Engin Akyurt from Pixabay

Chapter 1: Love Unconditionally—Image by stokpic from Pixabay

Chapter 2: Live Fearlessly—Image from Shutterstock: Mauricio Graiki

Chapter 3: Work Purposely—Image by carodoc from Pixabay

Chapter 4: Choose Compassionately—Image by Gaertringen from Pixabay

Chapter 5: Accept Nonjudgmentally—Image of Gracie Ann and Jillian by Jeff Janssen

Chapter 6: Learn Continuously—Image by macdeedle from Pixabay

Chapter 7: Serve Selflessly—Image from Shutterstock: Jesus Cervantes

Chapter 8: Appreciate Regularly—Image by Steve Howard from Pixabay

Chapter 9: Forgive Fully—Image by Jeff Janssen

Chapter 10: Trust Completely—Image by Jeff Janssen

Bring Heaven to Earth—Photo by Davide Cantelli on Unsplash

"Death is not extinguishing the light;
it is only putting out the lamp because
the dawn has come."

RABINDRANATH TAGORE

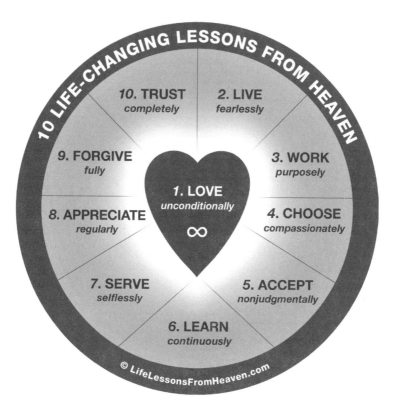